Philosophy and Practice of Organizational Learning, Performance, and Change

New Perspectives in Organizational Learning, Performance, and Change
JERRY W. GILLEY, SERIES EDITOR

Philosophy and Practice of Organizational Learning, Performance, and Change by Jerry W. Gilley, Peter J. Dean, and Laura L. Bierema

Assessing the Financial Benefits of Human Resource Development by Richard A. Swanson

The Manager as Change Agent by Jerry W. Gilley, Scott A. Quatro, Erik Hoekstra, Doug D. Whittle, and Ann Maycunich

Philosophy and Practice of

Organizational Learning, Performance, and Change

Jerry W. Gilley

Peter J. Dean

Laura L. Bierema

New Perspectives in Organizational Learning, Performance, and Change

PERSEUS PUBLISHING

Cambridge, Massachusetts

Many of the designations used by manufacturers and sellers to distinguish their products are claimed as trademarks. Where those designations appear in this book and Perseus Publishing was aware of a trademark claim, the designations have been printed in initial capital letters.

A CIP catalog record for this book is available from the Library of Congress.
ISBN: 0-7382-0461-7
Copyright © 2001 by Jerry W. Gilley

Perseus Publishing is a member of the Perseus Books Group.
Find us on the World Wide Web at http://www.perseuspublishing.com

Perseus Publishing books are available at special discounts for bulk purchases in the U.S. by corpora-tions, institutions, and other organizations. For more information, please contact the Special Markets Department at the Perseus Books Group, 11 Cambridge Center, Cambridge, MA 02142, or call 617-252-5298.

Set in 10.5 point Minion by Perseus Publishing Services.

First printing, June 2001
1 2 3 4 5 6 7 8 9 10—03 02 01

Publisher's Note

Organizations are living systems, in a constant state of dynamic evolution. New Perspectives in Organizational Learning, Performance, and Change is designed to showcase the most current theory and practice in human resource and organizational development, exploring all aspects of the field—from performance management to adult learning to corporate culture. Integrating cutting-edge research and innovative management practice, this library of titles will serve as an essential resource for human resource professionals, educators, students, and managers in all types of organizations.

The series editorial board includes leading academics and practitioners whose insights are shaping the theory and application of human resource development and organizational design.

Contents

List of Figures

An Overview of the Professional Practice Domains of HRD

Organizational Learning, Performance, and Change

Jerry W. Gilley

The field of human resource development (HRD) and the goals of its practitioners have changed dramatically during the past twenty-five years. Today, dedicated, determined HRD practitioners spend their time, energy, and effort helping their organizations to create the right learning environment, design performance management systems, and implement change initiatives. It is no longer acceptable to simply provide training programs and hope that employees will mysteriously improve their knowledge and skills and that organizational effectiveness will magically blossom. For most HRD practitioners, their primary aims are to alter an organization's structure, mission, strategy, leadership, managerial practices, and work environment. As a result of these new responsibilities, the philosophy and practice of HRD continue to evolve.

Although the importance and credibility of HRD practitioners have improved tremendously over the years, some contend that the field of HRD is more divided today than ever before (Bierema, 2000; Swanson and Arnold, 1996). During the past decade, HRD practitioners have aligned themselves with one of the following philosophical orientations: (1) organizational

1

learning, (2) organizational performance, and (3) organizational change (Gilley and Maycunich, 2000a). Each of these three philosophical orientations manifests itself as a professional practice domain in which HRD practitioners focus on learning, performance, or change activities. Thus, they embrace the philosophy and practice of their chosen domain. This affects practitioners' decisionmaking, priority setting, actions taken, behaviors, and practices. Such alignments are similar to what occurs when immigrants adopt the language, customs, practices, and culture of a new country.

Unfortunately, each domain is attempting to assert its influence over the direction of the field, which is affecting the interaction, cooperation, and partnerships among HRD practitioners. This is evident in comments such as "performance consulting is one of the premier bait-and-switch offerings in the training world's current product line" (Murphy, 1999, 104). Bierema (2000) believes that performance consulting masquerades the fact that there is no reliable technology for improving performance and leaves itself vulnerable to the age-old question "Why don't we get no respect?" A similar viewpoint was shared by a leading HRD academic who referred to a performance consultant as "one of them," as though being a productive, change-oriented HRD practitioner was a negative thing. On the other side of the ledger, learning-oriented practitioners are often referred to negatively as "trainers or adult educators" without regard for their contributions to changing the learning culture in organizations. Organizational change practitioners are commonly called "quant-jocks" who are more interested in statistical probability and correlational relationships than in improving the human condition within organizations. Such sentiments negatively affect the image of practitioners and the field and prevent the acceptance of a unified approach to improving organizational effectiveness.

Divisions within the field are also reflected in the growing separation among professional associations and societies, such as:

- American Society for Training and Development, which primarily embraces organizational learning through training;
- International Society for Performance Improvement, which embraces organizational performance; and
- Society of Industrial and Organizational Psychology, which embraces both organizational performance and change.

Furthermore, academic groups have separated into ideological fiefdoms. For example, the Academy of Human Resources Development emphasizes organizational learning and performance for the purpose of enhancing organizational results, whereas the Commission of Adult Education Professors emphasizes adult learning for the purpose of improving the human condition and society as a whole. Each provides research journals that reinforce these perspectives, such as the *HRD Quarterly* and *HRD International*, and *Adult Education Quarterly*, respectively. The International Society for Performance Improvement promotes performance improvement, performance management, human performance technology, and the role of performance engineers and consultants in their professional journal, *Performance Improvement*, and their research journal, *Performance Improvement Quarterly*. The American Society for Training and Development primarily advocates learning and development and sometimes promotes performance improvement through their professional journal, *Training and Development*, whereas Lakewood Publications provides a similar treatment in a professional magazine entitled *Training*.

Although it is perfectly appropriate to separate into practitioner groups in order to focus on a narrow specialization, it can be harmful when these practice domains become competitive and divisive. History is full of examples where such balkanization eventually fostered antagonistic and even hostile conditions. For example, religious and cultural conflict has resulted in genocide and destructive wars. Political conflict has led to dictatorships and repressive governments, which in turn brought about human misery and cultural destruction. These are extreme examples of divisive situations, yet they serve to remind us that rigidly defended viewpoints can lead to unintended consequences and negative outcomes.

The Aim of this Book

Of course, our situation is not nearly as serious as the ones just described, but it has become increasingly negative in recent years. At the center of the controversy are the HRD practitioners' assumptions about their role, responsibility, and approach to practice. As mentioned earlier, one's assumptions affect the choices, commitments, and actions taken. This is much like aligning oneself with a political party because it makes explicit one's assumptions regarding government's role, responsibility, and approach to society's problems. As much as it may be unavoidable to subscribe to a specific branch of HRD, it is best to avoid being locked into a philosophical identity that prevents the adoption of positive improvements within HRD practice.

Unless these assumptions are revealed and analyzed, it will be difficult for HRD practitioners to truly understand why they engage in the activities they do. Therefore, one of the aims of this book is to provide a better understanding of the assumptions that practitioners maintain so that they can be appropriately altered or adjusted. This is especially important when adopting a radical change such as an organizational transformation. Quite simply, one's assumptions affect the beliefs, policies, principles, and practices adopted, and so influence one's actions and behavior. Once assumptions are identified and understood, they are easier to alter and will have a measurable effect on the future choices, commitments, and actions of the HRD practitioners.

To fully comprehend the influence of assumptions, we must examine the relationship of assumptions to behavior. According to Brookfield (1992, 13), one way to think about assumptions is to consider them as "taken for granted" beliefs one has about reality. Another way is to view assumptions as the rules of thumb that guide one's actions. A third approach sees assumptions as a common set of beliefs and conventional wisdom one relies on when making decisions or electing to behave in a certain manner.

Schwinn (1996) believes that assumptions are an explicit set of conditions, principles, ethics, and expectations taken to be true about the basis for choosing actions and studying the consequences that follow. In other words, he concludes that assumptions are the anchors to which most decisions are linked. Therefore, it is critically important to identify practitioners' assumptions about HRD in order to understand their approach to practice.

According to Mink et al. (1993), the majority of change that occurs within individuals and organizations involves routines, activities, problems, issues, and specific circumstances; this is sometimes referred to as *first-order change*. The same is true for HRD practitioners. Most changes are directed at minor improvements and adjustments that occur naturally as practitioners gain experience and expertise. Therefore, the preponderance of first-order changes necessarily requires serious assumption testing on the part of practitioners.

Another type of change involves a fundamental shift in HRD practitioners. It questions their basic assumptions regarding HRD and addresses new and unknown elements of their philosophy and practice. This is sometimes referred to as *transformational change* or *second-order change* (Mink et al., 1993) and requires practitioners to conduct extensive assumption testing activities. Furthermore, second-order change requires the integration of new practices, processes, procedures, and values. These will transform practitioners' responsiveness, focus, service quality, and results.

Second-order change is necessary if HRD practitioners are to alter their practice activities. To facilitate this outcome, practitioners will need to examine the rich history of each of the professional practice domains of HRD. They will also need to incorporate the elements of each of the domains into their practice. Such a transition requires them to examine the type of interventions and initiatives they provide, as well as how they provide value-added service within the organization. It compels practitioners to adopt a different HRD philosophy whereby their efforts are dedicated to employees' continuous improvement based on their strengths (Buckingham and Coffman, 1999), the transformation of organizational systems (Burke, 1992), and improvement of professional practices (Rummler and Brache, 1998). Moreover, second-order change requires HRD practitioners to develop additional expertise and accept new responsibilities (Gilley et al., 2001). Finally, practitioners will also need to examine their competencies and determine whether they are sufficient to integrate and incorporate all of the elements of these three professional practice domains of HRD. Once this is determined, practitioners must create a development plan they can use to build on their strengths while managing their weaknesses (Clifton and Nelson, 1992).

A second aim of the book is to examine the similarities and differences between each of the practice domains. To accomplish this objective, we must examine the philosophical foundations of each domain and the implications that each has on HRD practice (Chapters 2–8). From our discussion it will become apparent that each domain has very positive attributes that can powerfully influence organizational effectiveness. Equally important, one must understand that no single domain of HRD possesses greater stature or effectiveness. In other words, each orientation provides a piece of the HRD puzzle but in no way represents the whole truth on how to improve organizational effectiveness.

We will not attempt to convince the reader of the superiority of any one domain but are instead dedicated to compare and contrast them. We will emphasize the similarities among domains while pointing out their differences. From our perspectives, it is more important to celebrate the similarities than promote our differences. In this way, we are determined to avoid the divisiveness that is so common among many of today's HRD academics and practitioners.

A final aim of the book is to examine the strengths and weaknesses of each domain. We will also identify the opportunities for each orientation to improve organizational effectiveness, as well as identify the threats that serve as barriers and prevent the proper implementation of each orientation (Chapter 9). In considering these issues, we will demonstrate the limitations of a single domain in enhancing organizational effectiveness. At the same time we will reveal the power of combining the approaches of each domain into one comprehensive approach in order to address any issue facing an organization and to provide HRD practitioners with multiple approaches to improving organizational effectiveness. Moreover, by combining these three practice domains, practitioners will be able to see the overlaps and linkages among learning, performance improvement, and change, which will provide a fresh perspective when addressing organizational issues, problems, and break-downs. Finally, we hope a three-in-one approach provides HRD practitioners with an understanding of the similarities of the domains, thus generating a more unified effort in improving organizational effectiveness.

An Introduction to the Three Professional Practice Domains of HRD

We would like to provide a short introduction to each of the practitioner practice domains of HRD. We have dedicated at least two chapters to each orientation, in which we examine the philosophical underpinnings of each domain and the effects these elements have on how they are practiced. Organizational learning is discussed in Chapters 2 and 3. Organizational performance is examined in Chapters 4, 5, and 6, and organizational change will be examined in Chapters 7 and 8.

Organizational Learning

HRD practitioners who embrace organizational learning believe that individual learning and development are the primary purpose of HRD. As Bierema (2000, 292) writes, "HRD is about *development*, not profit, and HRD practitioners need to carefully consider how their work impacts the human growth, not just the corporate wallet. It has also been argued that focusing on individual development has long term benefits for the individual, organization, and society." She points out that "there are long term costs associated with failure to provide the resources and infrastructure to support whole person learning such as turnover, mistakes and employees leaving to work for the competition. There are also social costs of such neglect that will impact lives, communities, and the environment." These comments nicely frame the philosophical beliefs of an organizational learning practitioner.

From an organizational learning perspective, practitioners are motivated to create learning cultures that foster continuous employee learning (Senge, 1990; Redding, 1994). This is based on a conviction that learning is key to organizational effectiveness. Moreover, they embrace the principles and practices of the learning organization (Senge, 1990), action learning (Marquardt, 1999), critical reflection (Argyris and Schon, 1980, 1996), and transformative learning (Mezirow, 1991), and their application within organizations. The philosophy of organizational learning is based on five orientations: liberalism, progressivism, behaviorism, humanism, and radical adult education (Zinn, 1983).

When confronted with performance problems within an organization, organizational learning-oriented HRD practitioners will typically rely on a learning solution as a way of addressing the issue. They perceive that learning is a prerequisite to performance improvement and change. Therefore, they believe that learning is essential when dealing with most organizational problems and embrace the formal design, development, and implementation of learning interventions as their primary purpose within an organization (Knowles, 1970). Such practitioners place great value on group learning as a way of bringing about organizational change (Marquardt, 1999; Watkins and Marsick, 1993). Formal learning transfer activities are used to enhance individual learning and application on the job (Broad and Newstrom, 1992). Organizational learning practitioners embrace the integration of action learning (Marquardt, 1999), transformative learning (Mezirow, 1991), and self-directed learning activities (Knowles, 1975) in daily practice. Finally, these practitioners believe that the design and facilitation of successful training programs will enhance their credibility within an organization (Heron, 1989).

Organizational Performance

Organizational performance-oriented HRD practitioners believe that performance improvement and management are the essential components of HRD (Swanson, 1995; Rummler and Brache, 1995). They maintain that practitioners need to analyze performance problems, isolate the cause of performance breakdowns, and recommend or design interventions to address them (Gilbert, 1978; Mager, 1975; Harless, 1970). Furthermore, they believe that training is *not* the intervention of choice in most performance improvement situations (Silber, 1992). Rather, they believe that management action is the most appropriate approach to improving organizational performance (Stolovitch and Keeps, 1999). Additionally, they utilize system theory, behavioral psychology, and knowledge management when examining performance shortfall (Brethower, 1999).

Performance-oriented practitioners believe that their primary responsibility is to utilize the human performance system as a way of improving organizational effectiveness (Fuller and Farrington, 1999; Rosenberg, 1996). They contend that compensation and reward systems, organizational structure and culture, job design, and the motivational environment should be designed to reinforce performance change and improvement (Rummler and Brache, 1995; Gilbert, 1978). Performance-oriented practitioners believe that they are responsible for discovering efficiencies within an organization through analysis activities (Rossett, 1999b; Swanson, 1994). These practitioners advocate the principles and practices of human performance technology (Jacobs, 1987), performance consulting (Robinson and Robinson, 1996), and performance engineering (Dean, 1999b), and even advocate creating separate performance improvement departments dedicated to performance analysis, consulting, and evaluation (Robb, 1998). They believe that their credibility is affirmed when the overall performance of the organization improves (Dean, 1999b).

Organizational Change

Organizational change-oriented practitioners believe that alterations in the organization's culture, structure, work climate, mission, and strategy are the more important activities performed by HRD practitioners (Gilley and Maycunich, 1998; Kissler, 1991; Burke, 1992). They adopt a systemic and strategic approach to improving organizational effectiveness, embrace the principles and practice of organizational development as their primary orientation, and play the role of change agent within the organization (French and Bell, 1995). They contend that organizational change is the aim of their efforts and that organizational learning and performance often improve as a result of such intervention (Nadler, 1998). Change-oriented practitioners contend that organizational development is a full-time activity and requires an independent group of practitioners to implement it by focusing on permanently altering the organization's culture (Burke, 1992). Operationally, they work closely with senior executives, division and department managers, and line managers. These practitioners believe that they demonstrate their credibility and effectiveness by bringing about change within the organization and managing its implementation (Ulrich, 1998).

One of their primary responsibilities is to help organizations and its members absorb change without depleting the organization's or the individual's energy. Patterson (1997) refers to this quality as resilience. Such HRD practitioners are challenged to strengthen employees' adaptability to change, both personally and professionally. When this end is achieved, such employees are referred to as "resilient employees" who are "positive, focused, flexible, organized, and proactive," according to Conner (1992, 238).

Conner (1992) and Patterson (1997) suggest that resilient employees demonstrate a special adaptability when responding to uncertainty. They believe that resilient employees have a high tolerance for ambiguity and need only a short time to recover from adversity or disappointment. Conner (1992, 240) states that resilient employees engage change rather than defend against it (i.e., they are proactive). Such employees realize when change is inevitable, necessary, or advantageous and use resources to creatively reframe a changing situation, improvise new approaches, or maneuver to gain an advantage. Resilient employees take risks despite potentially negative consequences; draw important lessons from change-related experiences that are then applied to similar situations; respond to disruption by investing energy in problemsolving and teamwork activity; and influence others to resolve conflicts (Conner, 1992, 240).

Burke (1992, 177–178) believes that the effectiveness of a change-oriented practitioner, sometimes referred to as an organizational development change agent, depends on his or her ability to tolerate ambiguity. Gilley and Maycunich (2000a) argue that these practitioners improve their organizational impact and influence by demonstrating business understanding, political awareness, and organizational consciousness. Such practitioners are in a unique position to serve as employee champions because they help employees identify legitimate work demands and thus help workers set priorities (Ulrich, 1997). These practitioners must have knowledge of HRD practices, partnering and negotiating skills, organizational understanding, client relationship building, and organizational development skills. They must accept a variety of responsibilities, each designed to maximize the effectiveness of change initiatives and achieve change goals (i.e., improve communications, enhance client relationships, improve organizational performance capacity, enhance the organization's culture, and improve work environments).

Organizational Change and Culture. Much has been learned in the last few years about culture change and the central role of HRD practitioners in its accomplishment. According to Ulrich (1997, 169–170), five steps embody the essence of the change-oriented practitioners' role in successful culture change: (1) define and clarify the concept of culture change; (2) articulate why culture change is central to business success; (3) define a process for assessing the current culture, the desired future culture, and the gap between the two; (4) identify alternative approaches to creating cultural change; and (5) build an action plan that integrates multiple approaches to cultural change. These will be discussed in Chapter 8.

Organizational Effectiveness: The Ultimate Objective of HRD

Whether change occurs in a large organization or system, a small division or department within an organization, or an individual employee, the primary purpose of change is to improve the organization and make it more effective

(Burke, 1992). This is the primary objective of HRD regardless of one's professional practice orientation. We believe that by adopting a three-in-one approach, such that organizational learning, performance, and change are blended into a comprehensive but integrated approach, HRD practitioners will be more effective in facilitating and promoting organizational effectiveness.

Unfortunately, improving organizational effectiveness is not easy. In fact, the evaluation and measurement of organizational effectiveness are one of the biggest obstacles facing an HRD practitioner. The oldest and most widely used way of measuring organizational effectiveness is to determine whether the organization has achieved its strategic and operational goals (Fallon and Brinkerhoff, 1996). Measuring effectiveness in terms of the extent to which the organization accomplishes its goals is but one way of examining this concept. Effectiveness can also be measured in terms of an organization's ability to acquire needed resources to accomplish desired results, such as computers needed to improve quality and efficiency or additional human resources to complete deliverables on time (Gibson, Ivancevich, and Donnelly, 1997). Furthermore, effectiveness can be defined in terms of how smoothly departments operate (i.e., absence of conflict, turnover, and absenteeism), or the extent to which organizations are able to satisfy their stakeholders' needs and expectations (i.e., employees, other managers, organizational leaders, and internal and external customers). In this latter approach, organizational effectiveness is measured in terms of stakeholder satisfaction with the use of deliverables as well as their perception of the correctness of their decision to have an ongoing relationship with their operational unit (Fallon and Brinkerhoff, 1996).

Though it may be difficult to agree on one way of measuring organizational effectiveness, such effectiveness is certainly an important part of organizational life. Consequently, HRD practitioners need to adopt an acceptable or appropriate way of determining organizational effectiveness in order to have a unified goal that all organizational members strive to achieve.

Conclusions

Each of these three professional practice domains is complex, in both substance and implementation. Additionally, the assumptions and beliefs of practitioners differ greatly depending on their orientation. As a result, many disagreements exist regarding how to enhance organizational effectiveness, which have negative impacts on the field of HRD and its practitioners. This prevents the adoption of a unified approach toward organizational improvement.

Although each domain has its strengths, each also has its limitations in enhancing organizational effectiveness. Therefore, identifying the philosophical underpinnings to HRD practice can provide practitioners with insight when addressing performance problems and organizational breakdowns. Once these are identified, HRD practitioners can blend the three practice domains in order to demonstrate overlaps and linkages among organizational learning, performance, and change. Such a synthesis will provide practitioners with a more focused strategy in their efforts to enhance organizational effectiveness.

Philosophy of Organizational Learning

Laura L. Bierema

The goal of this chapter is to outline the general philosophies underlying adult and organizational learning and illustrate how they manifest in human resource development applications. Specifically, this chapter examines the philosophical assumptions and values underpinning adult learning, illustrates how the philosophies are applied, examines the philosophy from both the learner and teacher perspectives, and highlights the contributions of each philosophy.

Houle defines adult education as

> The process by which men and women (alone, in groups, or in institutional settings) seek to improve themselves or their society by increasing their skill, knowledge, or sensitiveness; or it is any process by which individuals, groups, or institutions try to help men and women improve in these ways. The fundamental system of practice of the field, if it has one, must be discerned by probing beneath many different surface realities to identify a basic unity of process. (Houle, 1995, 47–48)

Learning is a complex phenomenon that has been studied for centuries. Merriam and Caffarella emphasize, "Learning defies easy definition and simple theorizing" (1999, 248), and illustrate how Plato and Aristotle influenced early investigation of learning through Plato's "rationalism," evident in Gestalt and cognitive psychology, and Aristotle's "empiricism," evident in early behavioral psychology. The scientific investigation of learning began during the nineteenth century with exploration of the mind, of knowing, and of behavior.

The study of educational philosophy has been rigorous for only the last two centuries, largely inspired in the last century by the writings of John Dewey (Elias and Merriam, 1995). Philosophy is concerned with the general principles of any phenomenon, object, process, or subject matter (Elias and Merriam, 1995). Principles are the fundamentals or basic structures used to understand phenomena. General principles of education might include aims and objectives, curriculum, subject matter, methods, analysis of the teaching and learning process, and the relationship between education and society. Merriam and Brockett (1997, 28) explain that the goal of philosophy is to make sense of the world, and it literally means "love of wisdom or knowledge." They state that "A philosophy of education is a conceptual framework embodying certain values and principles that renders the education process meaningful."

Elias and Merriam (1995) explain that philosophy has traditional subdisciplines of logic, epistemology, metaphysics, and ethics. Logic focuses on the rules for correct reasoning and thinking and on various forms of argumentation. Epistemology explores rules for determining whether or not information is truth, opinion, or falsehood. Metaphysics searches out the most general principles of reality. Ethics investigates rules of moral reasoning and conduct (1995, 3). Philosophy helps practitioners and researchers to identify issues and make good decisions. Philosophy demands reflective practice, inquiry into thought and action, and a holistic, systems perspective. Elias and Merriam observe that all philosophies incorporate political and social dimensions. They also note that few adult educators pay attention to educational philosophy and its implications:

> The educator is generally more interested in skills than in principles, in means than in ends, in details than in the whole picture. The philosophy of adult education does not equip a person with knowledge about *what* to teach, *how* to teach, or how to organize a program. It is more concerned with the *why* of education and with the logical analysis of the various elements of the educational process. (Elias and Merriam, 1995, 8; emphasis in original)

Elias and Merriam (1995) argue that understanding educational philosophy distinguishes professional educators from paraprofessionals and beginning teachers. True professionals not only know what to do, but why they do it. They seamlessly merge theory and practice and embody truly reflective practice.

Multiple perspectives have influenced the emerging human resource development (HRD) field, and learning is no exception. Although there is not agreement about the role of adult education and learning in HRD, learning is considered of great importance by HRD scholars. Ruona (1999, 2000) interviewed ten HRD scholars about their philosophy and perspectives on the field and found similarity among their views about learning. All scholars felt that learning was at the heart of HRD, a process that occurs at multiple levels and is a valued aim of the profession. The scholars in Ruona's study also classified HRD as a helping profession seeking betterment in the various organizational contexts in which HRD is practiced. She found a bias toward individual development, and learning and development. Notably, she reported a waning in the learning–performance debate that has characterized the field to date. She also found several areas of disagreement around whom HRD serves. Ruona concludes that serious dialogue about the philosophical frames of the HRD field is in order as the field continues to emerge.

Philosophical Frame of Adult Education

Elias (1982) recognizes that one of the most difficult problems addressed by philosophers is the relationship between philosophy and action, or between theory and practice. He traces the history of theory and practice and the often tenuous relationship between the two. He offers a description of four elements present in the theory–practice relationship: explanation, criticism, direction, and imagination. Explanation happens through a theory or philosophy explaining a practice. Educational theories aim to explain the ends and objectives of practice, and also inform activities that are appropriate to educational goals. Practice, on the other hand, helps to improve the understanding of theories and provides concrete examples for explaining them. Theories also criticize practice. They test practice based on established criteria and question the goals and rationale of various educational programs. Educational assumptions are questioned. Through practice, theory can also be criticized. Often theory is insufficient for explaining reality or for offering adequate answers. Theories also serve the vital role of directing action, and may function to establish practice guidelines. Practice is also directive in that it raises questions and issues for both theorists and researchers to pursue. Practice may reveal inconsistencies that need to be answered through research and theory development. Imagination, the fourth element of the theory–practice relationship, is a more creative, intuitive way of considering this dichotomy. Theory is often created through imagining an explanation for phenomena. This can lead to idealistic theories that do not work well in practice, but it can also lead to theoretical breakthroughs and radical reorganizing of reality. Just as theory imagines practice, so too does practice imagine theory, often to the chagrin of theorists. This may occur through the generation of new ideas as educators seek practical solutions.

A key process in bridging the theory-to-practice gap is to understand the *why* in our practice. Philosophy offers an opportunity to reflect on the why. Why should we care about philosophy? Merriam and Brockett (1997) offer several reasons. First, developing awareness of underlying values and assumptions provides guidelines for making decisions and creating policy. It is important to recognize the connection between assumptions and values and their impact on curriculum and instruction. Understanding individual philosophy also helps one to communicate it more effectively in interpersonal relationships. Articulating a philosophical standing allows educators to contribute to the field through raising questions about ethics and practices. It separates professionals from paraprofessionals. Finally, a philosophical stance functions to bridge theory and practice.

Philosophical frameworks of adult education have been proposed by Apps (1973), Beder (1989), and Elias and Merriam (1995). This chapter will rely on the Elias and Merriam framework to provide an overview of the various philosophical perspectives. Educators interested in assessing their individual philosophy should refer to Zinn's (1983, 1991) PAEI, Philosophy of Adult Education Inventory. Five philosophies of adult education will be shared and introduced in the chronological order of their emergence. These philosophies include liberalism, progressivism, behaviorism, humanism, and radical adult education. The philosophies are summarized in Figure 2.1.

Liberal Adult Education

Liberal education is rooted in classical Greek philosophy (i.e., Socrates, Plato, Aristotle). It is the oldest and most enduring educational philosophy in the Western world, and is also known as classical humanism, perennialism, rational humanism, and general education (Elias and Merriam, 1995). Liberal education values a highly cultivated intellect and views learning as a leisure activity. Merriam (1995) describes it as aiming to produce a complete human being and contrasts it with vocational or technical education, which aims at earning a living or making money. Livingstone (1995, 3) argues that the aim of liberal education is "the making of men; and clearly it is different from a technical education which simply enables us to earn our bread, but does not make us complete human beings." In Aristotle's words, "in education it makes all the difference *why* a man does or learns anything; if he studies it for the

FIGURE 2.1   Five Philosophical Frameworks of Adult Education

	Liberal (Arts) Adult Education	Progressive Adult Education	Behaviorist Adult Education	Humanistic Adult Education	Radical Adult Education
Purpose(s)	To develop intellectual powers of the mind To make a person literate in the broadest sense—intellectually, morally, spiritually, aesthetically	To promote societal well being: enhance individual effectiveness in society; to give learners practical knowledge and problem-solving skills	To promote skill development and behavioral change and ensure compliance with standards and societal expectations.	To enhance personal growth and development; to facilitate self-actualization	To bring about fundamental social, political and economic changes in society through education
Learner(s)	"Renaissance person" cultured always learning, seeking knowledge, and developing conceptual and theoretical understanding	Learner needs, interests, and experiences are key elements in learning People have unlimited potential to be developed through education	Learner takes an active role in learning. Learners practice new behavior and feedback Learners significantly influenced by environment	Learner is highly motivated and self-directed Learner assumes responsibility for learning	Equality with teacher in learning process Personal autonomy Create history and culture through collective reflection and action
Teacher	The "expert" transmitter of knowledge Authoritative Clearly directs learning process	Organizer Guides learning through experiences that are educative Stimulates, instigates and evaluates learning process	Manager Controller Predicts and directs learning outcomes	Facilitator Helper Partner Promotes learning but does not direct it	Coordinator Suggests but does not determine learning direction Equality between teacher and learner
Concepts/ Key Words	Liberal arts Learning for the sake of learning Rational, intellectual education General, comprehensive education Traditional knowledge Classical humanism	Problem-solving Experience-based education Democratic ideals Lifelong learning Pragmatic knowledge Needs assessment Social responsibility	Competency-based Mastery learning Standards-based Behavioral objectives Trial and error Stimulus—Response Feedback Reinforcement	Experiential learning Freedom Individuality Self-directedness Interactive Openness Authenticity Self-actualization Empowerment Feelings	Consciousness-raising Praxis Noncompulsory learning Autonomy Social action Empowerment "Deschooling; Social transformation
Methods	Lecture Dialectic Study groups Contemplation Critical reading Discussion	Problem-solving Scientific method Activity curriculum Integrated curriculum Experimental method Project method Cooperative learning	Programmed instruction Learning contracts Criterion-referenced testing Computer-aided instruction Skill training	Experiential learning; group tasks; group discussion; team teaching; self-directed learning; individualized learning; discovery method	Dialogue Problem-posing Critical reflection Maximum interaction Discussion groups Exposure to media and people in real life situations

(continues)

(continued)

	Liberal (Arts) Adult Education	Progressive Adult Education	Behaviorist Adult Education	Humanistic Adult Education	Radical Adult Education
People	Socrates Aristotle Plato Alder Rousseau Piaget Houle	Spencer Dewey Bergevin Brameld Sheats Lindeman Benne Blakely	Watson Skinner Thorndike Tyler	Rogers Maslow Knowles Tough McKenzie	Holt Kozol Freire Illich Shor Ohlinger Perelman
Educational Practices	Great Books Society Paideia Proposal Center for the Study of Liberal Education Elderhostel Chautauqua	ABE ESL Citizenship education Community schools Cooperative extension University without walls	APL Vocational training Teacher certification Military Religious indoctrination	Encounter groups Group dynamics Self-directed learning projects Human relations training Esalen Institute	Freedom Schools Freire's literacy training Free schools Social action theater
HRD Applications	Education Assistance HBR Classics	Experiential learning Situated Cognition Vocational education Employee involvement Quality Circles	Management by Objectives Human Performance Technology WBT ISD Vocational Training	Learning organizations Dialogue Action Learning Career Development	Diversity Initiatives Networks (women's, gay/lesbian) Action Learning Technologies Multicultural Program Antiracist Initiatives

SOURCE: Adapted from Lorraine M. Zinn, *The Philosophy of Adult Education Inventory (PAEI)*© (1999).

sake of his own development or with a view to excellence, it is liberal" (Livingstone, 1995, 4).

Merriam and Brockett (1997) characterize liberal education as valuing the acquisition of knowledge, developing a rational perspective, and enhancing the ability to analyze critically. Liberal education is concerned with "What is the good life and how are we to attain it?" (Elias and Merriam, 1995, 25). Classical influences are visible in liberal education philosophy through Socratic methods of questioning assumptions and knowing the truth, Plato's quest to promote learning as an individual's radical encounter with a truth outside himself, and Aristotle's view of education as a formation of habits and development of practical and theoretical wisdom.

Elias and Merriam (1995) conclude that the educated person in the liberal perspective possesses the four components of a liberal education, a rational or intellectual education that involves wisdom, moral values, a spiritual or religious dimension, and an aesthetic sense. They suggest that a liberal education is rational and intellectual. Its goal is to convert information into knowledge, and knowledge into wisdom. Information is a collection of facts, but having information does not make one educated. Knowledge is a synthesis of facts or a grasp of information that one is able to communicate to others. Wisdom is a truly educated state and comes in two forms: practical and theoretical. Practical wisdom is the ability to apply information and knowledge to daily life. Theoretical wisdom is the ability to consider the deepest principles of a subject matter and reorganize their connection and relationship to other areas. There is tension between practical and theoretical wisdom, evident in the present-day gulf between theory and practice in many fields.

Liberal education has been criticized as being elitist. Traditionally, liberal education was pursued by the upper class as a means of becoming cultured. Lower classes were not viewed as needing liberal education to carry out their service roles to the higher class. Learning for work is not a concern of liberalists. Rather, they are concerned with learning for life. This is why liberalists tend to react with a high degree of negativity toward vocational education.

Liberal Applications.   Liberal education is content driven and views philosophy, religion, and humanities as superior to the sciences. Technical and scientific values are criticized in this tradition. The scope of liberal education is broad, valuing the conceptual and theoretical understanding of information. It goes beyond memorization and transmission. Dialogue is a valued tool through which concepts and meanings are clarified. Intuition and contemplation are also valued. Elias and Merriam (1995, 33) summarize Fredenberg's functions of liberal education for adults:

1. Teach persons the value of freedom and help them become competent to use it.
2. Help learners to respond appropriately to the difference between the objective and the subjective; between the events in which they participated in and their feelings about them.
3. Increasing the range of human experience to which one could respond.

Contemporary examples of liberal education would be a traditional liberal arts college program, the Elderhostel model of learning, the great books program, some organizational educational assistance programs, and organizational philosophy drawing on classical theory (see, for instance, *Harvard Business Review's* classic article series). Hirsch's 1988 book *Cultural Literacy: What Every American Needs to Know* offers an attempt to illustrate the content that a liberal education should have. Bloom's *The Closing of the American Mind* (1987) discusses the failures of American universities to uphold traditional liberal education and speculates that this would result in an erosion of justice, human rights, and other civil liberties.

Zinn (1983) describes the learner in liberal education as a "Renaissance Person" who is cultured, continually learning, and seeking conceptual and theoretical understandings of knowledge. The learner in this tradition is passive, relying on the expertise of the educator to transmit his or her knowledge to the learner. The learner would pursue an understanding of the classics and not necessarily seek learning that would be useful for work or practical matters.

Liberal education is highly teacher-centered, viewing the teacher as a subject matter expert who must impart her knowledge and wisdom to students. Experiential learning or learning through discovery is not favored in this tradition. Lecture is the preferred instructional method, and teachers are expected to be scholars. Teachers would have little concern with creating learning-centered teaching or environments. Rather, they would focus on themselves and the content.

Contributions of Liberal Philosophy. Merriam and Brockett (1997) suggest that adult liberal education has been overshadowed by other philosophical traditions that are more congruous with contemporary concerns. Today's liberal educators regard behaviorists as suspect in their attempts at behavior change through behavior modification and learning reinforcement. Liberal influences in adult education are being undermined by the movement toward career and vocational education, and a strong behaviorist orientation of contemporary education theory and practice. Although vocational education is disregarded by liberalists, the liberal philosophy has progressed to bring knowledge of liberal learning to working women and men and eventually developed into university and college extension programs.

Progressive Education

Rooted in progressive movements in politics, social change, and education, progressive education is concerned with the relationships between education and society, experiential learning, vocational education, and democratic education. Progressivism's impact on adult education philosophy and practice has been more influential than any other school of thought. Adult education's growth paralleled a movement toward progressive education in the United States. Adult education theorists who espouse progressive principles include Knowles, Rogers, Houle, Tyler, Lindeman, Bergevin, and Freire. Progressive adult education takes many forms, including adult vocational education, extension education, citizenship education, family education, and education for social movements. Basic principles of adult education were derived from progressivism, such as learner needs and interests, the centrality of experience to learning, pragmatic and utilitarian goals, and a commitment to social responsibility in education.

Progressive education's origins can be traced to rationalist, empirical, and scientific thought that emerged in Europe and became prevalent in the United States. Industrialization brought an increasing faith in education for solving social, political, and economic problems (Elias and Merriam, 1995; Perkinson, 1977). Progressive education is responsible for the addition of vocational education to the traditional liberal arts curriculum. Elias and Merriam (1995, 47) note, "the highest ideal of the progressive movement was education for democracy, defined by Dewey as people engaged in joining activity to solve their common problems." John Dewey is regarded as the father of progressive thought in education and his writings, particularly *Democracy and Education* (1916), are seminal works. Democratic values characterize the philosophy of progressivism. In a departure from the liberal education viewpoint, Dewey argued "an occupation is a continuous activity having a purpose. Education through occupations consequently combines within itself more of the factors conducive to learning than any other method" (1916, 308). Lindeman (1961) describes assumptions of his progressive view of adult education as (1) inclusive of all aspects of life; (2) putting meaning into the whole of life; (3) approached through real-life situations, not subjects; and (4) using the learner's experience as learning resources (Merriam, 1995).

Progressive education does not view the individual in isolation. Rather, it is concerned with creating educated individuals who help improve society. Bergevin (1995, 38) describes it this way: "An individual cannot really become a person outside the social order."

Progressive Applications.   The impact of progressive philosophy is visible in most adult learning programs. Merriam and Brockett (1997, 35) outline three dimensions of pragmatism that appealed to educators:

• The acceptance of empirical rationality for understanding and solving social problems.
• The reliance on experience rather than authority for one's source of knowledge.
• The allowance of social action and social reform as a legitimate concern of politicians, educators, and philosophers.

The basic operational principles of adult progressive education include:

1. A Broadened View of Education. Education is not viewed solely as formal schooling, but includes all informal and incidental learning in society that involves teaching values, attitudes, knowledge, and skills. Education in this sense is viewed as *lifelong* and incorporating a practical, pragmatic, and utilitarian curriculum that values experience and the interaction of the individual with the environment as core teaching methods.
2. A New Focal Point in Education. Progressive education shifted its focus away from the teacher to the learner. This new view of the learner as central corresponded with a shift in the view of the human person. Progressives view humans as neither good nor bad, but rather born with unlimited potential to develop and grow. Growth is a lifelong process.
3. A New Educational Methodology. Elias and Merriam observe, "How we teach is intimately related to why we teach and what we teach. Progressives saw value in learning the methods that have been used by others, but they laid more stress on the individual teacher developing his or her own method of teaching suitable for the group being taught" (Elias and Merriam, 1995, 59). Progressive educators applied scientific methods to discovering knowledge through problemsolving, project, or activity methods.

4. A Change Relationship Between Teachers and Learners. Progressives believe that learners engage in learning for themselves and the role of teachers is essentially to facilitate this process. Progressive educators are responsible for organizing, stimulating, instigating, and evaluating the complex education process. Knowles's contribution in popularizing the concept of andragogy falls under progressive education.

5. Education as an Instrument of Social Change. Elias and Merriam argue, "Progressives believed that the function of education was not merely to prepare learners for fitting into the existing society, but also to provide a means for changing society. . . . education was to foster creativity and stability as well as individuality and social consciousness" (Elias and Merriam, 1995, 66). This social action component inspired Myles Horton's Highlander Folk School in Tennessee. Elias and Merriam describe the progressive ideal in social action: "Education for social change, but always respecting the freedom of individuals to be true to their own convictions and commitments" (Elias and Merriam, 1995, 59–68).

Learners in this progressive philosophical framework are active participants and their needs, interests, and experiences drive the learning process. Learners are viewed as having unlimited potential to be developed through education.

Progressive educators organize and guide learning through experiences that are educative, stimulating, and investigative. Educators both instigate and evaluate the learning process. Educators in the progressive framework cater to the needs of the learner, perhaps even at the expense of themselves. The progressive adult educator is a facilitator of a learning process that is practical and invigorating and that helps learners develop problemsolving and practical skills. They also actively seek learner feedback and input to the learning process.

Contributions of Progressive Philosophy. Progressive education is responsible for education reform and it has significantly shaped adult education methods. The shortfall of progressivism has been to place too much faith in education to accomplish social change and being too optimistic in the impact and outcomes. Elias and Merriam (1995) believe that few adult educators have adopted the social drive of progressivism and that few education philosophers would align solely with this movement. Progressivism's impact has been through its learner-centeredness approach and methods. Socially conscious, activist adult education was embraced by radical educators such as Paulo Freire.

Elias and Merriam (1995) suggest that humanistic, radical, and behavioristic adult education are to some extent dependent on progressive education for their fundamental beliefs. Humanism adopted learner-centeredness, radicalism embraced social change, and behavioralism emphasized experimental and scientific dimensions of education. Examples of progressive education include Americanization, community education, employee involvement, and quality circles.

Behaviorist Philosophy

Behaviorist educational philosophy is grounded in behavioral psychology influenced by Thorndike, Pavlov, Watson, and Skinner. Behaviorism is concerned with control, behavior modification, and learning through reinforcement. Modern-day organizational practices such as total quality management, on-the-job training, management by objectives, and human performance technology have roots in behaviorism.

John B. Watson is regarded as the father of behaviorism. Behaviorism addresses overt, observable behaviors of organisms, and behaviorist researchers study both animal and human behavior in laboratory settings by applying the scientific method. Feelings, intelligence, and emotions are not regarded as observable or measurable and are not investigated in behaviorism. Behaviorists believe that all human behavior is caused by prior conditioning that is influenced by the environment. Humans are viewed as having little or no control over environmental factors that influence behavior. Thus, creating an optimal environment for learning is a major focus of behaviorists.

Elias and Merriam (1995) trace antecedents of behaviorism to three philosophical traditions. The first is *materialism*, the theory that reality is explainable by laws of matter and motion; materialism rejects spiritual and intellectual explanations of observed reality. *Scientific realism and empiricism* is the second tradition and was introduced into Western thought by Francis Bacon. This inductive method examines information through the senses only. The third tradition is *positivism*, traceable to Auguste Comte and his belief that knowledge is not derived through theology or traditional philosophy, but through scientific observation and measurements of facts. Thorndike made significant contributions to behavioristic educational philosophy through his description of learning as a process of association. He is credited with the stimulus–response theory based on the notion that organisms, when presented with a stimulus, form a connection or response with it. Skinner established contemporary behaviorist philosophy and believed that "To develop a better world, the environmental forces that control behavior need to be identified" (Merriam, 1995, 57). Skinner did not believe that changing human nature itself offered leverage in facilitating behavioral change. Elias and Merriam describe his view of psychology's purposes as "to understand, predict and control human behavior" (1995, 85). Thus the job of the behaviorist educator is to define the desired behavior and produce people who behave in those ways.

Behaviorist Applications. Behaviorism in education manifests in several ways. Behaviorists are interested in inculcating values that mirror those of society. There is a deemphasis on individualism and competition and an emphasis on cooperation and interdependence. Behaviorists attend to the environment and strive to control behavior through positive reinforcement (versus negative). Education has been significantly influenced by the use of behavioral learning objectives. Learning in behaviorism is defined as a change in behavior. Objectives in this sense tend to specify the conditions or stimuli under which students are expected to perform, identify the desired behavior, and establish the criteria for judging the resulting behavior. Behaviorism has had its chief influence in adult education in the areas of program planning and curriculum design (Elias and Merriam, 1995). Tyler's (1949) program development model has been highly influential in the development of other program development models derived by Houle (1972) and Knowles (1970). Learning definitions generally incorporate concepts of behavioral change and experience. The underlying assumptions of behaviorism are (Merriam and Caffarella, 1999):

- Observable behavior rather than internal thought processes is the focus of study.
- The environment shapes behavior (what one learns is determined by the environmental elements, not by the individual learner).
- The principles of contiguity (how close in time two events must be for a bond to be formed) and reinforcement (any means of increasing the likelihood that an event will be repeated) are central to explaining the learning process.

Merriam and Caffarella (1999) cite several educational practices that can be traced to behaviorism, such as instructional design, behavioral objectives, instructor accountability, programmed instruction, and competency-based education. Vocational training and technical and skills training would fall under the auspices of behaviorism. Today's performance-based HRD also has deep ties with behaviorist theory and practice. Elias and Merriam (1995) identify several instructional methods that have been influenced by behaviorism: competency-based education, criterion-referenced instruction, programmed instruction, teaching machines, contract learning, Personalized System of Instruction (PSI), Individually Guided Education (IGE), and Individually Prescribed Instruction (IPI). Regardless of the method, responsibility for learning lies with the learner.

Learners, as in progressivism, take an active role in learning that is organized from a behaviorist philosophy. Learners are encouraged to learn and adopt behaviors, skills, and competencies. They receive ongoing feedback about their performance of the desired behaviors within specific environments.

The role of the teacher in behaviorism is to foster behavior that promotes the survival and success of both individuals and society. Teachers are responsible for eliciting desired behavior and minimizing undesirable behavior. Behaviorist educators involve learners in the mastery of behaviors by planning, managing, organizing, and controlling the learning process.

Contributions of Behaviorist Philosophy.   Elias and Merriam (1995) conclude that there is no adult educator or program that is exclusively behavioral, but that the influence of this philosophy is readily apparent in the programs, policies, and practices of adult education. Behavioral learning objectives are very common. They note:

> Regardless of the extent to which one concurs with Skinner's underlying philosophical assumptions or plans for restructuring society, one can make use of the techniques and principles of behavior proposed by this school of psychology. Behaviorism has, in fact, had a significant impact upon various facets of our society. (Elias and Merriam, 1995, 86)

Humanistic Adult Education

Humanistic adult education is grounded in existential philosophy and humanistic psychology that value freedom and autonomy, active cooperation and participation, and self-directed learning (Elias and Merriam, 1995). Humanistic educational practices include: learner-centered training, group dynamics, team building, group processes, sensitivity training, encounter groups, and self-directed learning. The goal of humanistic education is:

The development of persons—persons who are open to change and continued learning, persons who strive for self-actualization, and persons who can live together as fully-functioning individuals. As such, the whole focus of humanistic education is upon the individual learner rather than a body of information. That is not to say that humanistic education lacks substance. It is the approach to material and person within the educative process that is emphasized. (Elias and Merriam, 1995, 122)

Humanism can be traced to classical China, Greece, and Rome expressed through religion, education, and psychology and to the philosophy of Aristotle and Plato. Humanists value the freedom and dignity of the individual and, unlike behaviorists, emphasize the affective and emotional aspects of personality. Humanists also value what is not seen, rather than seeking only observable behavior as a measure of learning on which behaviorists rely. Modern humanism emerged as a protest to industrialism and the advancement of science and the behavioristic philosophies associated with these phenomena.

Because humanists are influenced by humanistic psychology, they are interested in the human potential for growth. They focus on both affective and cognitive learning and trace influences to Freud's theories of psychoanalysis. Humanists depart from Freud and behaviorists by rejecting the notion that human nature is predetermined by either the environment or the subconscious. Instead they regard humans as inherently good and in control of their own destiny. Humanism's impact on adult education is most evident through the practices of self-directed learning and experiential learning. Psychologists Abraham Maslow and Carl Rogers have had the greatest influence on humanistic practices in adult education, and Knowles' theory of andragogy is grounded in humanistic psychology.

Elias and Merriam (1995), quoting Patterson, review two major principles influencing humanism from earlier educators, including developing human potential and promoting a good relationship between the teacher and student. They outline the differences between behaviorism and humanism according to Wandersman (1976). These include: scientific versus intuitive; means versus ends; external behavior versus internal emotion; behavior change versus insight; and manipulation versus humanization. Humanism's basic assumptions include:

1. Human Nature Is Naturally Good. Humanists believe in the inherent goodness of humans and the potential for humans to become highly developed individuals and citizens if given the opportunity through nurturing environments and the freedom to develop.

2. Freedom and Autonomy. Humanists believe humans are truly free creatures who make choices that are not subject to external forces or internal urges.
3. Individuality and Potentiality. The uniqueness of each person is acknowledged and valued.
4. Self-Concept and the Self. The self is the sum total of attributes making an individual unique, such as attitudes, body, values, feelings, intellect, and emotions. The self-concept is a person's subjective evaluation of who she or he is. It influences behavior and the ability to develop.
5. Self-Actualization. Maslow (1954) popularized the term self-actualization, meaning a lifelong quest for personal growth and the fulfillment of human potential.
6. Perception. Behavior is a result of the selective perception of the individual. Seemingly objective stimuli can be interpreted differently by individuals. This principle is central to the philosophy of phenomenology and the idea that perception is reality. For humanists, perception explains behavior and behavior can only be understood through and in engagement with the individual's perceptions and world.
7. Responsibility and Humanity. Although humanism has a strong emphasis on the individual, there is also a strong sense of responsibility to humanity. Humans are expected to self-actualize for the benefit of society. (Elias and Merriam, 1995)

Rogers's model of client-centered therapy has been extremely influential in adult education. He argued that teaching was overrated and advocated that the goal of education and role of the educator are to facilitate learning. His influence is seen in the shift toward a personal, reciprocal relationship between the teacher and learner.

Humanism Applied.   Self-development is not viewed in isolation from others in humanistic education. Learners create knowledge through cooperative interaction with groups in a supportive setting. Methods such as discussion, small group projects, and use of committees and teams are common humanistic teaching strategies.

Humanistic education has several components, including student-centeredness and teachers as facilitators of learning (not the sage on the stage, but rather the guide on the side). Humanism values the act of learning as a unique personal undertaking. The humanistic curriculum strives to develop self-actualizing persons. Elias and Merriam argue that, "Teaching a curriculum, then, is not the goal of humanistic educators. The curriculum functions as a vehicle which, if creatively employed, can promote the real goal of humanistic education—the development of self-actualizing individuals" (1995, 128). Humanistic philosophy has been highly espoused by Malcolm Knowles and his andragogy framework to describe adult education. The model is grounded in self-concept, self-direction, and learner autonomy.

Humanism is popular owing to its similarity with democratic values and its voluntary nature. It is evident in HRD practices in many forms. The decade-long trend of learning organizations is grounded in a humanistic philosophy that values the individual and seeks to foster both self and collective learning. Several scholars have offered models of the learning organization (Dixon, 1994; Watkins and Marsick, 1993; Pedler, Burgoyne, and Boydell, 1991; Senge, 1990). Action learning models also have a strong humanistic base (Revans, 1983). The tool of dialogue is another process that traces its roots to sensitivity training and the process of affective disclosure and sharing.

Contributions of Humanism. Humanism has had more impact than behaviorism on education in the United States during the mid-twentieth century (Elias and Merriam, 1995). It has shifted away from the control orientation of behaviorism to create an approach to learning that is learner-centered and learner-controlled, and it has redefined the role of the instructor. Humanism also strives to help humans reach their ultimate potential through self-actualization.

Radical Adult Education

Radical adult education is rooted in radical movements over the last three hundred years: anarchism, Marxism, socialism, and left-wing Freudianism (Elias and Merriam, 1995). The Anarchist tradition includes contemporary educators Paul Goodman, Ivan Illich, and John Ohlinger. The goal of anarchism is to preserve personal autonomy to the degree possible: "The heart of education according to the anarchist is the development of individuals able to choose, free of dogmas and prejudices, their own goals and purposes" (Elias and Merriam, 1995, 141). The tradition considers this goal impossible to achieve within government-sponsored education systems. The Marxist–Socialist tradition seeks education that produces free and autonomous individuals through revolutionary social changes that shift society away from capitalist forms to socialist forms of government. The Freudian Left advocates that many individuals are prevented from acting in their own self-interest because of imposed authority structures traceable to stages of early child development. Solutions in this tradition include sexual freedom, changes in family organization, and libertarian methods of child rearing and education.

Radical Applications.   The goal of radical education is radical social change. Educational efforts focus on the forging of social, political, and economic change through learning and social action. The work of Paulo Freire and his push for radical conscientization to raise the awareness of the oppressed is one example. Radical education falls outside conventional educational philosophy because it does not accept that meaningful change can occur within existing social structures. Rather, society must be radically restructured to foster true change. Progressives and humanists seek educational solutions to social reform. Radicals seek profound social changes.

Paulo Freire is the most famous and celebrated radical educator. Elias and Merriam (1995, 147–148) suggest that "Many important elements in Freire's general and educational philosophy are indicated with these words: vision of man and world, dialogue praxis, teacher–learner relationship, analysis, the liberation of man, and the Marxist concept of denouncing and announcing world views and consciousness." Freire believed that the opposite of humanization was oppression, that social change could be facilitated through praxis, or action with reflection, and that there was a relationship between levels of individual consciousness and social organization. Through a process of conscientization, the oppressed become aware of their oppression and learn strategies for challenging it. Freire viewed conscientization as a social activity engaged through dialogue with others on experiences of reality. Critics charge Freire with being too idealistic, and not addressing the internal struggle that may accompany conscientization.

Freire was highly critical of traditional education and coined the term "banking education" to represent the passive transfer or depositing of knowledge from teacher to student that was devoid of critical assessment. He believed that banking education robs the learner of autonomy and imposes a hidden curriculum, and suppresses the consciousness of students.

Freire offered an alternative to the traditional banking method of education through libertarian, dialogic, and problem-posing education. He viewed education as political action.

Those truly committed to liberation must reject the banking concept in its entirety, adopting instead a concept of men as conscious beings, and consciousness as consciousness intent upon the world. They must abandon the educational goal of deposit-making and replace it with the posing of the problems of men in their relations with the world. (Elias and Merriam, 1995, 143)

HRD applications of the radical philosophy may be found in some organizational diversity efforts, networks to support women and people of color, and the application of action learning technologies. The learner in this philosophy has equality with the teacher (and other learners) in the learning process. Personal autonomy is respected and learners are viewed as knowledge constructors. Learners create history and culture by combining reflection with action and through this process critically assess their context. The radical educator functions as a provocateur who suggests but does not determine the direction for learning. Equality between teacher and learner is highly valued and sought after.

Contributions of Radical Philosophy.   Elias and Merriam (1995) regard radical adult education as having little impact on the practice of adult education in the United States, and cite several reasons for adult educators' intolerance of it. First, adult education occurs within traditional institutions that have conservative values and social structures. Second, adult educators tend to be concerned with individual and personal change instead of structural change in society.

Radical adult education philosophy has provided a critical lens for assessing educational practices, yet this perspective is rarely embraced by HRD practitioners or scholars (Bierema and Cseh, 2000). The radical philosophy regularly raises questions about whose needs are being served by organizational programs and strives to eliminate structural inequality.

Contemporary Learning Frameworks

Although Radical Philosophy is not widely practiced, it provides key lessons in promoting organizational change, and is having an important influence on Learning Philosophy and Practice. Contemporary Frameworks have the potential to reshape the emerging field of HRD. This section illuminates contempory learning frameworks, including the importance of awareness of the learning environment, situated cognition, critical theory, and feminist pedagogy. Workplace educators are keenly aware of learners, but may be less cognizant of the environment or contextual impacts on learning. The learning environment might be the atmosphere among a few colleagues at training. It could be the customs of a work team, or the culture of an entire organization.

The learning environment is also affected by the larger social context within which it is situated. Caffarella and Merriam (2000) provide a framework for linking the individual learner and context. They suggest that such an integrated perspective enriches the learning experience and challenges educators and program planners to understand learners as individuals and be aware of the contextual dimensions affecting learners, instructors, and the instructional process.

The philosophical perspective that has contributed most significantly to the study of context is radicalism. The concepts of context and positionality, situated cognition, critical theory, and feminist pedagogy offer insights into deepening awareness and practice in educational environments.

Context and Positionality

Context is the social system that permeates the thinking and actions of all human beings within a particular social situation. Schools, organizations, communities, and nations have a context. Individuals act and learn through a process of interaction with the context. Positionality is how a person's race, class, and gender affects his or her experience within context. A person's success within a given context depends on her interaction with other individuals in the context. For instance, a woman of color may find that her efforts to advance in an organization are constantly thwarted by a culture that functions to promote and protect white men. White male participants in training may be given more attention by an instructor who calls on them more often, makes eye contact more frequently, and encourages their participation more regularly than the women.

Although contexts and experiences differ, they hold the potential for dramatically improving learning and even organizing our learning as described by Merriam and Caffarella:

> Adult learning in context has a structural dimension which acknowledges that our society has become highly multicultural and diverse and that political and economic conditions often shape the learning experience. It is no longer a question of whether in adult learning situations we need to address issues of race, class, gender, culture, ethnicity, and sexual orientation, but rather a question of how should we deal with these issues, both in terms of who presently constitutes the majority of learners, at least in formal adult learning activities, and who should be involved. We need to know the backgrounds and experiences of our learners, as individual learners, but also as members of socially and culturally constructed groups

such as women and men; poor, middle-class, and rich; and black, white, and brown. These socially constructed notions of who our learners are and who we are as educators and subsequent power dynamics should be given the same attention in teaching and learning, planning, and administrative functions of the technology of our practice. (Merriam and Caffarella, 1999, 196)

Adult life is usually situated in the context of work, family, and community. In addition to their daily roles, adults are lifelong learners in continual interaction with the context. Jarvis (1992, 11) explains, "Learning . . . is about the continuing process of making sense of everyday experience." He also observes that motivation for learning may not lie within the learner but within the dynamic tension existing between the learner and the sociocultural world.

Situated Cognition

Situated cognition holds promise for further explaining adult learning (Merriam and Brockett, 1997). In situated cognition, the context is preeminent and central to understanding adult learning. What we know and the meanings we attach to our knowledge are socially constructed. Wilson (1993) outlines three principles of situated cognition: learning and thinking are generally social activities; thinking and learning abilities are deeply influenced by the availability of situationally provided tools; and thinking is influenced by interaction with the context in which the learning occurs.

Consider an organization that is merging with another organization. How people learn and think about the merger are social activities and a significant amount of time will be spent in conversation about the changes around the water cooler or in meetings. The learning about the merger will be influenced by the availability of tools in the situation, such as information from management, news reports, rumors, and information from people at other organizations who have experienced similar situations. The learning that happens in the context of a merger is significantly different from the learning about a merger in the abstract, such as from a business textbook, since it happens within the situation and is laden with emotion, circumstance, and human interaction.

Critical Theory

Critical theory is based on the argument that true learning occurs only when people who have been marginalized in society based on positionality (race, gender, social class, sexual orientation, and so forth) are given a voice in the learning process. Popular education is characterized by a critical perspective, evident in the work of Myles Horton and Paulo Freire. Critical theory challenges adult educators to aid the creation of developmental, learner-centered, and emancipatory educational institutions concerned with individual development. Freire worked with the poor in Brazil to help them recognize that they lived in a system (or context) that was preventing them from moving out of poverty. Through awareness and then control over their learning, meaningful change was accomplished regarding this problem. The U.S. labor movement is another example of giving voice to a marginalized class. Through the efforts of the labor movement we now enjoy (and take for granted) things like a five-day workweek, paid vacation, health benefits, and pensions.

Feminist Pedagogy

Feminist pedagogy is derived from radicalism and a belief that adult educators have an ethical responsibility to create environments in which people can explore how context and positionality structure their lives and experiences. A full understanding of this interaction requires an exploration of structured power relations. This means helping learners see how race, class, and gender influence the degree of opportunity, power, or control they have in particular contexts (family, workplace, or personal life). Learning about structured power relations also involves exploring the unspoken rules about how individuals are supposed to act depending on their background with people of different status (Cunningham, 1988; Freire, 1971; Tisdell, 1993).

Feminist pedagogy shares critical theory's critical perspective and commitment to giving voice to the oppressed, but takes different forms. Tisdell (1993) identifies liberatory and gender models of feminist pedagogy. Liberatory models critique structural inequality and how the interlocking systems of race, class, and gender combine to oppress various groups in society. This model seeks structural changes in power relations for lasting change. Gender models deal with women's socialization on the personal and psychological levels, but lack a systemic analysis.

A poststructural pedagogy or a positional pedagogy (Tisdell, 1995, 75) examines how "various positionalities—the gender, race, class, sexual orientation—of both the participants and the instructor matter and have an effect on the learning environment." This perspective problematizes the power and authority of the teacher and considers the ramifications of redistributing this power. Tisdell focuses on connections between "the individual and the intersecting structural systems of privilege and oppression" and connections between "one's individual (constantly shifting) identity and social structures" (Tisdell, 1998, 146). Further, Tisdell describes how these connections might lead to change in an adult learning setting:

> As learners examine how social systems of privilege and oppression have affected their own identity, including their beliefs and values, the "discourse" is disrupted, thus shifting their identity, as well as increasing their capacity for agency. For example, if one has embraced societal prescriptions of particular gender roles (or race roles, or sexual roles that are exclusively heterosexual), and one becomes conscious of and examines the social construction of such roles, and identity is likely to shift, and one could develop new ways of acting in the world. One also begins to see that there are different "truths" and perhaps not one "Truth," and that social systems have allowed members of privileged groups to control what has counted as "knowledge" in determining the official curriculum through the politics of the knowledge production process. (Tisdell, 1998, 146)

Maher and Tetreault (1994) conducted research on feminist educators and identified the themes of mastery, voice, authority, and positionality as important for creating learning environments for diverse learners. Mastery is when learners interact with the content and each other in ways that facilitate the interpretation of meaning and construction of personal and collective understandings of the information being studied. The interpretation is participated in by all members of the learning group and all perspectives are respected. Voice is a feminist metaphor for women's awakenings. Helping learners find voice means creating a space where teachers and students can speak from their identities based on ethnicity, gender, race, religion, sexual orientation, and social class. It involves both the discovery and shaping of voice with the influence of multiple perspectives. Authority is an issue for both students and instructors. Teachers must decide how to give up authority to promote student responsibility for learning and facilitate the creation of knowledge. This forces the instructor to reconsider her definitions of "good" teaching. Knowledge is valid when it accounts for the knower's specific position in any context, one that is always defined by gender, race, class, and other socially significant dimensions. Position, more than any other factor, influences the construction of knowledge, and positional factors reflect relationships of power both within and outside the classroom itself. Educators working from a radical, feminist philosophy strive to integrate these principles into their work.

Contemporary Frameworks: The Bottom Line

The practice of radical HRD philosophy embracing a critical or feminist perspective is predictably rare, since analyzing structured power relations in the workplace would be viewed as threatening by management and shareholders. Lack of support for, or even suppression of, heightening awareness about this phenomenon, however, maintains and reinforces the traditional power relations that may serve to oppress people based on race, class, and gender. To function competently in HRD one must accurately identify organizational context and inherent political interests. It would also require workplace educators to reflect on their own positionality and consider how it influences themselves and other people. Learning environments affect people, and it is the responsibility of the workplace educator to ensure that all voices are heard and respected.

Learning Philosophy in HRD

The HRD field draws on multiple philosophies to inform both theory and practice. There is not agreement on a particular perspective in the field, and likely a blend of philosophical traditions will inform and shape HRD in the future. McLean's approach captures this multiplicity: "My philosophic approach to human resource development is to look for multiple rather than single answers to questions, affirming the importance of ambiguity and recognizing the multiplicity of theories, construction, missions, beliefs, values and ideals that exist within HRD" (2000, 39). Watkins's (2000) core beliefs about the field of HRD are driven by three foundational elements: (1) central to the field is the challenge of fostering learning and change in an organizational context; (2) practitioners of HRD are helping professionals; and (3) the structural location and configuration of HRD define its mission, role, and scope. Holton (2000) offers three views of learning. Learning as a humanistic endeavor aimed at helping humans reach their maximum potential and self-actualization. Learning as a value-neutral transmission of information that parallels Dewey's pragmatic approach to education as instrumental in solving problems. And, finally, Holton suggests that learning as a tool for societal oppression has been overlooked by HRD scholars. In this regard, he notes political and social movements that may brainwash the populace and silence voices of the minority and the oppressed.

Kuchinke (1999) proposes a system of classifying philosophical schools of thought in HRD based on the nature of the developmental activity involved:

	Person-Centered	Production-Centered	Principled Problem-Solving
Philosophical Roots	Humanistic: (Maslow, Rogers) Romantic Idealism (Rousseau) Existentialism	Behaviorism (Skinner) Libertarian (Smith, Friedman)	Cognitive-developmental: (Kohlberg) Pragmatism (Dewey, James) Radical Humanism Aktouf) Postmodernism: Kincheloe)
Aims of Human Development	To develop the self Allow "inner good" to unfold Remove barriers to maturation	Competently and efficiently fulfill organizational roles Increase performance as defined by organization	Integration and synthesis of internal and external demands Dynamic balance of competing claims Self-development through performance
Assumptions about Human Nature	Inborn wisdom and goodness Health equals happiness	Needs and wants determined by society or culture Health equals adjustment	Ability to integrate internal and external demands Experience is paramount Health equals adequate cognitive understanding
Assumptions about the Nature of Organizations	Person-oriented Optimal organizational functioning through happy people'	Goal oriented Goals determined by owners Human capital employed to achieve goals	Stakeholder oriented Temporary and dynamically changing configuration of needs and wants of various stakeholders
Examples	Hierarchy of needs Two-factor theory Spirituality Meaning of work Quality of worklife	Industrial training Performance technology	High involvement organizations Learning organization

FIGURE 2.2   Comparison of HRD Philosophy and Practice

person-centered, production-centered, or principled problemsolving. (See Figure 2.2.)

Responsible HRD practice demands that practitioners critically reflect on the philosophies underlying their thought and action. Yet, in practice, the most effective approach will be a philosophical blend. Cunningham describes how practitioners negotiate philosophy:

Philosophical systems are symbolic abstractions of relationships which are idealistically constructed on selected assumptions. Only philosophers can be purists. When philosophy systematically and consciously informs their practice, practitioners do not operate in a world which conforms to their assumptions. They compete with alternative philosophies and alternative practices. In the area of practice, the educator must negotiate philosophy. Choices are made as to what can be deleted or altered with the least damage to the intended outcomes. It is not problematic that inconsistencies occur when a thoughtfully conceived system of values is put into practice. What is worrisome is that continuing educators develop and operate programs without a clearly visualized set of values in which the adult learning and societal well-being are central concerns. (Cunningham, 1982, 85)

Conclusions

The practice of learning in any context is not a neutral act. Learning professionals have a professional and ethical responsibility to be reflective practitioners who consider the philosophical foundation of their practice. A philosophically grounded educator is distinctive and distinguishable from a paraprofessional, or someone who has no philosophical or theoretical framework for his or her practice.

This chapter has introduced five philosophical traditions that have had the most impact on adult education. Liberal education values education for the sake of education and pursues the classical literature and arts that make a person "cultured." Progressivism, in a departure from liberalism, introduced a pragmatism to education and placed a high premium on experiential learning. This philosophy is responsible for much of the innovation in teaching methods and the move toward becoming more learner-centered. Behaviorism is concerned with creating optimal learning environments and predicting and controlling learner behavior. This perspective views learning as a change in observable behavior and has had wide influence in the design of educational goals and instruction. Humanism values the good in every individual and is focused on the cognitive and affective aspects of learning. This tradition fosters a more equal relationship between the teacher and learner and gives a significant amount of control to the learner for planning and evaluating learning experiences. Humanism views the learner as having unlimited potential for growth and the role of the educator as facilitating this growth. Radicalism introduces an analysis of social context based on race, class gender, and other positionalities. This tradition expands our view of education from individual to societal matters and regards education as a means for restructuring society. The chapter concluded with a review of contemporary learning frameworks that promise to influence the philosophy and practice of learning. In Chapter 3, we will review common organizational learning practices and illuminate the philosophical underpinnings of these practices.

Practice of Organizational Learning

Laura L. Bierema

Workplace learning is traceable to the 1700s. Rooted in the industrial revolution, workplace learning has been shaped by social events such as World War II, the growth of behaviorism, the American Civil Rights movement, technology, and the emergence of global economies (American Society for Training and Development, 1994a, 1994b). It includes job-related instruction (training), strategies for improving performance (human performance technology), human resource development, and what learners do (West, 1996). The field of workplace learning "helped temper the inhumanity of mass production, . . . broker the marriage between business and the social sciences, . . . open a profession to women, . . . and permeate public debate on economic competitiveness and performance" (American Society for Training and Development, 1994, 5). Workplace learning is coming of age during a time when information is the currency of the new economy, attention has shifted from training to learning (American Society for Training and Development, 1994a, 1994b), and the field of human resource development is maturing. These advances provide evidence that organizations are making workplace learning and development a priority. Organizations are always seeking change and growth, yet change does not simply happen. Without learning there can be no change. Thus, learning is pivotal in the quest to seek organizational effectiveness for individuals, teams, and ultimately the organization itself.

Learning in the workplace is shifting from formalized, short-term instruction by an expert to informal, strategically focused learning facilitation by stakeholders and internal employees. This change parallels the just-in-time (JIT) manufacturing movement. This JIT learning is evident in the development of learning organizations and action learning teams across corporate

From Training		To Learning
Focus on short term	➡	Focus on lifelong learning/development
Skill based	➡	Core competency based
Driven by individual request	➡	Driven by corporate strategy
Concentrates on managers and executives	➡	Concentrates on all employees
Assessment done by HR and/or managers	➡	Assessment done by affected individuals
Training happens offsite	➡	Learning happens anyplace
Training is scheduled periodically	➡	Learning happens in real time
Training based on knowledge delivery	➡	Learning based on creating new meaning about sharing experiences in workplace
Instructor driven; designed by specialists	➡	Self-directed
Generalized, prescriptions	➡	Specific, trainees determine
Trainers deliver, trainer-centered	➡	Facilitated jointly, learner-centered

FIGURE 3.1   From Training to Learning (ASTD 1994)

America, England, and Australia. Figure 3.1 highlights these shifts. Learning is also becoming more closely linked with organization strategy. This trend is expected to continue and become even more important when the results of training are being measured.

Workplace learning is influenced by philosophy, theory, and, of course, practice. This chapter addresses practical approaches to workplace learning and illustrates how adult learning philosophy and theory promote the understanding of learners, develop awareness of learning environments, improve the design of educational programs, help facilitate learning, and create infrastructure for capturing and sharing learning.

Drawing on the previous chapter and framework of adult learning philosophy, this chapter explores learning practices in organizations and links them with relevant philosophical frameworks. The five philosophies addressed in the previous chapter were liberalism, progressivism, behaviorism, humanism, and radicalism. Few HRD practices fall neatly into the liberal framework other than the study of classical management literature or employee educational assistance programs. Nor are there any purely progressive HRD practices, although progressivism has had a momentous impact on the development of adult learning theory. Refer to Figure 3.1 for a summary of the practical applications of learning in the workplace.

Understanding Learners

Adult learning philosophy and theory have provided a foundation for understanding both the cognitive and emotional aspects of the learner. This section reviews how we understand learners according to development, memory and intelligence, andragogy, and diversity.

Development

As adults move through life, learning transpires with each transition. Psychological developmental theories help explain the learning process, and Merriam and Brockett (1997) distinguish phase and stage theories of development. Phase theories use the metaphor of seasons to represent the life cycle and suggest that learning and developmental tasks are associated with each stage. For instance, the phase of adolescence or early adulthood carries with it certain developmental tasks such as leaving home or becoming financially independent. Examples of a phase theory include Levinson's *The Seasons of a Man's Life* (Levinson and others, 1974) and Sheehy's *New Passages* (1995).

Stage theorists view development as moving through progressively higher and more complex forms, such as from immaturity to maturity or from simple to complex forms of life (Cross, 1981). Movement through stages is not chronologically linked to the life cycle and development through them may occur at different paces depending on the individual. For instance, the ability to think critically is not necessarily associated with a particular chronological age or life phase, but is a developmentally higher stage than a learner who accepts everything at face value without questioning it.

Developmental perspectives can provide insight to adult educators by illuminating how life circumstances trigger the motivation to learn. "Recognizing that participation in adult education is often a response to a developmental change or crisis, educators are in a position to understand the learner from a holistic perspective" (Merriam and Brockett, 1997, 145). Triggers of learning might be a personal crisis such as divorce or disease; it could be a life change such as becoming a parent or moving to a new city. A developmental change in an organizational context could be a shift in strategy, a reorganization, or a merger. All of these triggers act as learning catalysts.

Clark and Caffarella (1999) point out that adult development is a twentieth-century phenomenon that continues to evolve. They recognize the difficulty in defining adult development and explore biological, psychological, sociocultural, and integrative perspectives in explaining development. Drawing from a variety of developmental theorists, Clarke and Caffarella consider that development involves sustainable change over time that creates irreversible and novel results. Development also involves increasingly higher, more integrated levels of functioning. Biological development is concerned with adults as physical beings who change physiologically through natural aging, environmental conditions, health habits, accidents, or diseases. Psychological development is concerned with internal developmental processes. Several developmental concepts are derived from psychology, including ego development, cognitive and intellectual development, sequential development, life events and transitions, and relational development. Sociocultural development considers the developmental aspects of social roles (parent, spouse, partner, worker, and friend) and the timing of roles in social life. Social aspects of positionality (race, gender, social class, ethnicity, sexual orientation) are also receiving more attention in their significance to adult development. The integrative perspective views adult development as too complex and multifaceted to be understood from just one frame, and examines the intersections between biological, psychological, and sociocultural development to understand adult development.

Memory and Intelligence

In the early twentieth century, intelligence was believed to decline with age. Today, controversy continues over whether intelligence declines with age, remains stable, or remains stable and increases (in some areas) (Merriam and Brockett, 1997). The rise of emotional intelligence (Goleman, 1995) has underscored an important idea regarding intelligence: That there is more than one kind. Memory is viewed as the acquisition of knowledge, the storage and retention of knowledge, and the retrieval or recall of knowledge.

Andragogy

Although there is no single theory of adult education, andragogy has had a major impact in the development and practice of it. Merriam and Brockett (1997) suggest that the term andragogy "belongs" to adult education, although they trace its origins to Europe as far back as 1833 and date the first U.S. use to 1927. The term gained popularity through the work of Malcolm Knowles in the late 1960s and early 1970s. Andragogy is a series of humanistic principles about instructing adult learners based on the premise that pedagogy (principles for educating children) is not sufficient for adults. Knowles (1986) describes andragogy as a theory, yet today it is more commonly regarded as a set of assumptions and techniques that support the adult learning process (Darkenwald and Merriam, 1982). The assumptions underlying andragogy include:

1. "*The need to know*. Adults need to know why they need to learn something before undertaking to learn it."
2. "*The learners' self-concept*. Adults have a self-concept of being responsible for their own decisions, for their own lives. Once they

have arrived at that self-concept they develop a deep psychological need to be seen by others and treated by others as being capable of self-direction."

3. *"The role of the learners' experience.* Adults come into an educational activity with both a greater volume and a different quality of experience from youths." This accounts for a wide range of individual differences among adult learners, the need to use experiential techniques in the learning process, and is more of a challenge when the learning involves new thinking and change. Finally, adult identity is linked with being valued and respected in the learning process.

4. *"Readiness to learn.* Adults become ready to learn those things that they need to know and be able to do in order to cope effectively with their real-life situations." An especially rich source of "readiness to learn" is the developmental tasks associated with moving form one developmental stage to the next.

5. *"Orientation to learning.* In contrast to children's and youth's subject-centered orientation to learning (at least in school), adults are life centered (or task-centered or problem-centered) in their orientation to learning."

6. *"Motivation.* While adults are responsive to some external motivators (better jobs, promotions, higher salaries, and the like), the most potent motivators are internal pressures (the desire for increased job satisfaction, self-esteem, quality of life, and the like." (Knowles, 1990, 57–63)

Pratt (1993) credits andragogy with making a significant contribution to adult education, but argues that its wide and noncritical acceptance is cause for concern. He suggests that andragogy has not advanced our understanding of the learning process. He does not regard it as either a theory or a unifying concept. Andragogy has also been criticized because of its focus on individual learning and lack of group or social analysis.

Diversity

Understanding learners is grounded in respecting their diversity and designing instruction that meets their varied needs. Sensitivity to the diversity of learners means that consideration is made for age, disability, and learning styles. Workplace educators must also be sensitive to groups based on race, gender, and social class. The dynamics of these social positions was discussed in the contemporary frameworks section of Chapter 2. Embracing diversity in workplace learning is a learner-centered approach grounded in humanism. Unfortunately, many educational experiences are designed with disregard for the adult learner, as when content-expert trainers sweep into a training session, dispense their infinite wisdom to the neophyte participants, and depart. Such instructor-centered training tends to both disregard the experience and knowledge that adult learners bring to the session and slight the diverse learning needs of adults. Learning professionals, whether designing or evaluating training, should be aware of adult learner needs and invest only in educational experiences that cater to adult learners. This is of vital importance, as it is estimated that as much as 80 percent of training does not transfer from the training environment to the workplace (Broad and Newstrom, 1992). Robinson (1994) summarizes various philosophical frameworks that focus on the purposes for adult learning:

- Personal growth and development
- Personal and social improvement
- Organizational effectiveness
- Cultivation of the intellect
- Social transformation.

Although most businesses may be interested in workplace learning only for its contribution to organizational effectiveness, they fail to realize that employees learn constantly, and that learning is usually beneficial to the organization regardless of the reason it is undertaken. Drawing on adult learning theory, Bierema (1996) argues that organizations sometimes fail to recognize the value of attending to employees personal and professional development. Whole-person development may help retain employees longer and keep them more productive. She suggests that organizations need to promote individual growth, cultivate cultures that value learning, and design organizational infrastructure that supports learning as well as the capturing and sharing of it with the rest of the organization. Caffarella (1994) assembled several points related to adult learning that are important to consider when planning or delivering instruction to adults. These points are summarized in Figure 3.2.

Understanding Adult Learners: The Bottom Line

Understanding and respecting adult learners are critical abilities for workplace educators. Insight into the learning process provides educators with the tools and knowledge to create educational experiences that transfer to the work context and facilitate the adoption of change. Understanding learners

✔ Adults can and do want to learn, regardless of their age.

✔ Adults have a rich background of knowledge and experience. They tend to learn best when this experience is acknowledged and when new information builds on their past knowledge and experience.

✔ Adults are motivated to learn by a mixture of internal and external factors.

✔ All adults have differing preferred styles of learning.

✔ For the most part, adults are pragmatic in their learning. They tend to want to apply their learning to real life.

✔ Adults are not likely to willingly engage in learning unless the content is meaningful to them.

✔ Adults come to a learning situation with their own personal goals and objectives, which may or may not be the same as those that underlie the learning situation.

✔ Adults prefer to be actively involved in the learning process than passive recipients of knowledge. In addition, they want the opportunity to be supportive of each other in the learning process.

✔ Adults learn both in independent, self-reliant modes and in interdependent, connected, and collaborative ways.

✔ Much of what adults learn tends to have an effect on others (for instance, on work colleagues and family).

✔ Adults are more receptive to the learning process in situations that are both physically and psychologically comfortable.

✔ What, how, and where adults learn is affected by the many roles they play as adults.

✔ Adults are often internally asking the questions, "Why am I learning this?" and "How will I use this in the future?" Be sure that this information is covered.

✔ Build in time for reflection.

✔ How does the content relate to the learner's experience? Often the learners will be able to answer this for themselves if asked.

✔ Attend to diverse learning needs.

✔ Conduct frequent process checks to ensure that learning needs are being met. Ask, "How could your learning be better supported by yourself? Your colleagues? Your learning facilitators?" Be sure to respond to any feedback offered by the participants.

✔ Vary the format to attend to multiple learning styles.

✔ Seek learner input to the design and flow of the learning.

✔ Challenge learners to consider how the wider context affects their learning. Think of this as a learning facilitator as you plan.

---

*Adapted in part from: Caffarella, R. S. (1994). *Planning programs for adult learners: A practical guide for educators, trainers, and staff developers.* San Francisco: Jossey-Bass.

FIGURE 3.2   Adult Learning Principles

also helps to foster their individual development. Sensitivity in this area requires that educators not only seek practices that appeal to them, but also apply a variety of strategies that will reach diverse learners.

Designing Educational Programs

Understanding learners and organizational context are the first steps toward designing educational programs that promote effective adult learning. His-

Tyler's Questions:	Knowles' chapters in *The Modern Practice of Adult Education*
1. What educational purposes should the school seek to attain?	1. Assessing needs and interests in program planning
2. What educational experiences can be provided that are likely to attain these purposes?	2. Defining purposes and objectives
	3. Designing a comprehensive program
	4. Operating a comprehensive program
3. How can these educational experiences be effectively organized?	5. Evaluating a comprehensive program
4. How can we determine whether these purposes are being attained?	Knowles, M. (1970). *The Modern Practice of Adult Education: Andragogy versus pedagogy.* New York: Association Press.
Tyler, R. (1949) *Basic Principles of Instruction.* The University of Chicago Press	

FIGURE 3.3   The Classic Educational Design Models of Tyler vs. Knowles

torically, the design of instruction has been most significantly influenced by behaviorist philosophy. Recently, other philosophical frames have begun to influence the instructional program planning process.

Lawson (1998) notes that successful educational programs depend on taking a systematic approach to delivering instruction that is effective for both the participants and the organization. Programs designed to correspond with the organization's strategy and employees' needs are most effective. This result can happen only if attention is paid to the learning system from the identification of a possible training need to the assessment of organizational results. Nearly all instructional models incorporate the steps of analyzing needs and selecting solutions, designing and developing nontraining solutions, deriving instructional outcomes, designing and developing instruction, implementing instruction, and monitoring and improving the process (Mager, 1997).

The instructional design process used to create most educational programs is grounded in behaviorism and, to a lesser degree, humanism. Cervero and Wilson (1994) classify such programs as classical because they are rational and have profoundly influenced instructional design for over fifty years. Ralph Tyler (1949) and Malcolm Knowles (1950) are credited with developing these classical models, which are summarized in Figure 3.3.

Sork (1997) summarizes the contributions from the Tyler and Knowles models as follows:

- Honoring the learners' experience, perspective, and expectations.
- Recognizing the importance of diversity.
- Involving stakeholders in planning.

Classical	Naturalistic	Critical
◆ Diagnostic ◆ Sequential learning experiences ◆ Create optimal learning conditions ◆ Based on appropriate methods and techniques ◆ Provide human and material resources ◆ Measure learning outcomes	◆ Plans in non-formulaic fashion ◆ Makes defensible judgments in context ◆ Formulates decision points ◆ Devises alternative choices ◆ Driven by values ◆ Considers pros and cons of alternatives ◆ Chooses "best" alternative intuitively ◆ Examines planning practice	◆ Commits to moral standard of equality ◆ Understands society's political and ideological streams ◆ Recognizes that decisions are ethical and political, *not technical* ◆ Seeks social, cultural, political, economic reconstruction ◆ Incorporates emancipation and social justice ◆ Views planning as a process of negotiating power interests

FIGURE 3.4   A Comparison of Classical, Naturalistic, and Critical Planning Framework

- Understanding the importance of context in which planning occurs.
- Basing programs on the needs of learners.
- Clarifying the aims or goals of the workshop.
- Incorporating workshop processes that actively involve learners.
- Choosing facilitators or instructors and instructional resources with great care.
- Promoting application of learning as a central theme.
- Attending carefully to administrative details.
- Caring for the physical and emotional needs of participants.
- Assessing program outcomes in addition to learner satisfaction.

Cervero and Wilson (1994) criticize the classical models for being too technical and view program planning from three perspectives—classical, naturalistic, and critical. These program planning frameworks are outlined in Figure 3.4. Their concern is that classical models do not accurately reflect reality because they ignore the human element of power dynamics and the negotiation of interests in the planning process. Cervero and Wilson argue that the training planner's role is to negotiate often disparate and incompatible interests while simultaneously mitigating power dynamics. They also challenge program planners to consider whose interests are being served by educational programs and to be aware of all stakeholders in the process. Consider a management team concerned about quality performance who asks human resources to conduct a quality training. Let's say the real problem is that management is not communicating specifications in a timely fashion to the employees and this is the root cause of the problem. Because managers may be trying to protect themselves from embarrassment or responsibility, the planning process may be a struggle over purposes and content. There are several conflicting interests in this simple example. Management is interested in saving face; everyone is interested in pleasing customers. Employees are interested in doing their jobs well and not getting blamed for every single quality problem. HR is caught in the middle trying to please the interests of both employees and management, not to mention individual, personal interests such as a favorable performance review or promotion. HRD professionals are faced with these dilemmas daily and make program planning decisions to negotiate interests, power, and responsibility. The classical model offers little guidance in negotiating power dynamics at the planning table. Although Cervero and Wilson offer an alternative perspective on program planning, the classical model is still widely applied. The next sections will explore the steps of designing training according to common classical planning models.

The Instructional Systems Development (ISD) Model (a.k.a. ADDIE)

The ISD model is the most widely used framework for designing instruction. Molenda, Pershing, and Reigeluth (1996) describe this model's qualities as *systematic* with sequential steps, *systemic* with attention to the whole organization, *reliable* or replicable from one site to another, *iterative* in that the design cycle repeats during a given project, and *empirical* in that data are collected and used to guide the design process. The ISD model is often referred to by the acronym of ADDIE, indicating the recurring steps of Analysis, Design, Development, Implementation, and Evaluation (Figure 3.5). ADDIE originated from the work of the United States Air Force around 1965 under the name "Instructional Systems Development." Gagne was one of the major players in those efforts. The ADDIE model steps are described in the following sections.

Analysis. Analysis is the first step of the ADDIE model. It involves identifying a need for intervention. This step identifies the problem to be solved and assesses whether or not training is the appropriate response. Deciding whether or not to train is vitally important, as training is often prescribed for problems that cannot be fixed by training, such as bad management, malfunctioning equipment, or unclear expectations. Nontraining interventions may be called for when the problem can more easily be solved by reassignment, job aids (e.g., simple instructions on equipment), management changes, or equipment modifications.

Once it is determined that training is a viable solution, performance deficiencies must be identified. These deficiencies are identified through needs analysis, which involves collecting data on the problem through individual or

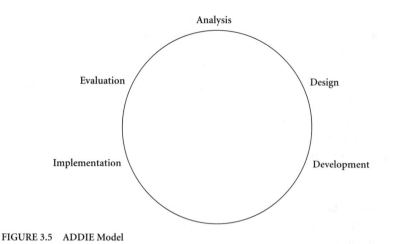

FIGURE 3.5   ADDIE Model

group assessments, observation, interviews, surveys, focus groups, professional literature, performance appraisal, or other data collection methods. The data help identify performance gaps between actual and desired performance. The learners, setting, and jobs may also be analyzed. For example: A plant supervisor works with the training manager to define a problem as rejected parts that are not meeting quality standards. They decide to analyze the problem and potential need for training by interviewing employees. They create a set of interview questions and identify a sample of employees to interview. After the interviews are conducted and answers are analyzed, the results reveal that new equipment was installed, but employees were never formally told how to operate it. Because the machinery is highly complex, training is identified as the best response to the problem. Other options would be less effective at improving quality performance.

Once the needs assessment is complete, the information should be presented to stakeholders and support to proceed should be secured. Task analyses are often done at this point, along with analyzing potential learners and writing training objectives. A training proposal should be developed that will guide the design process.

Design.   Design is the second step of the ADDIE model. The design step assumes that the needs analysis identified a legitimate reason to invest in training. Design involves identifying learning objectives (based on the needs analysis), determining performance measures, and sequencing the objectives. Sequencing involves moving the learner from lower- to higher-level skills, and from simple to complex concepts and tasks. For instance, in computer training, the learner would learn the simple task of how to navigate around a data base before moving to the complex process of writing programs. By the same token, the technical aspects of the computer operation would be investigated before ethical issues were evaluated.

Objectives writing is very important. Lawson (1998) suggests that training objectives fall into three categories of skill development: attitude (affective), skill (behavioral), and knowledge (cognitive). The instructional designer also has to make instructional and logistical decisions. These decisions include: teaching or instructional strategies, participant grouping, training environment, teaching methods, and content. For example: The purpose of the training is to familiarize employees with new equipment. The objectives might be (a) to operate the equipment correctly and safely and (b) to understand basic repair and troubleshooting. The participants could be grouped according to shift or in smaller groups of equipment operators in order to keep production moving during training. The environment could be in-plant, on the specific equipment, or at a technical training site. The methods might include lecture, demonstration, and practice. The sequencing would be from simple to complex, or from general operation to repair.

Development.   Development is the next stage of the ADDIE model. During this step, a prototype of the learning process is created. This may include developing facilitation and participant manuals, audiovisual materials, and other tangible materials that will be used in training. It also involves determining program formats, schedules, facilities, and staff needs during the event. Budgets and marketing issues need consideration as well. This phase may also include pilot testing of the materials and activities. There may be several revisions in the development of materials before the final materials are produced and ready for training. For example: A pilot group of machine operators could be trained to test the design. The participants then provide feedback and improvement suggestions. The trainers would revise the training before the rest of the machine operators received training.

Implementation.   Implementation is the fourth stage of the ADDIE model. Implementation involves the actual delivery of the training to the intended audience. For example: The training is rolled-out to the machine operators.

Evaluation.   Training evaluation is the step of the ADDIE model that is regularly overlooked or haphazardly applied. Many times evaluation is not considered until the training is nearly over. The time to think about evaluation is not at the end of training, but at the beginning of the design process. Why evaluate? Lawson (1998) identifies several reasons: determining whether the training met its stated objectives, assessing the value of training, identifying areas in which the training can be improved, targeting appropriate audiences for future programs, reviewing and reinforcing key learning points for participants, and selling the program to management and participants. Evaluation can be done during the training, at the end of the session, or after the training. Building on Kirkpatrick's (1995) four-level model of evaluation, assessment usually considers:

- Level 1: Reaction—Did participants like the program?
- Level 2: Learning—What skills and knowledge did participants gain?
- Level 3: Behavior—How are participants performing differently?
- Level 4: Results—How was the bottom line affected?

The four-level model of evaluation has been criticized for failing to measure return on investment (ROI) in training. Evaluation is increasingly being measured by looking for ROI performance. Human resource professionals need to ensure that training is evaluated, and that its value is communicated to the organization.

Before administering an evaluation the trainer needs to decide the purpose of the evaluation, such as assessment of training, potential follow-up, or behavioral results. Once the purpose is determined, it must be decided what to measure to assess it, and what sources of information are appropriate. For instance, if you want to measure the results of a customer service training, you could measure the number of complaints and could look at written complaints, or contact customers. You also have to decide how to gather information and determine when to conduct the evaluation. Finally, political issues must be assessed.

Learning Transfer: The Missing Component of the ADDIE Model

Learning transfer is the effective and continuing application of newly acquired knowledge, skills, and attitudes to the job. It is often referred to as the "so what" or "now what" phase of the learning process. "So what does all this mean and how can what was learned be applicable to my situation?" (Caffarella, 1994).

Learning transfer is influenced by several factors, including the learners, program design and execution, program content, changes required to apply learning, organizational context, and community and societal forces. Since adults wonder how they are going to use this information when they get back to work or back home, it is important that they be given some strategies to be sure this occurs.

Action Item	Interim/Key Steps	Others Whose Help is Needed	Target Date	Priority Assess when sheet is full

FIGURE 3.6   Action Planning for Learning Transfer

One way that learners can be assisted in their application of training is to give them time to reflect on what they have learned, and how they can use it after they leave. It is remarkable how, after only five or ten minutes, participants will often discover their own strategies to apply the tools they have discussed during the training. Reflection can be difficult, however, as many participants come from fast-paced environments where even stopping and gazing out a window for a few minutes to think is viewed as wasted time. They may need acknowledgment that this is a difficult task for some people, and encouragement to stick with it. Trainers often sacrifice a few moments of reflection for the coverage of a few more points. This is to be avoided. Chances are, the participants have reached saturation point. Instead, have them consider how they will apply what they have learned and raise questions about points that may have been unclear.

Action Planning.   The creation of a written action plan so that participants have a well-thought-out strategy to apply their information will give them a jump start toward application. Consider having participants complete the matrix in Figure 3.6 as they participate in the training. In addition to action planning, here are twenty-five tips for training transfer that I've assembled over the years.

25 Tips for Training Transfer.

   1.   Have participants develop an action plan, as discussed above.

2. Have participants craft a learning letter to their supervisor.
3. Create a network of course graduates (this could be electronic).
4. Schedule brown bag lunch sessions to share lessons learned.
5. Create a slogan or acronym to reinforce key points. For instance, "ya gotta be flexible!" or ADDIE.
6. Create a job aid for reference back on the job.
7. Involve managers prior to the training with tips on how they can help trainees get the most out of training.
8. Hold the course over several weeks with application "homework" in between sessions and reports on progress at the sessions.
9. Have participants do a force field analysis on applying learning at work before the end of the training.
10. Create posttraining learning groups or "buddies" to help each other after the class.
11. Have participants keep a journal after the course and meet periodically to compare notes on what is and is not working.
12. Have teams from across the organization participate in the training.
13. Offer training to whole departments and create collective strategies for application.
14. Have participants write letters to themselves and send them at a later date.
15. Have participants complete pre- and posttraining assessments.
16. Hold a 30-day posttraining debriefing on application with trainees and management.
17. Give managers a checklist of observable behaviors to look for after class.
18. Have participants create a vision or image of their learning.
19. Use music, poetry, or video clips to underscore points. These will serve as reminders of the training.
20. Have trainees "train" on what they learned.
21. Give participants a bibliography of books, periodicals, Web sites, and videotape or audiotape programs that will help them to maintain and enhance their skill.
22. Encourage participants in keeping the information they want to focus on visible either in their planner, on their bulletin board, or on their screen saver.
23. Give the participants time to spend with a "buddy"—someone they work with who will let them know when they are successfully using the skills.
24. Prior to the session give the learning objectives to the participants' supervisor. Ask the supervisor to discuss with them what he or she

would like them to learn during the session and why they are attending that particular class.

25. Use a Stop–Reflect timeout to consider how the learning can be applied to the job at various points throughout the session.

Planning Educational Programs: The Bottom Line

Designing educational programs is not a neutral act. Although models that have ignored context have been widely influential and applied for over fifty years, responsible program planners must continually ask, "Whose interests are being served?" when they plan programs. They must be cognizant of the power relations and interests and take responsibility to negotiate in an ethical manner. Again, they must question their educational philosophy and make an effort to move from behaviorism to more radical forms of philosophy that better accommodate our increasingly diverse world.

The previous sections have provided a general overview of the role, design, and facilitation of learning in organizational context. The next section addresses the challenge of training and employee development.

Rapidly Changing Environments

Learning facilitators have to respond to a rapidly changing environment characterized by technology advances, diversity, restructuring, and human performance management. Finally, training functions must adopt a customer focus.

Technology

Technological advances show no signs of slowing, and skill requirements will continue to change based on these advances. Training must assist the workforce in learning new technology. Further, trainers must learn to use the new technology that is widely available to conduct training. They need to be familiar with computer hardware, networking, multimedia software, and video conferencing, and be able to manage multiple-site training delivery.

Diversity

The news that the workforce is diverse is hardly met with a raised brow. Trainers must design training that respects diverse cultures, learning styles, and needs, as well as deliver training that helps organizations address diversity issues effectively.

Restructuring

Corporate restructuring has kept a steady pace and whether organizations are downsizing or reorganizing, training issues and problems are inevitable. Common restructuring training needs to include new job skills, improved morale, outplacement, policy change, and change management.

Human Performance Management

The American Society for Training and Development (1997) predicts that emphasis on human performance management will accelerate in the future. They have noted a number of comprehensive performance management approaches, including gainsharing, team-based performance evaluation, and employee performance evaluation tied to business goals.

Adopting a Customer Focus

Training departments are increasingly responsible for developing a strategic focus, producing high-quality training with a short cycle time, using the latest technology, linking multiple sites, and demonstrating a return on investment. These high expectations demand that training professionals adopt a customer focus. To best meet the needs of the customer, trainers must make strategic decisions related to needs analysis, outsourcing, design, delivery, and evaluation of training.

Facilitating Learning

Workplace educators are in essence learning facilitators who apply an array of strategies to foster the development of individuals, teams, and the entire organization. This section highlights a variety of learning strategies used in organizations. Many of the most effective strategies are experiential in nature and thus influenced by progressive learning philosophy.

Experiential Learning

Experiential learning evolved out of progressivism. Several models of learning can be attributed to experiential models, including the Shewart learning cycle popularized by Deming and known as the PDCA (Plan, Do, Check, Act) cycle. Other experiential learning models include those of Kolb, Schon, and Revans. These models incorporate a process of reflection and action as essential elements.

On-the-Job Training

On-the-job training (OJT) is one of the oldest types of training. According to Levine (1997, 1), OJT is a "just-in-time delivery system that dispenses training to employees when they need it." It is usually delivered as one-on-one training. OJT is classified as unstructured or structured. Unstructured OJT is the unstructured training that happens in the workplace, such as one employee teaching another how to run a machine. The problem with unstructured OJT is that it is casual, haphazard, unmonitored, unrecorded, and usually hit-or-miss in its results.

Structured OJT has grown out of the quality movement and companies' quests to become ISO 9000 certified. Structured OJT involves designated trainers, skill checklists, consistency of delivery, tracking recording, and evaluation. Levine outlines seven components of an OJT system: management support, formal trainer support process, checklists, OJT training materials, train-the-trainer program, and tracking and report generation. Effective OJT programs have structure, objectives, accountability, preparation, consistency, and sensitivity to learner needs.

Informal and Incidental Learning

Marsick (1985) identifies several assumptions about adult learning in the workplace. Among these assumptions are the following: that learning in the workplace involves learning on-the-job more frequently than learning in the classroom; that a wide range of learning resources exists within organizations, including written materials, skilled and helpful individuals, and supportive groups; and that resources outside the organization may be used to learn things that will enhance job effectiveness, such as materials, individuals, groups, or other institutions. Carnevale (1984) defines informal learning as an unstructured approach toward learning work skills on the job, such as supervision, observation of other workers, learning from mistakes, reading, and self-directed study. Marsick (1987) describes informal learning as reflection-in-action, based on Schon's work (1983). She identifies three modes of informal learning: job assignments, relationships, and self-directed learning.

Marsick views education and training as delivery systems. Conversely, she defines learning more comprehensively as "The ways in which individuals or groups acquire, interpret, reorganize, change or assimilate related clusters of information, skills and feelings. It is also the primary way in which people construct meaning in their personal and shared organizational lives" (1987, 4). Marsick and Watkins (1990, 6) define informal and incidental learning as "learning outside formally structured, institutionally sponsored, classroom-based activities." Specifically, informal learning is experiential and noninstitutional. Incidental learning, a component of informal learning, is unintentional, an outcome of another activity. Both types of learning differ from formal learning in that informal learning is controlled by the learner; it occurs in a location outside the classroom and has unpredictable outcomes. Examples of informal learning include: self-directed learning, networking, coaching, mentoring, performance planning, and trial-and-error. Incidental learning is tacit, taken-for-granted, and implicit in assumptions and actions. Examples of incidental learning include: learning from mistakes, assumptions, beliefs, attributions, internalized meaning constructions about the actions of others, understanding organizational culture, and hidden curriculum in formal learning (Marsick and Watkins, 1990).

The problems with informal and incidental learning include that they may be limited by the problems that learners select to attack and the ways they relate them to their contextual experience, along with the level of their ability to synthesize learning over long periods of time over many separate learning outcomes. The benefits of informal and incidental learning are that they promote creativity, productivity, and critical reflection in the problemsolving process. Marsick and Watkins (1990) suggest that informal and incidental learning may occur on any of four levels: individual; group, such as a work group; organizational, spearheaded by top management; and professional groups, which are influenced by norms set outside organizations. Additionally, they observe that learning occurs from experience and from the context of the work environment.

Learning outside the classroom has been the subject of exhaustive research. Tough (1979) used the iceberg analogy to explain adult learning. Traditionally, attention has focused on the visible portion of the iceberg: the formal, professionally guided learning experience. Yet Tough found that a mere 20 percent of learning experiences occurred in a classroom setting. The remaining 80 percent of learning projects were self-planned and self-initiated. Not surprisingly, the most common motivation for such learning projects was the anticipated use of the skill.

Self-Directed Learning

Self-directed learning, or the process of adults controlling their own learning, was popularized in adult education by Tough's (1979) examination of the frequency and nature of self-directed learning activities among a sample of sixty-six adults. He found that 68 percent of all learning activities were planned, implemented, and evaluated by the learners themselves. Self-directed learning is a complex process in which learning depends on both the individual learner (Kasworm, 1983) and the social context (Brookfield, 1985). Merriam and Brockett (1997), drawing on the literature, outline three self-directed learning trends. First, self-directed learning is the most frequent process adults select for learning. Second, the propensity to be self-directed is strongly related to self-concept. Third, several other personality and social features are related to self-directed learning, and self-directed learning research has provided a more holistic view of the adult learner. One example of a teaching strategy that applies self-directed learning principles is the use of learning contracts.

Transformative Learning

Transformational learning theory has been a major influence on adult education during the past twenty years. Initially described as perspective transformation by Mezirow (1978), transformative learning explains a process of change that begins with a disorienting dilemma—a situation where previous patterns of thinking and action are no longer effective—and progresses through a process of challenging and revising assumptions that ultimately leads to a new self-concept. Clark (1993) describes transformative learning as something that shapes people, noting that after a transformative learning experience, learners are different in ways that both they and other people notice. Returning to the example of corporate mergers, going through a significant change such as this could prove to be transformative for learners in their view of their career, company, and even life choices. A woman may have to transform her thinking about her identity as an executive if she encounters a glass ceiling at the middle or upper management levels. The numbers of women leaving corporations to become entrepreneurs is likely evidence of a transformative learning experience that resulted in them quitting a job to pursue something else.

Action Learning

Action learning is the art of creating real results in real time. It is a process of accelerating people's learning about real work problems and/or desired outcomes within the actual work context. It involves getting relevant individuals together to work on organizational issues in a fashion that causes and values learning throughout the process. Since the learning is in the action, action learning is not intended to be a spectator sport. Furthermore, action learning is versatile in its application. It is useful on both individual and collective levels and attempts to strike a balance between action and reflection. It can be led by either a facilitator or a participant. This makes it an ideal approach for individual and organizational development. The general process of action learning follows a simple cycle of examining real work issues, applying a process of questioning and reflection on the issues, taking action on the issues, and repeating the cycle.

Action learning involves working on real problems, in real time, by the real people who are affected by them. It is essentially learning by doing. Pioneered by Professor Reg Revans and developed worldwide over the last forty years, action learning relies on a recurrent cycle of action and reflection. It is based on a formula derived by Revans: $L=P+Q$. L=learning, and requires P=programmed knowledge (routine knowledge in use) and Q=questioning insight. The process integrates research on what is obscure with action to resolve a problem, and personal and communal reflection.

Action learning teams are becoming common in organizations that have shifted from traditional training to a learning orientation. These teams are referred to as "sets" in action learning terminology. A set comes together to work on a common problem or as individuals seeking to work on individual problems with the group. The set is assembled based on diversity and the use of nonexperts. The set reflects on the problem, establishes a strategy to tackle it, and adjourns to take action. After a period of action, the set reconvenes to reflect on how the action worked, to consider lessons learned, and to chart strategy for further action. Sets can exist either until the problem is solved or indefinitely, based on organization need. The set is often facilitated by a set leader who assists the group in reflection on their actions. An example is the Electrical Fuel and Handling Division's Division Operating Committee. The general manager instituted weekly action learning sessions in place of one-on-one meetings with each of his executives. Through these action learning sessions, the group was able to explore individual and collective issues related to managing the business, and learn in the process.

Components and Characteristics of Action Learning. Marquardt (1999, 5) asserts that action learning programs derive their power and benefits from six interactive and interdependent components: (1) a problem, (2) the group, (3) the questioning and reflection process, (4) the resolution to take action, (5) the commitment to learning, and (6) the facilitator. He claims that the success of action learning relies on the effective interaction of these six elements.

Marquardt (1999) asserts that action learning groups help create learning organizations because (1) team members develop solutions to problems that serve as valuable information in future problemsolving episodes and (2) the body of knowledge and the pace of learning are increasing in user organizations. Marquardt and Reynolds (1994, 23) identify characteristics of action learning that contribute to forming learning organizations:

- Is outcome-oriented
- Is designed to systematically transfer knowledge throughout the organization
- Enables people to learn by doing
- Helps develop learning-how-to-learn skills
- Encourages continual learning
- Creates a culture in which learning becomes a way of life
- Is an active rather than a passive approach
- Is done mainly on the job rather than off the job
- Allows for mistakes and experimentation
- Develops skills of critical reflection and reframing
- Is a mechanism for developing learning skills and behavior
- Demonstrates the benefits of organizational learning
- Models working and learning simultaneously
- Is problem-focused rather than hierarchically bound
- Provides a network for sharing, supporting, giving feedback, and challenging assumptions
- Develops the ability to generate information
- Breaks down barriers between people and across traditional organizational boundaries
- Helps an organization move from a culture of training (in which someone else determines and provides the tools for others' development) to a culture of learning (in which everyone is responsible for his or her own continuous learning)
- Is systems-based
- Applies learning to other parts of the organization as appropriate.

Trends in Organizational Learning

There are several important trends in organizational learning, including the shift from training to learning, that have precipitated the development of the learning organization, among them linking training to organizational strategy, the emerging role of a chief learning officer in organizations, examining ethical behavior by HRD practitioners as a means of making decisions, and capturing intellectual capital.

Learning Organizations

The learning organization concept was introduced in 1990 with Peter Senge's book *The Fifth Discipline: The Art and Practice of the Learning Organization*. This concept has significantly influenced organizational learning and change efforts. West views it as "an opportunity for adult educators to participate in business and industry in a manner consistent with adult education principles" (1996, 51).

A learning organization is one that learns continuously and can transform itself (Watkins and Marsick, 1993). Senge (1990, 56) defines it as "Organizations where people continually expand their capacity to create the results they truly desire, where new and expansive patterns of thinking are nurtured, where collective aspiration is set free and where people are continually learning how to learn together." The learning organization has also been defined as a learning company, which is "an organization that facilitates the learning of all its members and continuously transforms itself" (Pedler, Burgoyne, and Boydell, 1991). Dixon (1994) writes that an essential aspect is "the intentional use of learning processes at the individual, group and system level to continuously transform the organization that is increasingly satisfying its stakeholders" (1994). A learning organization, systematically defined, is an organization that learns powerfully and collectively and is continually transforming itself to better collect, manage, and use knowledge for corporate success (Marquardt, 1996).

These definitions have several things in common. Particularly, they all emphasize that learning occurs at individual, group, and organizational levels to create transformation and achieve success for the organization and its stakeholders. The Electrical and Fuel Handling Division (now a part of Visteon Automotive Systems, a division of Ford Motor Company) realized unprecedented performance in its new product launch process through the application of learning organization principles to change their former process. Their ability to launch new automotive component systems under budget, early, and of high quality resulted in a turnaround for the business (Bierema and Berdish, 1996).

The following explanation furnishes some critical insight regarding the difference between learning organizations and organizational learning:

> A learning organization, systematically defined, is an organization which learns powerfully and collectively and is continually transforming itself to better collect, manage, and use knowledge for corporate success. It empowers people within and outside the company to learn as they work. . . . [In] learning organizations, we are focusing on the *what,* and describing the systems, principles, and characteristics of organizations

that learn and produce as a collective entity. Organizational learning, on the other hand, refers to how organizational learning occurs, i.e., the skills and processes of building and utilizing knowledge. (Marquardt, 1996, 19)

Characteristics of Learning Organizations. Marquardt (1996, 19–20) identifies a number of important dimensions and characteristics of the learning organization:

- Learning is accomplished by organizational systems as a whole, almost as if the organization were a single brain.
- Organizational members recognize the critical importance of ongoing organization—wide learning for the organization's current and future success.
- Learning is a continuous, strategically used process—integrated with and running parallel to work.
- There is a focus on creativity and generative learning.
- Systems thinking is fundamental.
- People have continuous access to information and data resources that are important to the company's success.
- The corporate climate encourages, rewards, and accelerates individual and group learning.
- Workers network in an innovative, communitylike manner inside and outside the organization.
- Change is embraced, while unexpected surprises and even failure are viewed as opportunities to learn.
- It is agile and flexible.
- Everyone is driven by a desire for quality and continuous improvement.
- Activities are characterized by aspiration, reflection, and conceptualization.
- There are well-developed core competencies that serve as taking-off points for new products and services.
- It possesses the ability to continuously adapt, renew, and revitalize itself in response to the changing environment.

Linking Training to Organizational Strategy

One of the problems with most training is that, in spite of the investment of money and time, no change results over time. Unless explicitly linked to strategy, even the best-designed and best-executed training will fail. Of course, this assumes that the organization has a clear strategy to link training to. Often, organizations are unclear about their mission and vision. The first step is to clearly specify these. The second is to link all educational activities to them. In addition to strategic linkages, training should have a future focus. Rather than ensuring that employees have the knowledge and skill that are helpful to the business today, organizations need to consider what information will help them in the future. Needs analysis takes on even greater importance when linking training to strategy. Needs analysis becomes an opportunity to assess how the organization is performing against its strategy, and to craft a performance-based plan to improve the situation. Strategic training is generally a team or collective process, because individuals who attend training often come up against cultural and political barriers that may prevent them from applying new knowledge to the organization.

The Chief Learning Officer

A scan of current job titles reveals hints that learning is taking hold in progressive organizations. Today titles like "Chief Learning Officer" or "Vice President of Organizational Learning" are becoming common. This shift is indicative of the heightened importance of learning in organizational life. Willis and May (1997) suggest that the concept of the Chief Learning Officer (CLO) exceeds traditional concepts of training and development. These executive-level positions are usually charged with facilitating learning and change in the organization; improving individual, team, and organizational effectiveness through integrated use of communication media, performance consulting, training, and organizational design; and supporting the business strategy and tactics. The rise of the CKO (Chief Knowledge officer) or CLO is at least token evidence of organizational commitment to the management of intellectual capital. Guns (2001) outlines the core competencies of the learning officer:

1. Set strategic priorities for knowledge management
2. Establish a knowledge data base of best practices
3. Gain the commitment of senior executives to support a learning environment
4. Teach information seekers how to ask better and smarter questions of their intelligence resources
5. Put in place a process for managing intellectual assets
6. Obtain customer satisfaction information in near real-time
7. Globalize knowledge management

Ethical Issues in Employee Training and Development

As in many emerging fields of practice, HRD and training have undefined and sometimes conflicting ethical standards. Nadler and Nadler (1994) raise some of the ethical issues in this field. One concern is HRD's focus on behavioral change. Does the organization have a right to change people's behavior? What is to be done when HRD programs include controversial material? Is HRD a form of brainwashing or therapy? What if HRD is used with antiunion intentions? Is it ethical to force employees to learn? What is the organization's responsibility to support the community through learning efforts? How can HRD address the growing diversity of the workforce?

Intellectual Capital

Intellectual capital is the collective brainpower or intellectual material such as knowledge, information, intellectual property, and experience that organizations can utilize to create wealth (Stewart, 1997). Many organizations seek to manage their intellectual capital in a manner that increases competitiveness and profitability.

Conclusions

This chapter has introduced several applications of learning and related them to their philosophical and theoretical roots according to how these traditions help us understand learners, develop awareness of learning environments, design educational programs, facilitate learning, and capture and share learning. Effective learning facilitators will understand these philosophies and recognize their manifestation in their individual thinking, action, and practice.

Philosophy of Organizational Performance

Jerry W. Gilley

Another critical practitioner practice domain is organizational performance. The first step in understanding the philosophy of organizational performance is to examine its terms. The term *organization* refers to a "formal institution arranged to pursue goals that could not be achieved by individuals acting alone" (Gibson, Ivancevich, and Donnelly, 1997, 492). The term performance is also critical. Rothwell (1996a, 26) believes that to *perform* means "to begin and carry through to completion; to take action in accordance with the requirements of; fulfill." Thus, the term *performance* is sometimes defined as an accomplishment, execution, outcome, or achievement, which denotes a quantified result or a set of obtained results. Within an organizational context, Gilbert (1978) contends that performance is defined as an "accomplishment" that is valued.

To understand the philosophical foundations of the organizational performance domain, we must consider several essential elements, including its origin, philosophical underpinning, and principles.

Origin of the Organizational Performance Domain

To fully comprehend the origins of the organizational performance domain, we must examine the early works of Gilbert (1978), Harless (1970), and Mager (1975). These works helped frame organizational performance and gave it a unique set of characteristics, principles, processes, and techniques. More importantly, the organizational performance domain is sometimes referred to as

Traditional Focus	Performance Focus
Focuses on what people need to learn; skill and knowledge is the end.	Focuses on what people need to do; skill and knowledge is a means to an end.
Event oriented.	Process oriented.
Reactive	Reactive and proactive
Seeks single solution through training.	Open to multiple solutions of which training is a part.
Sometimes independent of client.	Based on partnership with client.
Front-end assessment optional	Front-end assessment mandatory
Success measured on quality of solution (training event)	Success measures based on performance change and operational impact.

FIGURE 4.1   Characteristics of a Traditional and Performance Focus

human performance technology (HPT) and draws much from this philosophical perspective, including its orientation, operational practices, assumptions, and frameworks. Therefore, we need to examine HPT closely to gain a better understanding of the organizational performance domain.

According to Robinson and Robinson (1998), HPT is a subset of the human resource development field. They suggest that the best structure for focusing on performance includes alignment of the needs related to business, performance, learning, and work environment. The trainer becomes a performance consultant with the responsibility for partnering with learners to help them achieve improved performance (see Chapter 5). Robinson and Robinson (1998) contrast traditional training and performance training, as shown in Figure 4.1.

Definition of Human Performance Technology

Stolovitch and Keeps (1999) maintain that HPT is concerned with measurable performance and the structuring of strategies within the organizational system to improve performance. As a result, the HRD practitioner (also referred to as a human performance technologist) must identify and analyze factors within the organizational system that may affect performance and the consequences of employee performance (rewards and punishments) to uncover root causes of inadequacies so that a performance solution can be constructed to address them.

Rothwell (1996b, 5) describes HPT as a "systematic process that links business strategy and goals and workers' abilities to achieve them with a variety of interventions, including environment redesign, learning and training, and incentive system reconfiguration." The principal result is individual (human) and organizational performance improvement. He advocates that through causal analysis of performance problems or business opportunities, underlying causes are identified for which effective solutions can be generated for any given performance challenge. Stolovitch and Keeps (1992, 3) contend that "human performance technology is a field of practice that has evolved largely as a result of the experience, reflection, and conceptualization of practitioners striving to improve human performance in the workplace." They assert that the term "human" is included in the name to focus practitioners' efforts toward human performers in organizational and work settings.

The term *technology* can be confusing because it has multiple connotations. But when linked with the word *performance* and introduced into an organizational context, it implies a systematic and objective procedure for examining performance issues from both individual and organizational perspectives (Gilley and Maycunich, 2000a). Thus, "human performance technology is a field of endeavor that seeks to bring about changes to a system, in such a way that the system is improved in terms of the achievements it values" (Stolovitch and Keeps, 1992, 5).

According to Dean (1999b), the conceptual domain of organizational performance (HPT) can be defined by three key aspects: (1) functions to manage the development of human performance systems or other management operations, (2) functions to develop human performance systems, and (3) the components of human performance systems. Thus, HPT is the development of human performance systems and the management of that development, using a systems approach to achieve organizational and individual goals.

Fuller and Farrington (1999, 94) believe that human performance technology can be defined as "a systemic and systematic approach to defining a business need or opportunity, identifying barriers to achieving the desired business result, implementing solutions to remove the barriers to performance, and then measuring bottom-line results." This approach differs from previous definitions in proposing additional considerations such as: (1) using a systematic approach, (2) defining a business problem or opportunity, (3) identifying barriers, and (4) removing barriers through interventions.

1. *Using a systematic approach:* HPT follows well-organized procedures, using a step-by-step approach, method, or system that is known for achieving results. By *systemic*, Rothwell (1996b, 15) implies that human performance improvement can be addressed in an organized, open systems approach, whereby the organization system absorbs

environmental inputs (people, raw materials, capital, and information), uses them in such transformational *processes* as delivering service or manufacturing products, and discharges them as outputs such as finished goods or customer services. Rothwell reinforces the obvious influence of systems theory.

2. *Defining a business problem or opportunity:* Fuller and Farrington (1999) believe that HPT as a process ensures that the organization knows what the problem or opportunity is that practitioners are trying to solve.

3. *Identifying barriers to achieving the desired business result:* Rothwell (1996a) suggests that present and future barriers that prevent an organization, process, or individual from achieving desired results must be discovered and analyzed to prevent them from interfering with the achievement of business results. Thus, performance-oriented HRD practitioners use process, performance, and causal analysis to assess the root cause of the problem or the real reason why an opportunity is not being realized (see Chapter 5). This is done to ensure that HRD practitioners go beyond identifying the symptoms of a performance problem and successfully isolate the real cause(s) to performance breakdowns and underachievement.

4. *Implementing solutions to remove barriers to performance:* HPT eliminates barriers to performance by offering a number of solutions (e.g., work environment, motivational factors, knowledge, and skills), since most performance problems or business opportunities require a combination of interventions. Rothwell (1996b) and Fuller and Farrington (1999) suggest that designing and developing cost-effective and ethically justifiable interventions will help organizations discover optimal, sensitive, and efficient means of solving past or present performance problems while also planning for future performance improvement opportunities. Additionally, the implementation of interventions includes installing and maintaining performance improvement solutions. Finally, performance-oriented HRD practitioners are responsible for *evaluating results* as a means of gathering persuasive evidence that demonstrates the solution's effectiveness.

Influence of Human Performance Technology

HPT is based on a number of underlying assumptions. These are well articulated by Geis (1986), and they remain largely true today.

1. HPT follows specific laws and can often be predicted and controlled (systems theory, motivation theory, behavioral psychology, cognitive science, knowledge management principles).
2. HPT must rely on practical experience as well as scientific research, since knowledge of human behavior is limited.
3. HPT draws from many research bases while generating its own.
4. HPT is the product of a number of knowledge sources: cybernetics, behavioral psychology, communications theory, information theory, systems theory, management science, and, more recently, cognitive sciences and neuroscience.
5. HPT is neither committed to any particular delivery system nor confined to any specific population and subject-matter area. It can address any human performance, but it is most commonly applied within organizational, work, and social improvement settings.
6. HPT is empirical. It requires systematic verification of the results of both its analysis and intervention efforts.
7. HPT is evolving. Based on guiding principles, it nevertheless allows enormous scope for innovation and creativity.
8. HPT cannot yet pretend to have generated a firm theoretical foundation of its own, the theory- and experience-based principles that guide it are molded by empirical data that have accumulated as a result of documented, systematic practice (Stolovitch and Keeps, 1992, 7–8).

HPT is also grounded in general systems theory as applied to organizations. Checkland (1972, 91) characterizes a system as "a complex grouping of human beings and machines for which there is an overall objective." Within HPT, systems refer to those that are results-driven, productivity-oriented systems, which makes HPT practice particularly valuable to organizations whose purposes and goals are generally clearly defined.

Every organization is part of larger system (Katz and Kahn, 1978). For example, all organizations are part of an industry, a society, and a global economy. Each of these systems places demands on the others. Demands for acceptable quality and quantity of products and services are most common, however, organizations must also satisfy demands for sustainable environments by promoting appropriate policies and actions or for global political stability by investing resources accordingly. Consequently, an organization cannot simply produce a product or service to satisfy its customers, but must produce actions and behaviors to satisfy other important elements of the larger systems.

HPT also has roots in behaviorism because it is concerned with measurable performance and the structuring of elements within the system to improve performance. "A cornerstone of performance technology is outcome signification, discovering valid, useful performance objectives and stating them in terms that are easily understood" (Ainsworth, 1979, 5). Once identified, interventions can be designed to effect change. Moreover, they are monitored and modified until the organizational system attains the required level of measurable performance.

An emerging influence on HPT is the cognitive sciences. This is primarily because the information age demands more mental tasks and activities from employees. Thus, HPT has become increasingly attuned to the lessons and insights that can be learned from cognitive sciences. The field of neuroscience has also become an important part of HPT because neuroscientists have discovered how memory is actually formed and what it takes to alter deeply entrenched behavior. Thus to influence employees' performance, HRD practitioners need to discover how brain chemistry, information-load limitations, and memory facilitators and inhibitors interface, interact, and integrate to affect performance (Alkon, 1992).

Another important element of HPT is motivation theory. Research evidence suggests that examination of both external and internal rewards provides a powerful means of influencing human performance. Keller (1999, 375) contents that a motivational system consists of "people, with their internal motivational characteristics, and the environment, with its tactics and strategies that affect goal-directed effort and affect." However, a motivational system cannot be understood unless one considers it in terms of how it is integrated into the larger system of influences on performance, which includes both internal, psychological factors and external, environmental factors. Keller (1999, 375) suggests that such a statement assumes that an adequate explanation of human behavior cannot be based solely on "behavioral observations or on inferences about human affect, attitudes, and cognition; rather, an adequate explanation must account for the influences and interactions of both."

Motivation can be represented by a person's initiative to pursue a goal, which is influenced by personal characteristics such as internal curiosity, motives, and expectations of success, and by environmental influences on the situation, such as job complexity, leadership style, and role match (Keller, 1999). When acceptable performance is demonstrated, a person is rewarded externally (financial rewards) or internally (satisfaction). Personal satisfaction will influence the person's desire to continue pursuing the same or similar goals. Satisfaction is influenced by the feedback and incentives received in relation to the actual level of accomplishment and by a person's perception of equity in relationship to the fairness of the consequences (Flannery, Hofrichter, and Platten, 1996). Keller contends (1999) that motivational influences must be considered in relation to other elements that influence one's capability and opportunity to perform well.

Economics, particularly those aspects dealing with human and intellectual capital, is also becoming a major part of the foundation of HPT. Swanson (1999, 11) believes that unless improvement in organizational performance is founded on economic theory, "organization development is reduced to individual development, team development, or the pursuit of change in the hopes of achieving improved organizational performance." He questions how a responsible organizational performance cannot include direct analysis, action, and measurement of economic outcomes. In short, interventions and initiatives must contribute to the viability and profitability of an organization.

Swanson identifies three economic theory perspectives that are most appropriate for performance improvement: scarce resource theory, sustainable resource theory, and human capital theory.

- *Scarce resource theory* contends that there are limitations to everything (money, raw materials, time, and human resources).
- *Sustainable resource theory* is much like scarce resource theory except that it focuses on the long term versus the short term.
- *Human capital theory* suggests that investment in human resources is essential to organizational success.

Stolovitch and Keeps (1999) warn that organizational performance should not be applied to all organizational systems because it is a results-driven, productivity-oriented process that may be inappropriate in social systems. They believe that it is particularly valuable for business and industry, where organizational purposes and goals are generally clearly defined.

Philosophical Underpinnings of Organizational Performance

Identifying, analyzing, and evaluating systems within an organization are essential parts of organizational performance. Fuller and Farrington (1999, 162) believe that this requires the ability to assess which elements of a system are related to one another and to determine which inputs, processes, and outputs from one element of a system interact with other elements of that system. Moreover, Rossett (1999b) suggests that performance-oriented HRD practitioners need to be able to predict which parts of a system are likely to be affected when another part of the system changes. Furthermore, they need to be able to use the *human performance system framework* to determine where making one change may affect other elements of a system (see Chapter 5).

Thus, organizational performance is grounded in general systems theory as it applies to organizations. It also relies on behavioral psychology and knowledge management as essential components of the foundation of the domain.

General Systems Theory

In the organizational performance world, HRD practitioners adopt a holistic philosophy of performance breakdowns. Thus, they examine breakdown (defined as a gap between desired and actual states) from a broader context of the organizational system in which it actually occurs. Though most performance breakdowns do not require a thorough examination of all operational systems, each is studied in relation to how it affects the achievement of the overall goals and mission of the organization.

To have a through understanding of organizational performance, every HRD practitioner needs to examine and apply the characteristics of open systems as described by Katz and Kahn (1978). They maintain that every organization, as a system, bears several essential characteristics. These characteristics form a framework for appraising an organization's internal environment, isolating performance problems, and identifying relationships critical to organizational effectiveness, and serve as a component of the philosophical underpinnings of organizational performance.

As previously discussed, organizations are totally dependent on the larger external environment in which they operate (Rothwell, 1996b). All organizations acquire resources from this environment and transform them into products and services demanded by the larger environment. This essentially complex process can be simplified by employing the basic concepts of systems theory.

Quite simply, systems theory analyzes which organization takes resources (inputs) from the larger system (environment), processes these resources, and transforms them into outputs for the consumers in the external environment (Gibson, Ivancevich, and Donnelly, 1997, 19). Thus, the transformation of inputs into outputs is the basic starting point in describing how an organization functions.

Internal and external organizational behavior can be better understood through systems theory. For example, a manager asks an employee to perform a certain task (input), the employee mentally and psychologically processes the request (input), accordingly performs an appropriate group of tasks (process), and at the completion of these tasks generates a product (output). Although this is a simple linear example, it demonstrates the impact of system theory on employee behavior. Under more realistic conditions, the work environment, motivational factors, the employee's knowledge and skills, managerial feedback, communication between manager and employee, performance standards, and job interference could influence the process and positively and negatively affect output (Gilley and Maycunich, 2000a).

Inputs.   Organizations obtain resources such as raw materials from their external environment. These are referred to as *production inputs* directly related to producing products or delivering services (i.e., transformation processes). *Maintenance inputs,* such as organizational policies and procedures, guide employees as they carry out their activities as members of the system.

All systems, from the most complex to the simplest (an amoeba), are open systems (Miller, 1978; Brethower, 1999), which means that they must import energy to survive. Thus systems are open, not hermetically sealed, perpetual-motion machines (Brethower, 1999).

Rothwell and Cookson (1997, 105) identify the following questions that can be used by HRD practitioners when examining an organization's importation of energy:

- What are the production and maintenance inputs of the organization as a whole? Of each part of the organization?
- How are those inputs changing to respond to external environmental change?
- How should those inputs change in the future to respond to external environmental change?
- How do present and future changes in inputs affect program planning efforts?
- How should present and future changes in inputs affect program planning efforts?

Throughput (Process).   The process of transforming raw materials (inputs) into products and services is known as throughput. Rummler and Brache (1995) refer to this as process, which describes the steps employees go through to create products and deliver services.

Again, Rothwell and Cookson (1997, 105) provide several questions that help HRD practitioners when appraising an organization's throughputs:

- What are the throughputs (transformation processes) of the organization? Of each part of the organization?
- How are throughputs changing to respond to external environmental change?

- How should throughputs change in the future to respond to external environmental change?
- How do changes in throughputs currently affect program planning efforts?
- How should changes in throughputs affect future program planning efforts?

Outputs.   The process phase is used to generate outputs in the form of products and services, which are used to exchange for units of value (financial remuneration, additional resources, outputs from other entities) with the external environment (Katz and Kahn, 1978). The quality and quantity of the outputs consumed by customers (external environment) determine an organization's profitability. Performance-oriented HRD practitioners can use the following questions to appraise an organization's outputs (Rothwell and Cookson, 1997, 106): What are the outputs of the organization? How are outputs changing in response to external environmental change? How should outputs change in the future in response to external environmental change? How do changes in outputs currently affect program planning efforts? How should changes in outputs affect future program planning efforts?

According to Katz and Kahn (1978), other characteristics of systems theory include:

- *Cycle of events* implies that the input–throughput–output cycle flows smoothly as long as the organization maintains its current (if effective) processes and procedures. However, change imposed by organizations to address breakdowns or eliminate performance barriers require HRD practitioners to examine the relationship among inputs, throughputs, and outputs to detect existing or desirable changes and their impact on present and future performance (Rothwell and Cookson, 1997).
- *Negative entropy* refers to the tendencies of an organization to move toward disorganization, chaos, and demise. Thus, HRD practitioners should take steps to avoid such imbalance within the organization.
- *Steady state and dynamic homeostasis* refer to the continuous inflow of energy from the external environment and a continuous export of the products of the system.
- *Differentiation* occurs when "diffuse global patterns are replaced by more specialized functions" (Katz and Kahn, 1978, 29). As a result, advanced organizations become more specialized and differentiated in the products and services (outputs) they provide to the marketplace (environment).

- *Integration and coordination* efforts are required by organizations in an effort to set priorities, establish organizationwide rules and regulations, increase organizational communications, establish performance standards, identify operating procedures, coordinate production scheduling, or establish quality improvement standards.
- *Equifinality* is the tendency of open systems to attain their objectives by various means. Unfortunately, this can cause confusion and conflict among members of an organization. Thus, performance-oriented HRD practitioners can help an organization avoid such confusion by asking how much variation exists in pursuit of common goals or results in the organization? How are those variations manifested? What are and what should be the impacts of these variations on performance improvement efforts at present and in the future (Rothwell and Cookson, 1997, 108)?

Brethower (1999) contends that all open systems must have mechanisms for channeling energy. For example, electronic systems are designed to power down in a crisis so as to preserve specific functions. Thus, energy channeling is a fundamental process enabling an organization to set priorities, establish alignment, identify whom they will serve, and to whom they go to for help should the need arise.

Brethower (1999, 70) further asserts that an open system operates within the constraints imposed by the availability of resources. Such constraints give rise to the principle of *subsystem maximization*, which concerns the impossibility of maximizing the functioning of both a subsystem and the total system at the same time. He adds that this principle "describes why priority setting is essential, and why internal competition can be extremely harmful, [and] . . . why vaguely insisting on *high standards* of performance can be counterproductive" (emphasis in the original). This principle asserts that individual and organizational goals should be in alignment, internal conflict be reduced, operational and strategic goals be clearly identified, and high-performance teams be developed.

Behavioral Psychology

In addition to general systems theory, behavioral psychology is a critical source for the organizational performance domain (Brethower, 1999; Dean and Ripley, 1997). Behavioral psychologists define behavior as the function of the interaction of heredity and environment. Thus, observable behavior is what performance-oriented HRD practitioners are concerned with and constitutes the criterion against which performance is to be assessed. This view excludes virtually all hypothetical constructs such as those found in self-theory and in Freudian theory, whereby humans are at the mercy of their "unconscious" or their drives, for these entelechies, if they exist, can be expressed in many ways.

Though behavioral viewpoints vary, most behavioral psychologists believe that a majority of human behavior is learned. Therefore, "behavior can be altered by manipulating and altering learning conditions" (Shertzer and Stone, 1980, 188). So organizational performance becomes the thoughtful arrangement of learning or relearning experiences to help individuals change their behavior in order to solve whatever problems they manifest (Brethower, 1999).

Thoresen (1966, 17) characterizes behavioral psychology in a fivefold statement. First, most human behavior is learned and is therefore subject to change. Second, specific changes in the individual's environment can assist in altering relevant behaviors, and as a result the performance improvement process seeks to bring about relevant changes in employee behavior by altering the environment. Third, social learning principles (e.g., reinforcement and social modeling) can be used to alter behavior (improve performance). Fourth, the effectiveness and outcomes of performance improvement interventions are assessed by changes in specific employees' behaviors on the job. Fifth, intervention procedures can be specifically designed to assist the employee in solving a particular problem rather than being static, fixed, or predetermined.

Brethower contends that what sets behavioral psychology apart from other psychological orientations is its focus on improving the specific performance of individuals in a targeted situation. He further suggests that:

> like other psychologists, behavioral psychologists study behavior; what makes behaviorists unique is that they seek to identify the variables that can be used to improve the performance of specific persons in specific settings at specific times. Behaviorists do research to identify essential variables, and they use that knowledge to modify variables and improve performance in real settings. . . . Behavioral clinical psychologists help clients identify functional and dysfunctional behaviors relevant to life tasks, and they help clients increase the functional behaviors and decrease the dysfunctional ones. (Brethower, 1999, 72–73)

Behavioral psychologists collect data before, during, and after an intervention, which allows them to make specific statements about specific instances of performance in specific environments. This is commonly referred to as a time-series research design (Rossett, 1999a).

Behavioral psychology is based on specific principles about the interaction of individual and environment. They embrace Thorndike's (1931) *law of effect*, which states that actions leading to immediate positive consequences are likely to be repeated (conversely, actions leading to immediate negative consequences are less likely to be repeated). LeBoeuf (1985, 9) supports this law in workplace settings: "The things that get rewarded, get done." It is clear that this law is important in the design of systems for motivation, recognition, supervision, and compensation. An often-neglected aspect of the law of effect is immediacy. Unfortunately, most organizations' rewards and recognition systems delay the positive consequences for performance for days, weeks, or months after their successful completion. This is a tremendous barrier to performance improvement because delayed recognition is much less powerful than immediate positive recognition.

Brethower (1999) believes that there is a link between behavioral psychology and general system theory. The link is very close: just as organizations are systems, so too are individuals (Ford, 1987). Taken together, general systems theory and behavioral psychology provide two important parts of the foundation for the organizational performance domain. The third is knowledge management.

Knowledge Management

Senge (1990) and Stewart (1997) conclude that knowledge management is a key goal for HRD practitioners. Knowledge management focuses attention on strategies for increasing value and accessibility and for soliciting information that resides in the organization and its people. Rossett (1999a) identifies several questions that help us organize the knowledge management process:

- How do we capture that information?
- How do we find what it is that savvy employees know?
- How do we make certain that this information reflects not just the obvious but also the more subtle, cultural aspects that are essential to success?
- How do we make this information available to more people, and how do we make it available in more ways?
- How do we begin to take advantage of technology?
- How do we ensure that the information is kept current?
- How do we define jobs, roles, processes, and systems in ways that "inform," "automate," "outsource," and "capitalize" effectively and flexibly?

Performance-oriented HRD practitioners will find themselves expanding both their questions and their solutions to reflect the emergence of knowledge management as an organizational priority.

Since all performance requires knowledge, individuals will create their own interpretations of incoming information based on their past experience and expectations. Additionally, performance is affected by an individual's ability to incorporate several thoughts at any one time. Therefore, every individual uses two types of knowledge for most thinking tasks: automated *procedural* knowledge and conscious *declarative* knowledge (Clark, 1999). These are used differently during problemsolving and expertise building. Procedural knowledge is used to help us execute a task whereas declarative knowledge helps us understand why things work the way they do.

Principles Underlying Organizational Performance

Jacobs (1987, 41) identifies ten important principles of human performance technology, which serve as a foundation for the organizational performance domain. These principles provide insight and direction for practitioners and also serve as a filter for excellence in practice.

Principle 1: Human performance and human behavior are different, and knowledge of their differences is important for achieving goals.

The first step in improving and managing performance is to define the term *human performance*. The term human is obvious—it refers to people, but in this context it refers to those in the workplace. As we discussed previously, performance means something performed, an accomplishment. Thus, human performance is synonymous with outcomes, results, or accomplishments generated by people in work settings.

Swanson (1999) defines performance as the outcomes of behavior. But Gilbert (1996) and Rothwell (1996a) caution us not to confuse performance with other terms like behaviors, work activities, duties, responsibilities, or competencies. *Behavior* is an observable action taken to achieve results. Stolovitch and Keeps (1992, 4) argue that "behavior is individual activity whereas the outcomes of behavior are the ways in which the behaving individual's environment is somehow different as a result of his or her behavior." On the other hand, *work activity* is a task or series of tasks taken to achieve results. Thus, a work activity has a definite beginning, middle, and end. A *duty* is a moral obligation to perform, and a *responsibility* is an action or a result for which one is accountable. A *competency* is an area of knowledge or skill that is critical for producing key outputs. Furthermore, a "competency is an internal capability that people bring to their jobs, a capability that may be expressed in a broad, even infinite array of on-the-job behaviors" (Rothwell, 1996a, 26). When identifying and evaluating competencies, one can typically determine the underlying characteristics shared by outstanding performers (Robinson and Robinson, 1996).

Gilbert (1996) cautioned HRD practitioners to avoid focusing on behavior rather than performance when he discussed a concept entitled "the cult of behavior." He refers to it and describes it as "the appeal to control or affect behavior in some way . . . there is little or no technology of ends and purposes. Indeed, behavior itself is viewed as an end rather than as a means to an end" (1996, 7). The cult of behavior typically manifests itself in one of three specific areas: work behavior, knowledge, and motivation. Moreover, HRD practitioners need to be on guard to ensure that they do not fall into this pervasive trap.

When expenditures of energy in the form of hard work are encouraged regardless of the results achieved by work efforts, the focus is on work process rather than outcomes. This refers to the work behavior cult. When caught in this trap, Fuller and Farrington (1999) contend that organizations encourage employees to work exactly like exemplary performers (benchmark) and to value activity rather than results. However, actual outcomes are not significantly increased, thus the organization is in danger of not achieving its strategic business goals.

When the knowledge is revered regardless of whether performance improves, an organization is reinforcing the knowledge cult. When caught in this trap, Fuller and Farrington (1999) argue that organizations overly emphasize employee development. Although employee development is important, it must be able to generate improved results to be of value. Additionally, placing highly developed employees in a dysfunctional work environment is counterproductive because such individuals will struggle to generate better results.

When organizations overly emphasize employees' positive attitudes and eagerness rather than focus on results or achievement, the motivation cult is present. Even though these are desirable outcomes, they are usually insufficient when performance is inadequate. Again, Fuller and Farrington (1999) suggest that this type of cult is evident in organizations that overemphasize the building of morale and teamwork.

Although it is a performance-oriented HRD practitioner's objective to improve performance, too much emphasis on behaviors can be dangerous. This is because organizations value performance, not behavior. Further, specific behaviors do not necessarily lead to desired results because of environmental and motivational factors. In fact, some employees display "correct" behaviors yet never achieve the desired level of performance, whereas others exhibit contrary behaviors and achieve superior performance (Fuller and Farrington, 1999).

Principle 2: Any statement about human performance is about organizational performance as well.

Many HRD practitioners fail to see the connection between human performance and organizational performance. These terms are often used interchangeably for separate outcomes, which leads to increased confusion and the misapplication of each. Therefore, it is necessary to arrive at an acceptable understanding of the relationship between these two concepts in order to reduce confusion and thus the effective use of each concept.

Regardless of the type of performance that takes place in an organization, the focus remains the same: The "employees" are engaged in activities that generate internal products and external deliverables that are used by the organization to achieve its revenue goals. Therefore, the common element in each performance activity is the individuals. They are the ones who are participating in learning and who receive the greatest benefit. The implication of this is that human performance lies at the heart of organizational performance. This is a "micro" perspective of organizational performance, which maintains that each employee contributes to the overall efficiency of the organization by his or her individual performance.

The "macro" perspective maintains an emphasis on the overall human performance system rather than on individuals within the system. Thus, organizational performance is the aggregate effort of individual employees as a result of maintaining systems alignment and integration such that desired business results are achieved. It requires performance-oriented HRD practitioners to possess performance management and systems thinking skills to bring about organizational change. Therefore, organizations need to maintain systems that reinforce and encourage exemplary performance. This includes making certain the policies and procedures and other work-related barriers do not interfere with an employee's performance. Moreover, internal competition for resources must be held to a minimum to avoid conflicts that interfere with achieving desired results.

Because there are both micro and macro views of performance, organizations generally maintain an individual performance process, which includes job description, job design, performance appraisal, and compensation review for each employee. Although managers are primarily responsible for these activities, the human resources department is responsible for their creation and maintenance. Organizations also maintain an organizational performance process, which is commonly known as a performance management system. Included here are human resources planning activities, job design, performance coaching and feedback, performance and causal analysis, environmental analysis and engineering, motivational analysis, developmental planning, performance appraisal (e.g., 360 degree evaluation), and compensation and reward programs. Senior managers and executives are mostly responsible for these elements.

Unless the micro and macro approaches are integrated and coordinated, they can be counterproductive. This is because each alone fails to recognize that the aggregate of human performance is in essence organizational performance. Thus, the elements used in managing and shaping human performance must be incorporated in the overall performance management system of the organization.

Principle 3: Costs of improving performance should be regarded as investments in human capital, yielding returns in the form of increased performance potential.

Another principle of organizational performance is that the investments needed to improve performance (e.g., employee development) are realized through the benefits received (e.g., improved quality, productivity, efficiency, profitability). It is important to identify such ratios in order to persuade organizational leaders that performance improvement interventions and initiatives yield positive results. Thus, such expenditures are not viewed as costs but rather as investments into human capital, which will ultimately benefit the organization. This can be determined in two ways: the return on investment (ROI) method and the cost–benefit method.

The return on investment method provides HRD practitioners with the expected return (benefits) on investments (costs) expressed as a percentage or in actual dollars. There are two ways of calculating ROI. First, the percentage method requires HRD practitioners to identify the benefits of improving performance in financial units and divide them by their actual cost. The higher the percentage the greater the benefit to the organization in financial terms. The second way of calculating ROI involves identifying the performance improvement value resulting from an expenditure in financial terms and subtracting their respective costs (Swanson, 1999, 815). With this method, the higher the number the greater the benefit. Of course, both methods can reveal a negative ROI.

The investment (cost) portion of the formula, such as the salaries of managers, employees, and HRD practitioners, the cost of facilities or equipment, and the opportunity cost (loss of productivity for participants' development or production costs), represents capital expenditures. ROI can be calculated at two different times during the intervention process prior to initiating a performance improvement intervention to estimate its potential cost-effectiveness, or it can be calculated afterward to measure achieved results. When the intervention benefits can be clearly documented and substantiated, ROI calculations are most useful and powerful. Also, the nature of the intervention can affect whether it is appropriate to calculate a return on investment.

One problem with the ROI method, however, is that most benefits derived for interventions cannot be quantified. HRD practitioners must identify the qualitative benefits (skills, intellectual capital, specialized expertise and knowledge, industry knowledge, human capital) that will be of the most importance to the organization in the future to overcome this problem. Additionally, they must provide a solid rationale for how various performance improvement scenarios will achieve the organization's desired end.

Two other methods for evaluating investments can be used: the payback period method and the future value method (Swanson, 2001; Swanson and Gradous, 1988). The payback method divides total performance improvement investment by annual savings to arrive at a time period (years or months) in which the intervention will be expected to "pay back" the original investment. To determine the long-term effects of more than one decision, the future value method is used. This approach is based on the premise that performance improvement investments have various returns, and therefore future value analysis indicates the future benefits of each investment option and illustrates the option with the highest return. On the basis of this information, HRD practitioners can provide organizational decisionmakers with information regarding the best way to allocate performance improvement resources.

The cost–benefit analysis model addresses the concerns of organizational decisionmakers for justifying the investment in improving performance (Kearsley, 1986). This method is also an excellent framework for comparing alternatives for future investment. Smith and Geis (1992, 153) state that "cost–benefit models lend themselves to decision making and often lead to a better understanding of the entire performance system."

The cost–benefit method takes one of four forms. First, it lists the cost factors to consider in comparing alternatives (alternative method). Second, HRD practitioners can divide cost by some outcome measure (ratio method). Third, practitioners can express benefits and costs in the same units (return on investment method). And fourth, they can calculate the relationship between the program and performance (consulting method).

Brinkerhoff (1987, 188–189) reports that six basic steps are involved in conducting a cost–benefit analysis:

1. Identify decisionmakers and their values. Indicate which people are to be included in the analysis and how different values are to be weighted relative to one another.

2. Identify alternatives and clearly understand the decision choices. When the alternative to program A is program B, use benefit–cost ratios that compare the two programs directly rather than ratios that compare each program to the null alternative of no program.
3. Identify costs, including all direct and indirect expenses as well as opportunity costs.
4. Identify benefits that individuals, groups, or organizational elements will enjoy as a result of the program.
5. If possible, translate the potential worth to beneficiaries and the possible costs in terms of some comparable data, such as dollars saved, absences reduced, productivity gains, and so on.
6. Aggregate and interpret valued effects. The various valued effects of a program can be combined in a calculation of net benefits or a cost–benefit ratio.

Principle 4: Organizational and individual goals must be considered to define worthy performance.
At the heart of organizational performance are the organization's strategic business goals and objectives, which focus performers' activities (Harless, 1974). Jobs that do not help an organization achieve its strategic business goals and objectives cease to be valuable. It is extremely important, therefore, to link all job design activities to these goals and objectives (Brinkerhoff and Gill, 1994).

Principle 5: Knowing how to engineer human performance and the conditions that affect it is as important as explaining why the behavior occurred.
Gilbert (1978, 1996) introduced the Behavior Engineering Model (BEM), which has governed many of the practices within organizational performance. The BEM is a holistic performance improvement model designed to provide a comprehensive framework for troubleshooting existing human performance problems or identifying possible solutions to such problems. The model distinguishes between two dimensions—the individual performer and the work environment—as well as three critical components for each—stimuli, response, and consequences. When examining performance, HRD practitioners should assess what affect the performer and the environment have on achieving results. They must also understand that within the BEM framework, stimuli incite action; response represents behaviors; and consequences are the results of behaviors (Rothwell, 1996).

At the performer level, Gilbert (1978, 1996) identifies three elements: knowledge (stimuli), capacity (response), and motives (consequences). By knowledge, Gilbert means systematically designed training that matches the requirements of exemplary performers and the opportunity for training. Capacity refers to the match between people and positions, good selection processes, flexible scheduling of performance to match peak capacity of workers, and prostheses or visual aids to augment capacity. Finally, motives include the recognition of workers' willingness to work for available incentives, assessment of workers' motivation, and recruitment of workers to match the realities of work conditions.

In the work environment dimension, Gilbert (1978, 1996) identifies three elements: information (stimuli), resources (response), and incentives (consequences). Information includes the description of what is expected of performance, clear and relevant guides on how to do the job, and relevant and frequent feedback about the adequacy of performance. Resources include tools, time, and materials designed to achieve performance needs, access to leaders, and organized work processes. Incentives refer to adequate financial incentives made contingent upon performance, nonmonetary incentives, career development opportunities, and clear consequences for poor performance.

Using the BEM, HRD practitioners can clear identify a stimulus–response–consequence process that may be used to improve individual performance and to arrange work environments that foster positive performance outcomes and business results. This approach serves as a template for analysis and recommendation, which serves as a systematic approach for improving both human and organizational performance. Gilbert suggests that HRD practitioners should begin their efforts by identifying the achievements that their stakeholders desire. Next, they should measure opportunities for improvements, and then select intervention that brings about performance enhancement (Rothwell, 1996a).

For Gilbert (1978, 179), any performance system can be analyzed from six vantage points:

- *The philosophical level*—the beliefs within which the organization functions.
- *The cultural level*—the larger environment within which the organization operates.
- *The policy level*—the missions that define the organization's purpose.
- *The strategic level*—the plans the organization has established to accomplish its mission.
- *The tactical level*—specific duties carried out to realize plans.
- *The logistical level*—all support activities that help performers conduct their duties (Rothwell, 1996, 34).

Analysis of each of these levels will help determine the effects of organizational and environmental factors on human performance.

According to Rosenberg, Coscarelli, and Hutchison (1999, 37), "Gilbert's model has been recognized for several important strengths. It identifies and classifies specific areas for performance impact, and each one can be altered to influence behavior." Such a model provides a way for identifying appropriate interventions for each area while it builds on the contributions of behavioral psychology by tying organizational performance directly to one of its strongest roots.

Rosenberg, Coscarelli, and Hutchison (1999, 19–23) suggest that several other techniques that help HRD practitioners understand how to engineer human performance and environmental conditions also affect performance. First, practitioners can employ *cognitive engineering* techniques. In this process, HRD practitioners draw on the knowledge and techniques of cognitive psychology and related disciplines to provide the foundation for principle-driven design of person–machine systems. Another process is *psychometrics*, which is the measurement of human achievement and the capabilities used to measure the performance capacity of individual employees. Next, practitioners can used *ergonomics and human factors* analysis to make certain that the design of systems complies with the requirements of users, such as computers, software, equipment, desk chairs, tools, equipment, and so forth.

Three systems can be helpful in addressing human and organizational performance problems: analytical, feedback, and intervention systems. Analytical systems will be discussed in greater detail in the next principle. Feedback systems include formal compensation programs as well as other motivation, incentive, and reward programs used to enhance performance. According to Tosti (1986), there are three critical characteristics of feedback: who gives it, what the content of the feedback is, and when and where the feedback is given. Intervention systems are used as a way of responding to identified causes of human performance problems or to opportunities for improving performance. These are often referred to as solutions, strategies, tactics, change initiatives, or learning activities.

Principle 6: Diagnosing problems requires analysis of the present system and examination of differences between it and an ideal system. Avoiding anticipated problems requires analyzing the planned system and modifying it to approximate the ideal.

According to Watkins and Kaufman (1996) and Rothwell and Kazanas (1998), analysis is the process of determining the seriousness and importance of learning, business, performance, and organizational needs. In other words, analysis reveals what gaps exist and helps determine their importance, severity, and why they exist. It could be said that analysis is essential in the formation of strategies used in improving organizational performance, without which development becomes a hit-or-miss proposition.

Harless (1970) realized that analysis often occurs too late in the instructional process. He believed it was critical to complete the analysis process before the design of an instructional program. Over time, front-end analysis became the first step in the instructional design process.

According to Foshay, Silber, and Westgaard (1986, 27), analysis addresses seven key issues:

- Objectives of an analysis.
- Target audience to be assessed.
- Sampling procedures to be used to select a representative group of people from the target audience for participation in the analysis.
- Data collection methods used to gather information.
- Specifications for instruments to be used during the analysis, and how they should be used; and the approvals or protocols and the interaction procedures to be followed with members of the organization during the analysis.
- Methods of data analysis to be used to analyze the information collected during the analysis.
- Descriptions of how decisions will be made based on the data.

Phillips and Holton (1995) contend that these issues vary in importance depending on project constraints and stakeholder expectations (see the Analysis section in Chapter 5).

Principle 7: Exemplary performance provides the most logical reference for establishing job performance standards.

Identifying performance standards based on exemplary performance allows organizations to regulate the quality of performance outputs and activities, avoid needless mistakes, and maintain consistency. Ultimately, this leads to better operational results. Performance standards also help managers to engineer exemplary performance and provide criteria by which to measure the quality of these deliverables. Without performance standards, managers, employees, and the organization will not be able to ascertain whether they have generated deliverables acceptable to internal and external stakeholders.

Rummler and Brache (1995) contend that performance standards represent excellence criteria used to measure product and service quality and worker efficiency. They provide measures that enable employees to compare their efforts and outputs to ascertain whether they are performing at acceptable levels. Quite simply, performance standards represent the targets used to measure the quality of employee outputs and the efficiency of their performance activities (Gilley and Maycunich, 2000a).

According to Berke (1990), performance standards based on exemplary performance should be achievable, specific, measurable, time-based, and written out. They should be easily understood by managers and employees. Such standards allow employees to monitor and correct their performance because they can measure for themselves how well they are performing and whether or not they are producing satisfactory performance outputs. As a result, performance standards encourage employees to continue to produce at an acceptable level. Consequently, they will do their jobs and know when they are doing them well.

Principle 8: Human performance problems have differing root causes that originate either from the person, from something in the environment, or from both.

By their very notion, human performance problems are generated by a variety of factors. Differing work process, task execution, and personal preferences can contribute to such breakdowns. Organizational culture, work climates, environmental factors, policies and procedures, and managerial practices can also contribute to human performance problems.

As a way of understanding the causes of human performance problems, organizations need to employ root-cause analysis. This analysis is an excellent tool for identifying "hidden causes" of human performance problems and organizational breakdowns (Rossett, 1999b). Moreover, root-cause analysis establishes a framework by which HRD practitioners can identify the real cause of organizational and performance deficiencies. Failure to identify the root cause of human performance problems and organizational breakdowns can result in wasted financial, material, and human resources.

Root-cause analysis is a brainstorming technique used to reveal all possible causes of human performance problems and organizational breakdowns. This is a bias-free technique that can help organizations make significant improvements in their performance and efficiency.

Gilley and Maycunich (1998, 212) identify several steps of root-cause analysis. They are as follows:

- Identify and agree on the definition(s) of the problem(s). For example, survey results and individual interviews may indicate that employees feel there are no opportunities for promotion.

- Identify possible causes of the problem. Utilize brainstorming and cause–effect diagrams to generate ideas. Write down all ideas; later the group will discuss and eliminate as appropriate.
- Verify causes with data. Use existing data or, if needed, identify additional data necessary to help decide which are actual causes of the problem. If more information is needed, identify what it is and who will obtain it.
- Check your conclusions about causes. Do people with knowledge of the issue or processes agree with the conclusions? Do the conclusions make sense? Is additional information needed to support the results?

Following these simple steps, HRD practitioners can help their organization through a process of determining the real reasons for human performance problems and organizational breakdowns. However, stand-alone root-cause analysis can be very unreliable; therefore, other analysis techniques should be used to support results (see the section on cause analysis in Chapter 5).

Principle 9: The performance of one subsystem affects the performance of other subsystems in somewhat predictable ways, requiring that root causes be analyzed at more than one level of the organization.

Rummler and Brache (1995) maintain that organizational structures are a collection of integrated systems (e.g., finance, manufacturing, human resources, and marketing). Through systemic analysis they discovered that human performance is influenced by organizational systems, and vice versa. They suggest that all organizational systems (and their subsystems) are influenced by a complex and ever-changing variety of outside forces. Rosenberg, Coscarelli, and Hutchison (1999) argue that organizational analysis is required to examine this interrelationship and the impact of external forces.

Rothwell (1996b) believes each part of an organization is a *subsystem* (part of the organizational system) interacting with a *suprasystem* (the environment external to the organization). Consequently, each part of an organization contributes to its mission. Furthermore, changes in one part of the organization will affect others. This reflects the interdependencies of open systems.

Burke (1992) identifies several interdependent systems that can affect human and organizational performance. The integration and interface between and among these systems can affect the efficiency of performance and its adequacy. Systems include:

- *External environment:* External political, financial, and marketplace forces.

- *Mission and strategy:* A collective understanding of the overall purpose and direction of the organization by its people.
- *Leadership:* Executive behavior and values that energize others to act.
- *Culture:* Collective beliefs and visible and sometimes hidden rules and practices that have been shaped by the organization's history and past momentum.
- *Structure:* The placement of people into positions that allows for an optimal alignment of authority and responsibility needed to achieve the organization's strategic objectives.
- *Management practices:* The management activity that draws on technical, financial, and human assets to carry out the organization's strategy.
- *Systems:* The procedures, written guidelines, and other mechanisms that constitute predetermined answers to guide people in decisionmaking. The budgeting process, reward system, and human resource flow processes are examples.
- *Climate:* The collective current impressions, expectations, and feelings of the members of local work units. These influence relationships in multiple directions throughout the organization.

Other elements that can affect human and organizational performance include:

- *Task requirements and individual skills/abilities:* The skills and knowledge required to be successful in a specific assignment, which can be considered a job–person match.
- *Individual needs and values:* The internal psychological factors that provide attraction to, and assign value to, specific outcomes. These can be tangible or intangible.
- *Motivation:* The force that propels humans toward desired objectives. This energy comes from such basic motives as achievement, power, affection, discovery, security, and freedom.

Principle 10: Many different solutions may be used to improve human performance. Selection of any one solution is dependent on the cause and nature of the performance problem, and the criteria used to evaluate a solution must include its potential to make a measurable difference in the performance system.

Regardless of the human or organizational performance problem, Silber (1992, 61) recommends that HRD practitioners can use five different types of performance improvement interventions. *Isolated training* is the simplest intervention. It is typically used to fix an isolated performance problem, such as the lack of required skills or knowledge needed to execute a job. The primary weakness of this approach is the overreliance on training as the only solution to improve performance. *Isolated performance* involves using job aids, minor environmental redesign, and incentives or motivational system changes that fix an isolated performance problem. The principal difference between isolated training and isolated performance is that the latter uses other approaches, techniques, and strategies to enhance employee performance. Both approaches, however, rely heavily on training as a means of correcting performance problems.

Total training incorporates a broad view of performance problems by addressing the entire human performance system (see Chapter 5) and the skills, knowledge, and attitudes required for performance adequacy. Once identified, more effective and efficient training can be employed to resolve a performance problem. By contrast, a *total performance* approach includes studying information, environment/work design, incentives/motives, skill/knowledge, and management problems and solutions before identifying a solution(s) that is most cost-effective and that generates the highest return on investment. In this way, a macro approach to improving performance can be introduced, one that improves human performance as well as the environmental conditions affecting performance (see Chapter 5). Finally, the *total cultural* approach incorporates techniques used to examine performance problems and solutions within the context of the whole organization's values and culture. This approach enables HRD practitioners to determine the influence of larger-scale affective issues that underlie performance. This approach also helps isolate events, incidents, and efforts that indirectly improve performance, such as managerial quality, managerial forthrightness, employee engagement, and work climates free from fear.

Conclusions

The philosophy of the organizational performance domain is grounded in the field of human performance technology. From this origin, the philosophical underpinnings and principles of the performance domain can be identified. These principles serve to guide practice in organizational performance as well as to identify the roles and responsibilities of HRD practitioners.

Practice of Organizational Performance

Jerry W. Gilley

The practice within the organizational performance domain is greatly affected by the philosophical underpinnings and principles previously discussed. Thus performance-oriented HRD practitioners think and react differently than those who have an organizational learning or change perspective. For example, when confronted with a discrepancy within an organization, the first reaction of a performance-oriented practitioner may be to conduct an analysis of the situation as a way of determining the cause(s) of performance problems, opportunities, and breakdowns prior to engaging in the design, development, selection, and implementation of an intervention. Although organizational learning practitioners often engage in needs analysis prior to implementing solutions, they seldom participate in comprehensive performance and causal analysis before initiating action. Moreover, performance-oriented HRD practitioners think of performance first, and learning and change second or third. Unfortunately, this can cause a bias in the selection of solutions, but this is their general orientation and predisposition.

Additionally, they embrace three frameworks to guide their practice: the A.C.O.R.N. Model, the Human Performance System Model, and the Organizational Performance Improvement Model (also referred to as the Human Performance Technology Model). Finally, practitioners function as either performance engineers or performance consultants and adopt the corresponding model (see Chapter 6). The competencies and skills of these two types of practitioners are very similar, but they do differ slightly, which we will examine below.

Analysis: The Heart of Organizational Performance Practice

Rossett (1999a, 139) contends that analysis provides the foundation for organizational performance practice. Hence the perspective of a performance-oriented HRD practitioner is to examine situations and contexts before providing recommendations. Practitioners believe that data collection is critical before decisions are made and involvement is essential before solutions are recommended. Regardless of what the analysis is called (assessment or needs assessment or training needs assessment or performance analysis or front-end analysis), it is important because it helps practitioners make better plans for serving their stakeholders. The analysis provides a fresh perspective of a performance problem or organizational breakdown and helps define and direct one's efforts. It provides insight into an organization's operations, culture, mission, workplace climate, managerial practices, policies and procedures, job execution and design, and the quality and expertise of individual employees' performance. Analysis gives HRD practitioners an opportunity to think strategically about stakeholders' requests and to select those that will facilitate the achievement of an organization's business goals and objectives.

Mills, Pace, and Peterson (1988, 5) define analysis as "the act and process of separating any material or abstract entity into its constituent elements, which involves determining its essential features and their relation to one another." They suggest that analysis is a process designed to set goals for HRD, develop direction for the HRD function and its practitioners, determine the driving forces within an organization, identify performance, management, and organization gaps, and establish purpose and priorities for HRD. Moreover, they contend that analysis is grounded in the philosophy of problemsolving, which is a process of recognizing differences between what is and what should be (a deficiency), and taking corrective action to narrow the gap between the two. Rothwell and Cookson (1997) believe analysis involves all of the activities associated with recognizing the existence of a problem, its causes, and consequences, and classifying the problem in terms of what interventions might reasonably be used to narrow the gap.

Rossett (1999b, 141) argues that other researchers, such as Harless (1974), Gilbert (1978), Mager and Pipe (1984), Brinkerhoff and Gill (1994), and Robinson and Robinson (1996), see analysis as complementary to the organizational performance domain because of five related beliefs:

- Training is not the answer to every challenge in the workplace.
- There is a wide array of interventions that can be used to enhance performance, such as job aids, selection strategies, compensation and incentive programs, reengineered processes, and job redesign, which combine to be known as a performance system or solution system.
- Matching appropriate interventions to the challenge, opportunity, or problem is a process that is based on analysis of a cause or causes.
- Analysis is a process that forces practitioners to become actively involved with individual employees, managers, organizational leaders and decisionmakers, the work environment, and the organization.
- Competitive pressures (e.g., the global environment and marketplace) require a continuous reexamination of the elements and systems that constitute an organization.

Silber (1992) and Rossett (1999a) believe that HRD practitioners engage in three primary activities when identifying actual performance. First, they use front-end or performance analysis to identify problems (problem identification). Second, they conduct needs analysis to determine the skills, knowledge, and abilities required to perform a job adequately. Third, they break a problem down into its component parts, identify and categorize related issues, and then isolate the cause(s) of the problem(s) (problem analysis).

Obstacles to Analysis

Although analysis is an important component of organizational performance practice, there are several obstacles that prevent its execution.

- *Lack of support for analysis:* Many organizations view analysis as a waste of time, energy, and effort because formal support for conducting analyses within the organization is not obtained. Gaining support for analysis is critical as it conditions the organization to the use of such activities prior to implementing costly interventions (Rossett, 1992).
- *Analysis paralysis:* This occurs because executives, managers, and employees fear that incompetence will be revealed, for which they will be held accountable, or are concerned that analysis will be viewed as an end unto itself, with little or no attempt to identify solutions designed to overcome serious problems (Gilley and Maycunich, 1998).

- *Lack of value of analysis:* All too often analysis is used to justify training activities and other interventions without demonstrating the value-added results that can be realized (Rossett, 1999a).

According to Rossett (1999b, 108), three strategies can be used to increase support for analysis. First, practitioners can conduct effective analyses and document what has been done and how it has contributed to the bottom line. Second, they can justify the use of analysis by demonstrating their importance (e.g., a physician doesn't prescribe treatment without first performing a cautious diagnosis). Third, they can avoid using terms such as analysis, needs assessment, or front-end analysis if management does not respond well to them (instead, use terms such as planning, study, or research).

Types of Needs

Robinson and Robinson (1996) argue that there are four common needs: business, performance, learning, and work environment. *Business needs* are expressed in operational terms such as goals for a unit, department, or organization, and represent the quantifiable data measures used to monitor the organization's "health." They identified two types of business needs: problems and opportunities. Business *problems* define a gap between what is actually occurring at the present time and what should be occurring operationally. Business *opportunities* focus on a future operational goal; no current problem needs to be fixed, but an opportunity needs to be optimized (Robinson and Robinson, 1996, 28). *Performance needs* describe what people need to do if business needs are to be achieved. These are on-the-job behavioral requirements of people who are performing specific jobs. Robinson and Robinson (1996, 25) maintain that *learning needs* identify what people must learn if they are to perform successfully. Learning needs represent areas where employees lack the skill or knowledge to perform satisfactorily. Hale (1998) asserts that *work environment needs* identify what systems and processes within the employee's work environment must be modified if performance and business needs are to be achieved. By addressing work environment needs, an organization has taken action to achieve performance needs(Gilley and Maycunich, 2000a).

Models of Organizational Performance Practice

Within the organizational performance domain, practitioners rely on several models to guide their practice. Three of the most influential are the

A.C.O.R.N. Method of `Analysis, the Human Performance System, and the Organizational Performance Improvement Model. Each of these frameworks provides direction and structure to the practice of organizational performance.

A.C.O.R.N. Method of Analysis

Gilbert (1978) suggests that one of the first steps in reengineering or process redesign is to establish or clarify, and then communicate, the mission of the organization. The organization's leadership and culture greatly and equally influence an organization's mission. Therefore, performance-oriented HRD practitioners (performance engineers and consultants) should answer the following questions when reexamining an organization's mission:

- What is our purpose?
- What direction do we want to strive toward?
- Who are our customers?
- What are we trying to achieve?
- What significance are we attempting to accomplish?
- What will our purpose be in the future?

When these questions are answered, organizations can clearly envision where they are going and how to get there, similar to how your eyes and brain work in harmony to get you across town or home from work.

The analysis of an organizational mission is a time-consuming, soul-searching process intended to bring about unanimity among all organizational members regarding what the business is attempting to accomplish. A mission provides the vision and expectations for the organization and its people and also provides a standard against which performance (behaviors and accomplishments) can be measured at each level of the organization (Dean,1999b, 13). Ultimate agreement brings about enhanced support within the organization. Gilley and Eggland (1992, 76) believe a mission statement acts as an "invisible hand which guides widely scattered organizational members to work independently yet collectively toward the realization of the organization's strategic business goals and objectives."

Once the organization's mission has been examined, performance engineers and consultants can analyze the strategy that is used to execute the mission. Strategy refers to how an organization intends to achieve its purposes over an extended period of time. Strategy helps identify the tasks and activities that an organization will undertake in order to define its direction as it manifests its achievements. It can be considered an organization's game plan to be embraced and executed by all members. It should remain flexible and adaptive and take into consideration unique circumstances and events, but always be focused on helping the organization achieve its desired purpose.

In performance-oriented organizations, the firm's mission and strategy are fully communicated to and understood by all members of the firm. It is common for employees and managers to work in concert with organizational leaders to construct the mission and implement its strategies. In this way, performance-oriented organizations are living by the concept that *people support what they create.*

As a way to ensure that a performance accomplishment is indeed a part of the primary goal—the job mission—of those assigned to carry it out, Gilbert (1978, 1996) provided a model entitled A.C.O.R.N. This is an acronym for the following five qualities:

- Accomplishment: Is the stated accomplishment a result, not a behavior?
- Control: Does the performer have the authority necessary to carry out the accomplishment?
- Overall objective: Does the accomplishment represent the real reason for the job's existence, or one of several tasks?
- Reconcilable: Is this accomplishment reconciled, or congruent with, the mission of the organization and the goals for carrying it out, or is it inconsistent?
- Numbers: Can the accomplishment be measured to determine practicality and cost-effectiveness?

According to Dean (1999b, 14), "an accomplishment can be tested against these qualities to determine if it accurately represents the job mission of an individual, team or function." When determining the missions of the organization, performance engineers and consultants can use these five qualities to examine the congruence of a given accomplishment. Dean (1999b, 17) suggests that the test be first applied at the policy level so that the overall mission of the organization can be validated, then applied at successively lower levels of the organization (see Chapter 4, Principle 5). This framework can be used to validate the alignment of missions across and within levels of the organization and to identify misalignment and suggest corrections in mission. It can also be used to establish control appropriate to achieve the organization's mission, thus creating a mechanism that can enhance employee empowerment and a procedure for assignment and reassignment of job responsibilities. Finally, this framework encourages measurement of the practicality and cost-effectiveness of current processes, and can be used to generate goals, standards, and measures for lower levels of the organization (Dean, 1999b, 17–18).

Human Performance System

The human performance system accepts that organizations are *open systems* that are absolutely dependent for success on their external environments (Rothwell, 1996b). Katz and Kahn (1978) discuss how open systems receive inputs from the environment, process them, and release outputs into the environment. Rummler and Brache (1995) describe inputs as resources used to produce products or deliver services; *processes* are the work methods applied to the inputs; and *outputs* are the results of processes, such as finished goods or services.

Fuller and Farrington (1999, 14) believe that the human performance system consists of organizational inputs, people, and their behaviors, all of which lead to performance, consequences, and feedback, which loops back through the system to the organization and the people in it, and so on. Moreover, the components of this system exist within an environment that also affects performance (Figure 5.1).

Organizational Inputs. The first element of the human performance system is organizational inputs. These are the raw materials, people, financial capital, and information needed to generate deliverables for internal and external stakeholders. Of fundamental importance is how an organization obtains information from its internal and external stakeholders regarding their needs and expectations. Such information permits the organization to improve and manage performance. Mismatches in this area can lead to loss of external customers, turnover among employees, and unproductive partnerships. Therefore, when practitioners evaluate an organization's informational input they may wish to pose the following questions:

- How is the organization obtaining information about the needs of customers, employees, and partners?
- How are decisionmakers and prospective change participants using that information?
- How should they be using that information to make adaptive or even proactive change to meet or exceed customer, employee, and partner requirements?

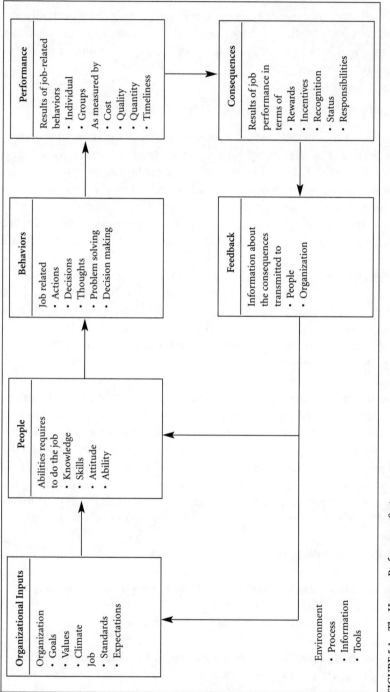

FIGURE 5.1 The Human Performance System

SOURCE: Fuller, J., & Farrington, J. (1999). *From training to performance improvement: Navigating the transition.* San Francisco: Jossey-Bass.

- How should performance improvement intervention support efforts to obtain and use information to meet or exceed customer, employee, or partner requirements (Rothwell and Cookson, 1997, 107)?

Fuller and Farrington (1999) contend that organizational inputs include business goals and objectives, values, guiding principles, and the overall work climate that affects the way employees operate within it. Additionally, organizations possess a culture, sometimes referred to as behavioral norms, that identifies how work is to be done and how members of the firm are to treat one another. Aronson (1995) asserts that those individuals who fail to abide by the culture are either punished (socially) by members of the organization, elect to leave because they don't fit in, or are dismissed for failing to demonstrate a willingness to adopt accordingly.

Job standards and *expectations* are the targets typically used to measure the quality of employee performance outputs and the efficiency of their performance activities (Rummler and Brache, 1995; Rummler, 1998; Gilbert, 1978, 1996). However, they can also be used to measure the quality of organizational inputs, which are used to generate outputs and excuse activities. Job standards represent the excellence criteria used in measuring the quality of organizational inputs, whereas expectations are used in measuring the anticipated consistency of inputs. Both are extremely important when improving performance effectiveness and efficiency. Nevertheless, job standards and expectations serve as targets for organizational leaders, employees, and HRD practitioners to guarantee that performance outputs are generated at an appropriate quality level and that performers have the best inputs with which to execute performance activities. Unless job standards and expectations are established for organizational inputs, performers cannot possibly generate performance outputs or execute performance activities that are acceptable to internal or external stakeholders.

People. How do organizations produce successful results? Simple. They understand the relationship between human resource planning, recruiting, selection, performance, and growth and development (see Figure 5.1). In essence, they had a plan for getting *the right people at the right place at the right time,* including employees, managers, HRD practitioners, and organizational leaders.

Effective organizations strongly believe in planning for future human resource needs and possibilities. They do so to improve business results and to remain at full alert, poised to meet competitive challenges. In such organizations, human resource planning, recruiting, and selection determine the type, quantity, and quality of human resources needed to foster organizational renewal and enhance competitive readiness. Thus, performance engineers and consultants and organizational leaders should engage in a series of related steps to guarantee that appropriate human resources are identified, recruited, selected, and developed to achieve performance success.

According to Gilley and Maycunich (2000b, 182), "human resource planning is a process of systematically organizing the future, of putting into place a plan designed to address upcoming performance problems or productivity and quality requirement." Such planning is integrated with the organization's strategic plan and other organizationwide initiatives, revealing a strong interdependency among human resource activities such as recruitment, selection, orientation, placement, performance management, the learning and change process, career development, and compensation and rewards. Absent an integrative approach, human resource planning is unable to secure the type and quality of employees needed to ensure organizational success.

The major influences of human resource planning include: business needs of the organization, competitive pressure, and future human resource requirements.

- Business needs: increased business revenue, profitability, quality, effectiveness, efficiency, safety, customer satisfaction, and so forth.
- Competitive pressures: every organization must respond to competitive pressure or be crushed by it. Therefore, organizations are continuously examining themselves to determine whether or not they can adequately respond to their competitors.
- Future human resource requirements: the necessity to forecast the number, kind, and type of employees required in the future (Gilley and Maycunich, 2000b).

In short, human resource planning is greatly influenced by these factors, requiring performance engineers and consultants and leaders to analyze their situation carefully and make projections accordingly.

An element of human resource planning is human resource forecasting. Its purpose is to estimate labor requirements at some future date (Cascio, 1995). Forecasting includes identifying the conditions inside an organization while simultaneously examining the external labor market as a whole to accurately project the quantity and quality of future human resources. Performance engineers and consultants and developmental organization leaders must carefully examine each of these components.

Once human resource planning efforts have been identified, performance engineers and consultants and organizational leaders need to undertake job analysis activities to identify the requirements for each job within the organization. These in turn create a solid basis on which to make job-related employment decisions (Schneider and Konz, 1989), helping organizations establish interviewing criteria, performance appraisal systems, and selection requirements for use in hiring and promotional decisions. Job analysis is also used to:

- clarify job requirements and the relationships among jobs
- forecast human resource needs
- identify training, transfer, and promotion requirements
- evaluate employee performance and conduct compensation reviews
- recruit future employees
- improve labor relations
- enhance career planning
- improve job design
- develop job classifications
- improve career counseling activities
- resolve grievances and jurisdictional disputes
- improve working methods
- identify job classifications useful in developing selection, training, and compensation systems (Cascio, 1995).

Behaviors. Behaviors are measured in terms of specific actions and are influenced by organizational inputs. Fuller and Farrington (1999) present how job-related behaviors can be observed via the actions, decisions, thoughts, problemsolving, and decisionmaking of individuals and groups. Ultimately, job-related behavior affects the achievement of desired business results.

Performance. At the heart of every job is the organization's strategic business goals and objectives that focus employees' efforts (Rummler, 1998). Jobs that fail to support organizational achievement of its strategic goals and objectives cease to be valuable (Gilley, 1998). Thus it is critical to link job analysis to these outcomes. Every job includes four elements: performance outputs, activities, standards, and competencies.

Performance is measured in terms of outcomes, such as reduced product costs, increased quality, or increased productivity. These are defined as performance outputs, which Rummler and Brache (1995) define as the tangibles and intangibles that employees are paid to produce. According to Gilley (1998, 91), performance outputs may represent "the number of sales calls made by telemarketing representatives, sales made per month by sales personnel, service claims handled by customer service representatives, the number of packages delivered per day by postal workers, and so on. Hence, outputs represent the hourly, daily, weekly, monthly, quarterly, and/or yearly expectations of employees in a specific job classification."

Employees engage in performance activities to generate performance outputs. It is the responsibility of performance engineers and consultants, managers, and employees to identify the activities required of employees. Each performance activity consists of micro tasks, which collectively form the components of an employee's job. One of the best ways of achieving this objective is to select exemplary performers and ask them to identify the tasks and the sequence used to produce their typical results. This is sometimes referred to as benchmarking.

Once performance outputs, activities, and standards are identified, performance engineers and consultants can identify the competencies that employees need to accomplish the organization's strategic goals. Gilley, Boughton, and Maycunich (1999) refer to these as *competency maps*. Such a map represents the identification of the knowledge, skills, behaviors, and attitudes that an employee possesses to complete job tasks that comprise performance activities. Competency maps are useful in recruiting and selecting employees for given job classifications, determining the growth and development activities in which employees must participate to master performance, and revealing employee strengths and weaknesses, thereby guiding the formulation of career development activities as well as performance growth and development plans.

The final element of performance is the *job description*, which demonstrates the relationship between performance outputs and activities. These should be written to achieve three goals: to clearly identify performance outputs for each job; to identify the performance activities required by employees to produce these deliverables; and to demonstrate the relationship between activities and outputs. Quite simply, a job description is simply a written document that describes an employee's performance activities and deliverables and the performance standards that must be met.

Consequences. According to Fuller and Farrington (1999), consequences may include rewards, incentives, recognition, status, power and authority, responsibilities, or compensation, and should be linked to job performance.

These constitute the typical compensations and reward system used in organizations to track and evaluate performance and assign rewards accordingly.

Compensation and reward systems are powerful incentives for improving performance, however, when used ineffectively they can be powerful de-motivators. When employees are rewarded for completing tasks that are unnecessary, less important, and unrelated to their jobs, it sends the wrong message. Thus, well-designed compensation and reward programs need to be linked to the organization's achievement expectations. In this way, organizations can continuously reward employees for improving their performance—putting into motion a developmental philosophy that enables the firm to achieve long-term success, enhance competitive readiness and renewal capacity, and improve performance capability. Effective organizations understand that rewarding employees for performance improvement is a wise investment in the future of all. Therefore, organizations should align the consequences of performance with organizational inputs. When these are out of alignment, employees are forced to choose between *what they are told to do* and *what actually gets rewarded* within the organization (Fuller and Farrington, 1999, 18).

Many employees fail to perform adequately as a result of a perceived disparity between their performance and the rewards they receive from the organization—known as a performance/reward disconnect (Gilley, Boughton, and Maycunich, 1999). In this case, desired organizational performance results such as loyalty, creativity, and entrepreneurship are ignored or punished in the workplace while other performance is rewarded. In other words, organizations communicate mixed messages by inadvertently rewarding performances they don't want or desire, such as individualism at the expense of coworkers or other departments. Improving performance requires a direct correlation between desired behaviors/actions and the rewards received. Research demonstrates that if people are rewarded for the right performance, the organization will get the right performance (LeBoeuf, 1985). As stated previously, this research suggests that the things that get rewarded get done. In essence, failure to reward proper performance behavior leads to undesirable results. Under these circumstances, employees will appear to follow organizational mandates, while spending most of their time doing what gets rewarded, which negatively affects the organization over the long term.

Feedback.   In the simplest terms, feedback is information about employee performance and the consequences of their performance. When employees are able to associate their work with specific consequences, they will modify their job-related behavior to optimize their performance. Without frequent, accurate feedback, however, employees are far less likely to improve their performance over time.

For a human performance system to function smoothly, managers need to communicate feedback in a way that encourages employees to improve their performance. Feedback should be delivered positively, which prevents employees from becoming defensive. It should be ongoing, not a surprise or a once-a-year event. That is, performance feedback should reinforce things that employees know about themselves and quickly recognize so they may make minor corrections in their job performance.

To be effective, managers need to secure appropriate and adequate documentation prior to sharing their observations with employees. In other words, implementing performance feedback requires a paper trail. However, recording every incident of performance feedback is unrealistic.

Thorough documentation of poor performance assures objectivity in dealing with the problem and the employee. On the other hand, accurate documentation of good performance justifies assigning new and more challenging work to employees. Precise, comprehensive documentation will place the managers and the organization on firm legal footing if an employee's performance leads to termination.

Gilley, Boughton, and Maycunich (1999, 74) identify a seven-step process that managers can use to provide their employees with feedback regarding incorrect or unproductive performance. First, demystify the performance problem by telling the employee exactly what was done incorrectly. Whenever possible, provide feedback immediately. Second, allow the employee to react and respond to feedback. This requires listening to the employee's response and observation of his or her nonverbal behavior. Third, once the employee's perspective of his/her performance is understood, offer concrete evidence of the poor performance. Be specific and clear in one's presentation. Fourth, attempt to identify the strength(s) possessed by the employee that may compensate for the weakness in performance. That is, commend something that the employee does well that will help overcome the weakness demonstrated. Fifth, identify the appropriate performance and have the employee demonstrate it. This may include the exact steps to be followed, changes to be made, or the way to go about improving or ensuring quality. Either way, managers' expectations must be clear. Sixth, review the downside of continuous poor performance. In other words, managers have a responsibility to communicate to the employee the consequences of poor performance (discipline, suspension, termination, etc.). It is a manager's responsibility to make certain the employee understands that poor performance will not be acceptable, and that change must be forthcoming. Seventh, make certain the employee understands that it is his/her responsibility to correct the performance and that he/she has "ownership" of the problem. The managers should help identify ways of improving performance or the skills and/or knowledge necessary for improvement. It is the responsibility of performance engineers and consultants to ensure that these seven steps become a standard practice within their organizations.

Environment.   According to Fuller and Farrington (1999), four environmental factors significantly affect performance: job processes, performance barriers, information, and tools. These environmental factors have the potential to seriously impede performance even if organizational inputs such as people abilities, behaviors, consequences, and feedback are of the highest quality. Many researchers believe that efforts to improve human performance must take into account the environments within which performance occurs. Rothwell (1996b, 32) identifies two environments that performance engineers and consultants should examine:

- The *organizational environment* is synonymous with the suprasystem. It is everything outside the organization (the external environment).
- The *work environment* is everything inside the organization (the internal environment).

Multiple Solutions Approach.   Fuller and Farrington (1999, 21) believe that "if people are to achieve top-level performance, all the components of their human performance system must be optimized." However, individual and organizational performance decreases when any of these components break down or are ignored. Performance engineers and consultants are than called upon to remove performance barriers by implementing appropriate performance improvement solutions.

Quite simply, the human performance system demonstrates the complexity of performance, its management, and its improvement. As a result, training by itself is an insufficient approach to improving performance. Many researchers (Dean, 1999b; Fuller and Farrington, 1999; Swanson, 1999; Gilley and Maycunich, 1998) have concluded that training can positively affect the people element of the human performance system, but it cannot fix breakdowns in the areas of organizational inputs, consequences, feedback, or the environment. Therefore, performance engineers and consultants are obligated to create interventions that address all of the broken elements of the performance system.

Rummler and Brache (1995, 25) believe that the human performance system is based on the premise that motivated and talented people who fail to perform adequately are usually the result of the organizational system in which they reside (e.g., organization, process, and/or job/performer level). They contend that organizations that effectively manage the human performance system should positively respond to the following questions:

- Do performers understand the outputs they are expected to produce and the standards they are expected to meet? (*Performance*)
- Do performers have sufficient resources, clear signals and priorities, and a logical set of job responsibilities? (*Performance*)
- Are performers rewarded for achieving job goals? (*Consequences*)
- Do performers know whether they are meeting job goals? (*Feedback*)
- Do performers have the necessary skills and knowledge to achieve job goals? (*Behavior*)
- In an environment in which the five questions listed above are answered affirmatively, do performers have the physical, mental, and emotional capacity to achieve job goals? (*People*)

Organizational Performance Improvement Model

Although many acceptable approaches to organizational performance exist, most involve a performance improvement process or system that includes performance analysis, cause analysis, and intervention selection, as shown in Figure 5.2. Deterline and Rosenberg (1992) developed the performance technology model in concert with this principle, but we have entitled it the Organizational Performance Improvement Model.

Performance Analysis.　Rosenberg (1996, 6) describes performance analysis as "a process of identifying the organization's performance requirements and comparing them to its objectives and capabilities." Performance analysis identifies what must be done to correct a specific performance problem and opportunities for improvement. Rossett (1999b) contends that performance analysis is a partnering activity with clients to help them define and achieve their goals. It involves reaching out for several perspectives on a problem or opportunity, determining any and all drivers or barriers to successful performance, and then proposing a solution system based on what is learned, not on what is typically done.

Performance analysis reveals the causes of a performance problem by examining why differences exist among performers and whether performance is acceptable or unacceptable, or below standard (Rothwell and Cookson, 1997). It also helps determine whether jobs are designed correctly, the rela-

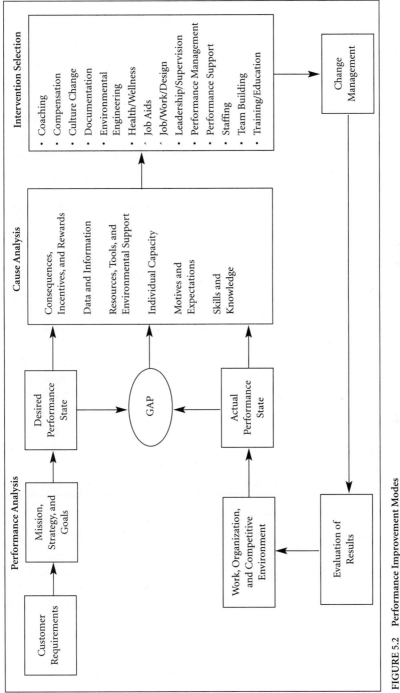

FIGURE 5.2 Performance Improvement Modes

SOURCE: Deterline, W.A. and Rosenberg, M.J. (1992). *Workplace Productivity: Performance Technology Success Stories*. Washington, DC: International Society for Performance Improvement Publications.

tionship between jobs, factors affecting performance, causal relationships, and the affects of motivational strategies.

This analysis, sometimes called *front-end analysis,* distinguishes performance deficiencies from learning and organizational needs (Harless, 1986). It focuses on identifying the causes of performance breakdowns and the impact of the work environment, motivational factors, and managerial impact on employee productivity and performance. Performance analysis is critically important because organizations cannot afford to waste scarce resources on interventions that fail to solve performance problems. Rothwell (1996a) argues that performance engineers and consultants lack the time to focus on learning activities when deficiencies do not stem from individual knowledge, skills, or attitudes. Instead, they should use their performance consulting skills to guide the organization in management actions that address the work environment or motivational factors.

According to Rossett (1999b), two broad types of information are required during a performance analysis: directions and drivers. First, *directions* are the performance and perspectives that the organization and its leaders are trying to incorporate. Two influences are common: optimal (or exemplary) performance and actual (or current) performance. Additionally, directions set the course for the performance improvement effort. These can be identified by prospective questions such as: What and why are you trying to accomplish? What do you want to see? What do your more effective people know or do? The other approach is to look at what is currently going on. Second, *drivers* are the things that block or aid performance. These can include skills, motivation, and work processes. It is important to understand the client's perspective on what's been getting in the way. In fact, Rossett (1999b) believes that drivers determine the solution(s) required to improve performance.

The goal of performance analysis is to measure the gap between desired and actual performance (Rossett, 1999b). As a result, performance engineers and consultants need to measure actual performance and conduct a comprehensive assessment of employees' current capabilities, the efficiency of organizational structure, the appropriateness of organizational culture, and its competitive position. The nature of the gap will determine the type of interventions used to bring actual and desired performance levels closer together.

Performance analysis provides an understanding of existing and desired conditions surrounding performance. As a result, Rossett (1996b, 13) identified four key questions that analysis answers:

- What results (performance outcomes) are being achieved?
- What results are desired?

- How large is the performance gap?
- What is the impact of the performance gap?

She (1999b) also identifies four kinds of opportunities for performance analysis. The first is a rollout, which is when new products or organizational philosophy is being introduced. The second is when a performance problem emerges. The third is when people development becomes an important issue within the organization. And the fourth is during strategy development initiatives where decisions about direction, values, and alignment are determined.

As a way of identifying and describing past, present, and future human performance gaps, performance engineers and consultants should assess desired versus actual performance. Several questions have been identified to guide such an effort:

- What is the desired situation versus the actual situation?
- What is the performance gap or difference?
- Who is affected by the performance gap? Is it one person, a group, an organization, or a work process?
- When and where did the performance gap first occur—or when and where is it expected to begin?
- When and where were its effects, side effects (symptoms), and aftereffects (consequences) first noticed?
- Have they been noticed consistently or inconsistently?
- How has the gap been affecting the organization?
- Have the effects been widespread or limited?
- Is the performance gap traceable to individuals, work groups, locations, departments, divisions, suppliers, distributors, customers, or others?
- What are the immediate and direct results of the gap?
- How much has the gap cost the organization?
- How can the tangible economic impact of the gap best be calculated?
- How can the intangible impact of the gap be calculated in lost customer goodwill or worker morale (Rothwell,1996b, 13)?

Unfortunately, the opportunity for mistakes in the performance analysis process increases with performance complexity. As a way of addressing this issue, Rossett (1999a) separated performance improvement need into three levels: primary, secondary, and tertiary. Primary needs are the specific improvements required (behavior or results) by performers to positively affect desired business outcomes, and secondary needs refer to those outside the control of performers but that will enhance their performance. Tertiary needs are environmental changes that are required to enhance performance. These include organizational structure, work climate, managerial quality, and work flow between different departments. This three-level need framework helps stakeholders understand that needs can be differentiated from situation to situation and that a particular performance improvement effort may require addressing more than one need simultaneously. This framework also allows performance engineers and consultants to assess the relative importance of needs at each level.

Rossett (1999b) identified eight strategies for speeding up the performance analysis planning process. She refers to them as "quick and dirty analyses" and summarizes the importance of soliciting and presenting opinions based on alternative interpretations discussed with the client. These strategies can help overcome "analysis paralysis" and reduce front-end time. The strategies are as follows:

1. Clarify the effort. (Know what you are doing.)
2. Re-purpose existing data. (Use existing data rather than gathering new.)
3. Use "straw" not tabula rasa. (Give your source something to respond to. Time is lost when people can't readily explain what they do or know. Offer the chance to agree, disagree, or elaborate rather than expect them to come forth with descriptions.)
4. Establish hypotheses; test them with sources. (Make educated guesses; test with experts.)
5. Establish a system for virtual analyses. (Be proactive; don't wait for the customer to ask for help.)
6. Generalize. (Use one source to frame possibilities; validate with others.)
7. Collapse the steps. (Bring key players together to answer critical questions at the beginning rather than build a systematic process.)
8. Rely on technology to speed the process. (Utilize Web sites and other electronic information data bases.)

A thorough evaluation of the performance analysis process ensures an accurate and complete needs identification. Each need, regardless of its level, must logically and validly relate to the desired primary performance improvement objective. Since performance engineers and consultants devote a significant portion of their time, energy, and effort to designing improvement interventions that address stakeholders' needs, it is critical that these interventions be on target. Dedicated performance engineers and consultants systematically revisit and reflect on the performance analysis process, double-checking for errors and oversights.

Cause Analysis. According to Rosenberg (1996), a common mistake made during the organizational performance improvement process is moving too quickly to adopt a solution or intervention (e.g., training). It is critical that the underlying cause(s) of a performance problem be identified. Each must be examined carefully to ascertain its contribution to a performance breakdown and the impact on performance.

Cause analysis uncovers the real reason(s) for why a performance problem or gap exists. Hale (1998, 9) contends that "cause analysis is also used to identify factors impeding and contributing to performance." Quite simply, cause analysis is used to determine the causes of a past, present, or future performance gap. Rothwell (1996b, 13–14) believes that determining the causes of performance gaps requires performance engineers and consultants to consider the following:

- Do employees have the knowledge, ability, skills, time, and other resources necessary to perform?
- What are employees' expectations of performance?
- Are employees motivated to perform adequately?
- Do performers possess the ability to perform their jobs correctly?
- What is the adequacy of environmental support and feedback?
- Are employees providing sufficient data and information regarding their performance?
- What are the rewards and incentives for performing correctly, and are they adequate to motivate acceptable performance?
- What are the results and consequences for performing inadequately?
- Are performers penalized or otherwise given disincentives for achieving desired work results?
- How well are people given the data, information, or feedback they need to perform at the time they need it? Are performers given important information they need to perform on a timely basis?
- How well are performers supported in what they do by appropriate environmental support, resources, equipment, or tools?
- Do performers have the necessary job aids and working conditions to perform satisfactorily?
- How well are individuals or groups able to perform?

- Do performers want to achieve desired results?
- What payoffs do they expect?
- How realistic are their expectations?

Answers to these questions will help determine the real reason(s) why human performance is inadequate, inferior, or both.

Intervention Selection.   Hale (1998) maintains that performance improvement efforts involving a simple fix, such as training alone, are not appropriate in a complex performance environment. In most situations, poor performance, that which has fallen below standards, occurs for a variety of reasons. Rummler and Brache (1995) believe that since performance problems are often multicausal, they may require a combination of interventions. Gilley and Maycunich (2000a, 275) conclude that "training combined with changes in the work environment (structure) or motivation strategy (compensation system) is more likely to be successful." When addressing complex performance problems, however, the rate of success and effectiveness increases if management engages in the training and provides the workforce with posttraining support, argues Rosenberg (1996). Therefore, performance improvement selection may require numerous interventions and changes across several layers and levels of the organization. The changes needed to bring performance up to an acceptable level may include training, performance coaching, motivational strategies, environmental change, and so forth (see Figure 5.2).

Robb (1998, 253) believes that prior to implementing solutions, performance engineers and consultants should engage in four activities. First, they should develop written agreements that outline the performance improvement interventions and how they will address the needs of stakeholders. Second, they should develop internal and external partnerships to help facilitate performance improvement. Third, performance engineers and consultants should develop the improvement actions that stakeholders will implement and support. Finally, they should identify the expected outcomes of an intervention as a way of determining how success will be measured.

Categories of Interventions.   Rosenberg (1996) argues that the best way to think about interventions and to work with them is to organize them by category. To this end, he suggests four major categories of interventions:

- *Human resource development* emphasizes improving individual employee performance via training, career development, individual feedback, incentives, and rewards.

- *Organizational development* centers on improving the performance of groups or teams. It involves organizational design, team building, culture change, group feedback, incentives, and rewards.
- *Human resource management* is concerned with coaching and managing individual and group performance, as well as recruiting and staffing. Intervention topics include supervision, leadership, succession planning, and personnel selection.
- *Environmental engineering* focuses on providing the tools and facilities for improving performance. Examples include ergonomics, job aids, electronic resources, systems design, job and organizational design, and facilities design.

To help determine the effectiveness of a performance improvement solution, Rothwell (1996b, 15) provides several key questions:

- How well did the intervention achieve desired and measurable results?
- How well realized were the forecasted and measurable improvements that were targeted for the intervention?
- What were the positive and negative side effects?
- What side effects of the intervention were noticeable?
- What lessons were learned from the intervention that could be applied in the future?
- How well has the intervention been adopted in the corporate culture?
- What best practices or lessons learned resulted from the intervention?

Change Management. An essential aspect of improving organizational performance is planning and implementing the intervention. This is sometimes referred to as change management. Of course, senior management's support is critical to successful implementation and can be assumed provided that a significant organizational performance problem is being addressed.

A performance improvement intervention may fail when organizational change isn't addressed adequately. This is because resistance to change can be a powerful obstacle, which is especially true when change affects the way people go about doing their jobs. Since change may challenge people's assumptions regarding their contributions and value within an organization, it may cause conflict between an employees' current state and their desired state. Therefore, it is important to carefully plan the intervention, manage resistance, and remove barriers to performance improvement. As a result, change management techniques are a critical aspect for successful implementation.

As summarized by Rothwell (1996a, 9), "a good solution that's poorly implemented becomes a poor solution."

The implementation of performance improvement interventions is an area in which performance engineers and consultants generally are the most comfortable and competent. The purpose of this phase is to close performance gaps using credible, stakeholder-identified and stakeholder-supported solutions (Hale, 1998). As a result, performance engineers and consultants will have reached their ultimate goal—improved performance in support of their organization's business goals.

Rothwell (1996b, 15) points out that performance engineers and consultants may assist employees, managers, and other stakeholders when installing an intervention. This requires them to:

- examine what the organization currently is doing to address the cause(s) of the human performance gap;
- determine what the organization should do in the future to address the cause(s) of the human performance gap;
- assess changes inside or outside the organization that may affect the intervention as it is implemented;
- clarify and emphasize how the intervention will help the organization meet its needs, achieve its mission, and realize its strategic planning goals and objectives; and
- identify the best sources of talent and resources to implement the intervention.

At the conclusion of this step, the organization should have a clear understanding of the desired outcomes to be achieved from the intervention. To be effective, however, any intervention requires a long-term commitment and constant oversight by performance engineers and consultants, stakeholders, and decisionmakers.

Kissler (1991) believes that performance engineers and consultants should monitor the intervention as it is being implemented by considering questions such as:

- How well does the intervention address the root cause(s) of human performance gaps?
- What measurable improvements can be shown?
- How much ownership have stakeholders vested in the intervention, and what steps can be taken to improve that ownership?

- How are changing conditions inside and outside the organization affecting the intervention?

This step assures that an intervention is properly monitored and managed in a way that is consistent with desired results.

Evaluation. Evaluating interventions allows performance engineers and consultants to determine whether the desired performance has been achieved. Evaluation reveals whether an intervention has made a difference, what activities were worthwhile, whether on-the-job behavior has changed, and whether changes in specific knowledge, skills, and attitudes have been sufficient to alter behavior. In short, evaluation determines if an intervention has closed the gap between the desired and actual performance state.

The principal objective of performance improvement interventions is to improve human and organizational performance, which results in increased organizational capabilities. Consequently, an evaluation of the organization's behavioral environment is required prior to designing a performance improvement intervention. After an intervention has been implemented, and employees have had significant time to internalize new knowledge, apply new skills, or incorporate change, another behavioral environment analysis should be conducted. The results can then be compared and conclusions drawn regarding the impact of the interventions on the environment. Finally, the behavior of employees who participated in the intervention should be compared to that of nonparticipating employees to obtain an accurate measure of program results.

Evaluation is also used to gather data on performance, to assess whether chosen solutions are producing desired results, and, if not, to determine how they can be modified to achieve the desired outcome (Rothwell, 1996a). Although evaluation appears to be the last step in the organizational performance improvement process, Rummler and Brache (1992) point out that evaluation should start at step one—*performance analysis*, where the performance to be improved is identified. They believe that evaluation procedures should be developed along with solutions and should be part of the ongoing management of the performance intervention. The data gathered and analyzed will determine whether the solution eliminated or significantly mitigated the performance problem. If the solution is deemed inadequate, treatment is discontinued or a new remedy is prescribed.

Rothwell and Cookson (1997) report that *evaluation* is the process of estimating the value of a planned learning experience. They suggest that evaluation involve two steps: comparing results and objectives, and appraising or judging the value of the differences assessed. In some respects, evaluation and analysis are similar activities in that both compare *what is* and *what should be*, and interpret the results of that comparison. They describe five intervention issues worthy of evaluation:

1. *Quality*—the value or utility of an intervention or initiative.
2. *Suitability*—the needs and expectations of sponsors and participants regarding an intervention or initiative.
3. *Effectiveness*—the impact or results of an intervention or initiative.
4. *Efficiency*—the costs and benefits of an intervention or initiative.
5. *Importance*—the long-term influence on an organization following an intervention or initiative.

Rothwell (1996b, 15) contends that an evaluation that is properly targeted at the subject of change (such as employee performance) and at the intervention (the means to an end) should answer these key questions: Did results match intentions? Was a human performance gap eliminated or a human performance improvement opportunity realized? Were organizational needs met?

Measurement Versus Evaluation. Laird (1985, 242) points out that it is important to distinguish between evaluation and measurement in that "*measurement* refers to the act of collecting information relative to the dimensions, quantity, or capacity of something while *evaluation* involves making judgments about ideas, works, solutions, methods, or materials related to the intervention" (emphasis in the original). The primary purpose of a judgment is to determine something's value or worth.

Rummler and Brache (1995) argue that without measures, managers have no basis for:

- communicating performance expectations to employees;
- knowing what is going on in their organizations;
- isolating performance gaps;
- providing feedback that compares performance to a standard;
- identifying performance that should be rewarded; or
- making and supporting decisions regarding resources, plans, policies, schedules, and structure.

Furthermore, Rummler and Brache (1995, 137) assert that, without measures, employees at all levels have no basis for "knowing specifically what is expected of them, monitoring their own performance and generating their own feedback, generating their own rewards and understanding what performance is required for rewards from others, or identifying performance improvement areas."

Purpose of Evaluation. Rothwell (1996b) contends that measurement determines how much change and how much improvement occurred, and answers the following questions:

- What were the impacts of the intervention strategy?
- What value was added in economic and noneconomic terms?

Guba and Lincoln (1988) provide several additional questions that will help determine the purpose of an evaluation:

- What decisions need to be made?
- Who has to make them?
- When will the decisions be made?
- Based on what criteria?

The answers to these questions reveal whether an evaluation is formative or summative.

It could be said that "evaluation is the process of delineating, obtaining, and applying descriptive and judgmental information . . . concerning some object's merit; as revealed by its goals, structure, process, and product; and for some useful purpose such as decision making or accountability" (Stufflebeam, 1975, 19). From this definition, two major purposes of evaluation can be put forward. First, evaluation involves *decisionmaking* to produce information for improvement and to guide choosing among possible modifications, which is referred to as *formative or proactive evaluation* (Rothwell and Cookson, 1997). This type of evaluation is characterized as developmental. It should be used as the basis for constructively modifying the intervention or initiative, not simply to keep it alive or, alternatively, to complete the process (Gilley and Eggland, 1989).

The second purpose of evaluation is to justify the intervention's value to employers, managers, organizational leaders, and the organization. This *summative or retroactive* evaluation purpose involves gathering information after program completion to describe and defend its achievements (Rothwell and Cookson, 1997). Quite simply, evaluation is used to establish accountability for the outcomes of an intervention. Thus, summative evaluations assess overall outcomes of an intervention and support a decision to continue or terminate the process. Performance engineers and consultants need to seek descriptive and judgmental information from everyone involved with the intervention and from those who influence or who might be influenced by the same.

Several important but less common purposes of evaluation can also be identified:

- fulfilling one's HRD responsibility regarding organizational performance improvement;
- improving the quality of the organizational performance improvement process;
- improving project management execution;
- educating organizational leaders about the values and benefits of organizational performance improvement;
- demonstrating one's capacity and capability; and
- improving intervention design and development, guiding HRD practice, and improving its effectiveness (Brinkerhoff, 1998).

Framework for Evaluation. Brinkerhoff (1998, 153) has developed a five-phase framework that can be used to evaluate the components of the organizational performance improvement model.

1. Analyze goals to determine the merits of the performance improvement intervention effort.
2. Audit the performance analysis process used in determining the performance factors and roles that must improved in order to achieve the business goal.
3. Evaluate the design of performance improvement interventions.
4. Analyze the implementation of the performance improvement intervention, including:

   A. Adequately steering the controls used to guide and direct the project;
   B. Assessing usage of implementation techniques;
   C. Providing accountability and documentation of project activities and results.

5. Determine the impact/results of the performance improvement intervention.

This framework can help performance engineers and consultants audit the accuracy of execution of the organizational performance improvement model.

Work, Organization, and Competitive Environment. Work, organization, and competitive environmental pressure greatly affect the actual performance state within an organization (see Figure 5.2). As Rummler and Brache (1995) write, when you put a good performer up against a bad system, the system wins every time. To that end, organizations need to focus serious attention on the socialization of employees into the workplace and to the organization as a whole. Gibson, Ivancevich, and Donnelly (1997) define socialization as a process by which organizations bring new people into the culture. Examination of socialization more closely reveals that some organizations implement more effective techniques of socialization than do others (where, all too often, employees are left on their own to sink or swim within the complexity of the organizational culture). Performance-oriented HRD practitioners have a responsibility to positively influence the socialization process as a way of improving organizational morale and thus performance.

Phases of Socialization. Feldman (1967) identifies three phases of socialization that predominate within organizations: anticipatory, accommodation, and role management. Each phase requires different tactics to increase an employee's chances of enjoying a successful career within an organization.

Anticipatory Socialization

Two questions typically arise in an employee's mind when he or she first considers working for an organization. What will it be like to work for the organization? Am I suited to the jobs available within the organization? Each question should be addressed by the organization prior to hiring the individual, since first impressions are typically lasting ones. Employees will feel a heightened sense of satisfaction and loyalty if addressed positively.

Accommodation Socialization

The second phase of socialization occurs after an employee becomes a member of the organization. Employees get to know the organization and its jobs as they really are during this phase. Over time, employees become competent performers on the job and active participants within the organization, which is often referred to as the break-in period. This period can be very stressful for most individuals. According to Gibson, Ivanevich, and Donnelly (1997, 38), four common activities constitute the accommodation phase:

- establishing new interpersonal relations with both coworkers and managers;
- learning the tasks required to perform the job;
- clarifying one's role within the organization via formal and informal groups; and
- evaluating one's progress toward satisfying demands of the job and the role.

If this is a positive period for employees, they will feel a sense of accomplishment and acceptance by coworkers and managers while gaining confidence in performing their jobs.

Role Management

The third phase is role management. This is the period in which conflict occurs once an individual has been fully integrated into the organization. Conflict may involve job performance, interpersonal relationships with coworkers or managers, inadequate development opportunities, insufficient job assignments, misinterpretation of rules or regulations, and so on. Role management socialization refers to the organization's ability to address and resolve conflicts between employees and the organization regardless of the root of conflict. If conflicts are successfully resolved, the employee will gain a positive organizational perception, while unresolved or negative resolution may cause resentment, poor attitudes, or lukewarm cooperation on the part of employees.

Characteristics of Effective Socialization.   Some organizations are more effective in socializing employees into their culture than are others. Typically such organizations understand the importance of recruiting employees using effective job interviewing techniques, followed by selection and placement using realistic career path projections. In this way, the organization addresses and resolves the issues that most concern employees prior to joining the organization.

Gibson, Ivanevich, and Donnelly (1997) believe that highly socialized organizations focus their attention on five different but affective activities:

- tailor-made and individualized orientation programs;
- social and technical skill training;

- performance evaluations designed to provide supportive and accurate performance feedback;
- challenging work assignments that stretch an employee's abilities and talents; and
- demanding but fair managers who practice effective performance coaching techniques.

Each of these activities is used to retain and develop new employees while reducing tension and conflict within the organization.

Organizations with a strong socialization ethic fully understand the damage that can be caused by conflict within the firm. As a result, performance engineers and consultants are commissioned to provide consulting services when conflict arises. Such organizations encourage managers to accept roles as career counselors and performance confronters so employees have a forum and persons with which to discuss career opportunities as well as difficulties on the job (Gilley, Boughton, and Maycunich, 1999).

Conclusions

Organizational performance practice is grounded in analysis. Moreover, such practice is based on three frameworks that are useful in guiding practice: the A.C.O.R.N. model, the human performance system model, and the organizational performance improvement model.

Emerging Practices and Roles in Organizational Performance

Jerry W. Gilley

There are several trends in organizational performance but the two that predominate are the emerging practices and roles. Most notable are the practices of performance engineering and performance consulting and the roles of the performance engineer and the performance consultant. Both rely heavily on analysis as a primary expertise in achieving results. The human performance system and organizational improvement model are critical frames for each orientation. There are important differences, which we will examine.

Performance Engineering

According to Dean (1999b, 10), "performance engineering consists of three phases of analysis: 1) determining desired accomplishments, 2) measuring the opportunities for improvement on desired accomplishments, and 3) selecting the techniques for performance improvement." Gilbert (1978, 1996) first embraced the idea of performance engineering when he elucidated his perspective of human competence. Originally, performance engineering was known as human performance technology, which we discussed in detail in Chapter 4. Today, however, performance engineering has evolved to become a very important element within the organizational performance domain.

At the center of performance engineering is the relationship among organizational mission, strategy, culture, and policy. According to Dean (1999b, 11), "the policy level is the one at which the goals of the organizational culture are translated into the mission of what the organization wants to achieve. The mission is represented—and achieved—by a collection of accomplishments. Identifying the mission of the organization is the point at which performance engineering begins."

Therefore, the organizational mission provides the context for the philosophical, cultural, and policy levels of the organization. Consequently, the three phases of performance engineering are applied at the policy level to help accomplish the organization's mission (the desired ultimate accomplishments). These phases are applied at all levels of the organization until there is reasonable certainty that all deficiencies in performance or opportunities to improve performance have been identified (Dean, 1999b, 11; Rummler and Brache, 1995; Rummler, 1998; Gilbert, 1978, 1996).

Phase One: Determining the Desired Accomplishments

During this phase, performance engineers work to determine the desired accomplishments of the organization as dictated by the organizational mission. This process is conducted throughout the entire organization and at every level. Dean (1999b, 11–12) contends that this is achieved by identifying the accomplishments that delimit the mission; comparing the mission to the context of the level above to determine its alignment with the mission of the organization; and revising the mission accomplishments at each level, if necessary, to achieve alignment (see Chapter 5). This also includes determining the requirements of the accomplishments and how they will be measured, and establishing exemplary standards for the accomplishments. Again, the A.C.O.R.N. (Accomplishment, Control, Overall Objective, Reconcilable, Numbers) framework, which we previously discussed, is used to ascertain the relationship of accomplishments to the organizational missions and whether they are achieved.

Phase Two: Measuring the Opportunities for Improvement

In this phase, performance engineers are responsible for making certain that the overall mission is aligned throughout the organization. Quite simply, this is a process of determining the congruence of separate, independent, and unattached organizational parts with that of the mission. Another important activity is the establishment of performance standards for outputs and activities as a way of generating and reproducing exemplary performance (Rummler and Brache, 1995). This is achieved by identifying the individuals who performed their job missions at the highest level of achievement (Dean, 1999b). As we discussed previously, this process has become known as benchmarking.

Dean (1999b, 12) believes that the process of measuring the opportunities for improvement includes:

- obtaining measurement data on the quality, quantity, and cost measures of accomplishments;
- conducting Potential for Improving Performance (PIP) analyses to indicate for which accomplishments the performance improvement opportunities may add the most value to the organization; and
- selecting the performance improvement opportunities that have the greatest potential for financial benefit to the organization.

Phase Three: Selecting the Techniques for Performance Improvement

During the third phase, performance engineers conduct an analysis to determine which solutions will be most appropriate in improving the performances identified in Phase Two (Dean, 1999b). The techniques used for gathering decision data include the behavior engineering model (see Chapter 4) and PROBE, a questionnaire designed for profiling behavior and identifying barriers to exemplary performance (Gilbert, 1982a, 1982b).

Using the data gathered with these two techniques, performance engineers can identify performance improvement solutions that will be most effective in closing the gap between typical employee performance and exemplary performance. These solutions can be categorized into three types:

- Environmental programs: more information, resources, or incentives;
- People programs: more knowledge and skills, improved recruiting; and
- Management programs: improved structures and standards (Dean, 1999b, 13).

Performance Engineers

Spitzer (1999, 163) maintains that performance engineers "are in the business of improving performance in organizations." Like other consultants who have no direct authority over organizational performance improvement, therefore, performance engineers rely on indirect influence by conducting analyses and recommending performance improvement solutions. In short, performance engineers work with individuals (employees) who operate within results-oriented systems for the purpose of enhancing their performance.

According to Stolovitch and Keeps (1999), performance engineers are responsible for identifying and analyzing stimuli within the system that may affect performance, responses that are emitted, and the consequences of those responses (rewards and punishments) in order to uncover root causes of performance inadequacy. Once this is done, an engineer can identify performance improvement solutions that enhance performance through the elimination of barriers to exemplary performance.

Performance engineers take a total system (systemic) approach to organizational performance, as opposed to making piecemeal interventions such as training activities. Stolovitch and Keeps (1999, 5) suggest that performance engineers adopt a "holistic viewpoint with respect to performance problems, which means that they examine any given problem (defined as the gap between desired and actual states) within the broader context of the subsystem in which it is situated, within other interacting subsystems, and, ultimately, within the overall system where it occurs." Even though not every performance problem requires performance engineers to thoroughly examine all systems, it does require them to examine each performance problem in relation to the mission of the organization, thus linking their actions to a context for improvement.

Performance Engineers' Competencies and Skills. Stolovitch, Keeps, and Rodrigue (1999a, 148) contend that performance engineers need not be expert in every step of the performance engineering process, but they all "should be able to conduct appropriate performance analyses, design/develop interventions, and establish operational plans for implementing, monitoring, and evaluating interventions with a high degree of skill and confidence." They state that the term "skill" refers to "a practical ability and dexterity; knowledge; understanding; ability; proficiency" and that they are grouped into two broad categories (technical and people skills) with two subsets each.

Category 1: Technical Skills

Technical skills are applied during Phases 1 and 2 of the performance engineering process. They are used to conduct performance and causal analysis, design and develop performance improvement interventions, implement interventions, perform change management activities, manage projects, and conduct evaluations. Two subset skills are required to accomplish these activities: analysis and observation skills and design skills.

Analysis and observation skills. Performance engineers must be able to examine a situation, dissect it into various elements, and determine and explain the relationships among them. They must be able to observe and then discern which elements of a job-related task, process, or situation have an impact on performance (Dean, 1999b, 148).

Design skills (creativity, logical thinking, and media knowledge). Performance engineers must have the ability to design, orchestrate, and logically sequence a series of activities (e.g., instructions, job aids, and incentive or feedback programs) that will solve the problem or improve performance. Design also requires knowledge of the most appropriate medium to be used for the situation (Dean, 1999b, 148–149).

Category 2: People Skills

People skills are applied primarily during Phase 3 of the performance engineering process. They are used to conduct stakeholder relationship building activities and interviews, project management planning, intervention identification and selection, evaluation activities, and follow-up and project termination activities. Two primary skills are required to conduct these activities: management and communication and interpersonal skills.

Management skills. Performance engineers must be able to ensure that the intervention plan is implemented as designed and that corrective actions are applied at appropriate moments. This requires organizational and project management competencies and skills (Dean, 1999b, 149).

Communication and interpersonal skills. Performance engineers continually communicate with clients, colleagues, client employees, and all other persons potentially affected by the scope of the work. Therefore they must be able to communicate effectively both orally and in writing.

According to Sink (1992, 566–567) and Stolovitch, Keeps, and Rodrigue (1999a, 158), performance engineers (originally referred to as human performance technologists) need to demonstrate six characteristics as a way of distinguishing them from other HRD practitioners.

- *Results-driven.* "Outstanding [performance engineers] are results-oriented. They solve human performance problems. . . . [They] do not become so intrigued with . . . the processes and procedures of [performance engineering] that they lose sight of the true problem and the desired results" (Sink, 1992, 566).
- *Investigative.* They possess the art of being able to ask "the critical few questions" and knowing where to look for information (Stolovitch, Keeps, and Rodrigue, 1999a, 158).
- *Know how to set and maintain standards.* From "the start of an intervention, the experienced [performance engineer] sets expectations for standards of quality . . . [and] institutes quality checks at all key points in a project" (Sink, 1992, 67).
- *Cooperative/collaborative.* "Successful [performance engineers] display and encourage collaboration with clients, subordinates, peers, and other practitioners" (Stolovitch, Keeps, and Rodrigue, 1999a, 158).
- *Flexible while maintaining key principles.* "Talented [performance engineers] easily adapt to new contexts and shifting priorities, deal with sudden constraints or increased scope, apply their systematic processes, and stay with what is best for the client and for the ultimate success of the project" (Stolovitch, Keeps, and Rodrigue, 1999a, 158).
- *Willing and able to add value.* "Successful [performance engineers] go beyond doing a good job by educating clients about performance improvement principles, providing them with new resources, or introducing them to technologies that have impact beyond the current project" (Stolovitch, Keeps, and Rodrigue, 1999a, 158).

Performance Consulting

Robinson and Robinson (1996) coined the term performance consulting to illustrate the roles and responsibilities of performance consultants and the approach they use to identify performance problems, isolate root causes, identify solutions, implement performance improvement solutions, and evaluate performance results and outcomes. Hale (1998, 9) defines performance consulting as the "practice of taking a disciplined approach to assessing individual and organizational effectiveness, diagnosing causes of human performance problems, and recommending a set of interventions."

Performance Consulting Process

Robinson and Robinson (1998, 715–716) identify a six-step performance consulting process.

- Partnership Phase: Activities include building mutually beneficial relationships with clients (stakeholders).
- Entry Phase: Alert the performance improvement department that there is an opportunity to work on a specific situation (e.g., performance problem, performance opportunity, substandard performance).
- Assessment Phase: Activities are associated with front-end analysis (performance and causal analysis).
- Design Phase: Activities include the design, development, and piloting of performance improvement interventions designed to resolve the problems or opportunities identified during the assessment phase.
- Implementation Phase: Various performance improvement interventions designed to change performance are implemented.
- Measurement Phase: This phase technically began with the assessment phase because measurement is really a front-end process. It involves measurement of the degree of performance change and the operational impact that has occurred.

Robb (1998, 234) presents a simpler performance consulting process consisting of three steps: (1) partnering with clients, (2) assessing performance, and (3) implementing interventions. He (1998, 235) believes that "performance consultants partner with clients to identify, build, and maintain a strong partnership relationship, assess performance to gather data, develop performance models, identify performance strengths, gaps, and causes, and analyze data for patterns and connections." Additionally, they need to collaborate with clients to identify impacts on business goals, and secure agreement on actions to be taken and measures of success. He also believes performance consultants are responsible for implementing interventions, managing and facilitating performance improvement efforts through internal and external partnerships, and measuring and reporting results. These activities are performed in order to secure performance results. Thus, performance consultants need to demonstrate on-the-job behaviors through which they can generate the required outputs, skills, and knowledge needed to perform successfully throughout the performance consulting process, and also to utilize systems, tools, and processes to do so successfully (Robb, 1998, 237).

Performance Consulting Model

Robinson and Robinson (1996) outline an eight-step approach to the performance consulting process. Each step is designed to help uncover the root cause of performance problems and identify appropriate performance improvement solutions. The steps are:

1. *Mapping the components of performance:* This is accomplished by creating a performance relationship, which is a vehicle for helping both performance consultants and clients understand the complex interrelationships of human performance (Robinson and Robinson, 1996, 53).
2. *Identifying business needs in operational terms:* Business needs should be identified in operational terms (Robinson and Robinson, 1996, 80–81). Thus, performance assessments must begin with a clear definition of business goals, objectives, and strategies for a unit, division, department, or entire company. These serve as the foundation to which all performance requirements will be anchored.
3. *Developing models of performance:* A model of performance consists of four components: performance results, best practices or competencies, quality criteria, and work environment factors. Performance models can be written in two ways: as best practices (benchmarking) and as competencies (competency maps).
4. *Identifying actual performance:* Performance consultants identify actual performance to establish a baseline for future comparisons through a process known as performance assessment, which is a three-phase diagnostic process (Robinson and Robinson, 1996). First, consultants obtain the client's perception of desired operational results and create operational measurement indicators. The outcome of this phase is an agreement with the client on business goals, initiatives, and challenges, and how they will affect employee performance requirements. Second, detailed descriptions are developed of the performance required to achieve desired operational results to secure agreement with the client on acceptable performance models. Third, performance consultants identify current performance strengths and gaps as compared to desired performance.

5. *Identifying factors influencing performance:* Performance consultants are responsible for identifying the factors that influence performance, including employees' knowledge, skills, and abilities, performers' actions and behaviors, managers' actions and behaviors, and organizations' actions and behaviors.

6. *Implementing performance improvement interventions:* Implementing these interventions is an area in which performance consultants generally are the most comfortable and competent. The purpose of this phase is to close performance gaps using credible, client-identified and client-supported actions (Hale, 1998).

7. *Managing performance consulting projects:* Consultants are responsible for planning, organizing, and monitoring performance improvement projects. Moreover, they may be called upon to communicate benefits at various stages of a performance improvement intervention, facilitate the removal of barriers, or resolve issues affecting the performance change process or project team (Gilley and Maycunich, 1998).

8. *Measuring and reporting results:* Using the impact measures agreed to in the assessment phase, performance consultants should measure the results of actions taken; act as broker for resources to measure results; or manage a project to design, develop, and implement the measurement process (Robinson and Robinson, 1996).

Performance Consultants

Performance consultants possess a very different perspective from traditional HRD practitioners in that their focus emphasizes helping organizations achieve goals and objectives by improving overall organizational performance. A performance consultant approach relies on performance management and systems thinking skills to bring about organizational change, with emphasis on the overall human performance system rather than on individuals within the system. From this perspective, performance consulting represents a "macro" perspective of overall organizational improvement. On the other hand, performance engineers primarily focus on conducting analysis activities and designing interventions (Rossett, 1999b; Dean, 1999a). This role is less complex and requires fewer skills and expertise than does performance consulting. Some contend that performance engineering is a subset of performance consulting, and specializes in front-end analysis (Wykes, 1998).

Fuller and Farrington (1999) stress that performance consultants partner with clients to provide services, determine what must be accomplished, and ensure that business problems are resolved to the client's satisfaction. Moreover, Robinson and Robinson (1996) believe that performance consultants are responsible for encouraging organizational leaders to take action to improve organizational performance. Consultants view the organization as a system containing inputs such as financial, physical, and human resources that produce outputs such as products and services through a series of business processes.

The principal role of a performance consultant is to enhance organizational performance and change; thus they must help the organization properly utilize its resources (inputs) by generating (through business processes) improved results (outputs). However, because of ever-increasing organizational complexity, ambiguity, and change, many performance consultants have difficulty attaining this role (Hale, 1998; Gilley and Maycunich, 1998; Robinson and Robinson, 1996). Consultants have little time for the pre-planned solutions that are so common in workshops and training-based HRD programs. Rather than leading clients through a carefully prepared training class, performance consultants investigate problems with creative zest. Additionally, to identify, isolate, and resolve performance problems, they conduct performance and cause analysis and design, develop, and implement solutions recommendations.

Robinson and Robinson (1996, 287) believe that performance consultants should serve as client relationship builders. In this subrole they partner with senior managers and organizational leaders to identify and contract performance improvement initiatives that address business needs. Further, they serve as performance analysts (performance engineers) in identifying the ideal and actual performances required to meet these business needs and in determining the causes of performance discrepancies (Rossett, 1999b; Elliott, 1998; Spitzer, 1992). Fuller and Farrington (1999) and Rossett (1999b) state that a performance analyst defines performance problems or issues to be addressed, determines gaps in performance, and recommends solutions for eliminating barriers to performance. Analysts also investigate the root causes of problems and of identified gaps in performance. When performance consultants serve as results evaluators, they identify and report the impact of an intervention on individual performance and organizational effectiveness.

Another subrole is that of performance consulting champion. In this subrole, they are responsible for spreading the word about the benefits of the performance improvement process. Performance consultants occasionally function as instructional designers (creating learning interventions) or organizational development specialists (managing change, restructuring the organization, or reengineering business processes). Once necessary solutions to performance problems have been identified, a consultant is responsible for developing intervention to resolve them. Once a solution is developed, they put them in motion—yet another subrole of performance consultants.

Since many projects are complex, performance consultants function as project managers to ensure that the project remains on schedule, within budget, and at an acceptable level of quality (Hale, 1998). Fuller and Farrington (1999, 153) point out that "whenever change is involved, people may have negative reactions to the change. Even if the change is widely perceived as positive, difficulties in making the change can occur. Someone should be managing the change process to ensure that the change as proposed will have the desired result and will transfer to common practice in the workplace." Performance consultants serving in this subrole act as change advisors.

Finally, Robinson and Robinson (1996) point out that the term performance consultant can also be used as a job title. So the *job* of performance consultants may involve all of the above roles. Additionally, one person may play the majority of these roles in many projects.

Performance Consultant Responsibilities. Performance consultants are responsible for many of the traditional organizational learning activities discussed in Chapter 3, but primarily provide guidance to performance improvement efforts used to improve organizational performance. Consultants must answer questions, provide guidance, and assist in solving problems that arise during the course of a performance improvement project. Robinson and Robinson (1996, 285) further contend that performance consultants are responsible for developing performance and competency models to identify performance gaps and for determining the causes of these gaps. They are also charged with measuring the impact of training and nontraining actions undertaken to change performance, advising management on business and performance needs, and identifying performance implications for future business goals and needs (Gilley and Maycunich, 2000a, 235). Performance consultants might also facilitate focus group activities—managing difficult participants, drawing out ideas from reticent individuals, and generally assuring that the best information is captured from the group.

According to Robinson and Robinson (1996, 254), consultants supervise how well skills are transferred to the workplace and how individual or group performance improves. They are also accountable for the degree to which training contributes to desired operational change and for the quantity and quality of client relationships.

Performance Consultant Competencies. The roles and subroles of a performance consultant require a set of skills and competencies if she or he is to function successfully. Robinson and Robinson (1996) argue that the skills that support successful performance in traditional training roles (e.g., instructors) may not be successful in performance improvement roles, and vice versa.

Rothwell (1996a, 149) believes that performance consultants must have the ability to identify the "importance of gaps between what is and what should be in the organization's interactions with the external environment." Rossett (1996b) adds that this ability is demonstrated by gaining an understanding of the organizational structure, culture, work climate, and policies and procedures to discover real or perceived problems. Moreover, performance consultants need to lead, coordinate, or participate in matching work requirements to worker competencies (Spitzer, 1992). To demonstrate this ability, consultants must discover answers to the following questions:

- What competencies *are* available among workers to function effectively in the organization's internal and external environment and to deal with work processing requirements?
- What competencies *should be* available among workers to function effectively in the organization's internal and external environment and to deal with work processing requirements?
- What gaps exist between worker competencies *required* now and those *available* now?
- What gaps exist between worker competencies required in the *future* and those available *now*?
- How important are the gaps in worker competencies?
- What consequences stem from—or are expected to stem from—these competency gaps (Rothwell, 1996a, 152–154)?

Nilson (1999) contends that performance consultants must also have the ability to compare an idealized vision of the future with organizational reality. Hale (1998) adds that consultants should be able to lead, coordinate, or participate in efforts at the work level to examine workflow, work processing, and the inputs, outputs, and transformation processes involved in producing the work or delivering services. This ability requires them to examine how work flows into a division, department, work unit, or team and to understand the raw (untransformed) states in which materials, people, and information also flow into these areas, argues Rothwell (1996a, 152). They must be able to ascertain how materials, people, and information *should* flow as well (Gilley and Maycunich, 2000a, 246–247). Next, Rossett (1999b) maintains that performance consultants need to identify the gaps that exist between what is happening and what should be happening and identify the consequences that stem from these existing gaps in workflow, as well as the importance of those consequences.

Furthermore, Rothwell (1996a, 178–180) asserts that performance consultants should also serve as strategic troubleshooters, that is, they should possess the ability to isolate strategic mismatches in the organization's interactions with the external environment. Moreover, they must have the ability to assess and benchmark other organizations in the industry or "best-in-class" organizations. Rossett (1999b) points out that consultants must be able to troubleshoot the causes of performance gaps between worker and other performance environments and the causes of gaps in the work or workflow.

In summary, eleven general capabilities are essential for a performance consultant:

1. *Business knowledge:* Effective performance consultants think like their clients. This requires an understanding of how things are accomplished inside the organization and how decisions are made (Brinkerhoff, 1998). Business knowledge includes awareness of how organizations operate and why they exist, including knowledge of business fundamentals, systems theory, organizational culture, and politics.

2. *System thinking skills:* Fuller and Farrington (1999, 162) believe that being a performance consultant requires the ability to identify, analyze, and evaluate systems within an organization. This also requires the ability to assess which elements of a system are related to one another and determine which inputs, processes, and outputs from one element of a system interact with other elements of that system.

3. *Interpersonal skills:* Consultants need to develop the ability to interact with executives, senior managers, and other managers from diverse functional backgrounds (e.g., finance, engineering, marketing, sales, manufacturing, facilities, information resources) in order to be effective. Fuller and Farrington (1999, 164–165) identify a variety of interactions that performance consultants are responsible for, which includes communicating the status of a project, presenting ideas persuasively, selling a concept or approach, holding an exploratory discussion to search for information one-

on-one or in groups, managing focus groups, and using appropriate and nonbiasing questioning techniques (e.g., asking open-ended and closed questions effectively, asking nonleading questions).

4. *Consulting skills:* Consultants must develop skills that enable them to enter into discussions with potential clients, determine what services and results clients require, and formulate contracts with clients (Fuller and Farrington, 1999; Nilson, 1999; Gilley and Maycunich, 1998; Hale, 1998).

5. *Project management skills:* Since every performance improvement intervention is a project, performance consultants must possess project management skills to lead such projects from beginning to end (Fuller and Farrington, 1999; Brinkerhoff, 1998; Gilley and Coffern, 1994).

6. *Change management skills:* Performance improvement requires a change in employees' skills and competencies, attitude toward work, or even in the organizational system for which performance occurs (Dormant, 1992). Fuller and Farrington (1999, 166–167) believe performance consultants need to develop change management skills so that they can implement and manage change, deal with resistance to change, and create work environments that are conducive to change. They need these skills to enlist the support and cooperation of organizational leaders, advocates, team members, and others involved with performance improvement. Moreover, Kissler (1991) states that consultants need to recognize and minimize weaknesses in an intervention, and recognize the stages of change and employ the appropriate strategies for each stage.

7. *Teamwork skills:* Hale (1998) notes that performance consultants must possess knowledge of teamwork and team building skills because performance improvement projects are often complex. These skills will help them manage projects, facilitate interventions, and develop support for causal analysis activities (Rossett, 1999b).

8. *Knowledge of performance technology:* The field of human performance technology acknowledges that employee performance is a function of many influences: feedback, accountability, skills and knowledge, rewards or incentives, motivation, and so forth (Nilson, 1999). Consequently, performance consultants should examine performance problems using the human performance system model (Rossett, 1999b).

9. *Partnering skills:* According to Robinson and Robinson (1996), consultants must take the initiative to establish trust with managers

and organizational leaders who are responsible for sponsoring, supporting, and implementing performance improvement within organizations.

10. *Performance relationship mapping skills:* Robinson and Robinson (1996, 53–54) say that performance consultants must be able to illustrate the relationship among business goals, performance requirements, training, and work environment needs, determine the performance needed if business goals are to be realized as well as the current capability of individuals to demonstrate this required performance, and determine the training and work environment actions needed to improve performance. This area of expertise is essential if they are to persuade organizational leaders of the complexity of the performance improvement process and identify the interdependent relationships among various elements that affect organizational performance.

11. *Performance model building:* Performance consultants must persuasively demonstrate the need for performance results, which become the basis for performance improvement models. Three types of models can be used when developing models of performance: performance results, best practices, or competency. A performance results model focuses on the outcomes that a performer must achieve on the job if the organization is to accomplish its business goals. A best practice model is based on identifying the tasks and activities that exemplary workers perform to achieve each of the performance results for a specific position. A competency model emphasizes the skills, knowledge, and attitudes required of employees if they are to achieve required results. The criteria used to measure performance, and the environmental factors affecting performance, differ with each model.

Performance Consultant Job Outputs.   Robinson and Robinson (1998, 717) contend that performance consultants are responsible for generating five important job outputs.

- Forming and growing partnerships with sustained clients.
- Identifying and qualifying opportunities for performance improvement.
- Conducting performance assessments, including performance models, competency models, process models, gap analysis, cause analysis, and data-reporting meetings.

- Managing multiple performance-change interventions.
- Measuring the results of performance improvement interventions.

Conclusions

Within the organizational performance domain, two types of practice have emerged: performance engineering and performance consulting. In concert with this development, two corresponding types of practitioner have evolved: performance engineers and performance consultants. They are essential to the continuous evolution of the organizational performance domain within HRD.

Philosophy of Organizational Change

Peter J. Dean

Organizations are dynamic and complex social systems formed to accomplish goals. Organizational change is a field of study that focuses on the organization as a system and how the framework of that system interfaces and influences the performance of the individual. Organizational design combines systems theory and qualitative and quantitative organizational analysis to help choose the best strategy for change, with the understanding that there is no one best design. Organizational design elements include the following:

Organization—A system of formal arrangements encompassing the interaction of the strategies, structures, and processes. These arrangements are designed in such a way as to optimize the learning interface between people and their work environment.

Continuous change—Learning that occurs in an incremental way usually motivated by cost-containment, efficiency, and evolutionary innovation.

Discontinuous change—Learning that occurs in a radical way driven by performance or technological problems, competitive shifts in the market, or political conditions.

Strategic vision—The response of the organization to the needs of the marketplace.

Structures—Structure addresses the division and coordination of tasks and the formal patterns of relationships among groups and individuals.

Processes—Processes define and measure the sequence of steps, activities, and methods to produce a specific goal or outcome.

Systems—Systems include all the procedures for budgeting, accounting, training, etc., that make the organization run. Systems use procedures, rules, policies, and practices that help control processes.

Performance—Both behavior, the actual observable activity, and its accomplishment, that which is left behind after the behavior occurs, define performance.

Cooperative learning—Workers learning and helping each other learn for a specific outcome.

Learning in organizations—Cooperative and reflective learning that occurs in response to the needs of the organization, thus helping the organization become self-designing.

However, an organizational designer attempts to bring about the best interface of these key elements in an organization. Other factors must be considered in organizational change. These include:

- the people performing their jobs;
- the measurement of the performance;
- the processes that make up the tasks being performed;
- the systems that comprise the processes; the arrangements of the hierarchy and reporting relationships that make up the formal structure;
- the informal structure that professionals create for themselves; and
- how the strategy of the organization aligns itself with all the aforementioned factors (Miles and Snow, 1978; Nadler, Gerstein, and Shaw, 1992).

These factors are underpinned by the following organizational behaviors of managers:

- recognition of individual differences in workers;
- accurate perception of performance;
- correct assumptions about the motivation of workers;
- use of information technology in organizational communication; and
- influence of conflict and collaboration on both group and team dynamics (Bowditch and Buono, 1997).

As a philosophy, organizational change stems from three approaches to changing systems, organizations, or institutions. (1) A rational approach streams from Aristotle's dialectic on the use of the scientific method. This approach is well documented in Chapter 2 of this volume in the discussions of

Aristotle, Watson, Skinner, Thorndike, and Tyler. (2) The second is a power-dominated approach in which the person leading the change is transmitting expert knowledge to cause attitudinal change, organizing and promoting data to cause attitudinal change, or directly controlling the attitudinal change from a distance through manipulation of situational variables. This approach, depending mostly on knowledge as a major ingredient of its power, can seem oppressive and forceful to those affected if it is misused by the leaders of change. Again, a good sense of this approach was documented in Chapter 2 in the discussion of the liberal, progressive, and behavioral adult education models.

These first two approaches offer solid theories for learning, but they may not be the source of primary interaction for leaders of change who help to bring about improvement in organizational systems. In fact, both approaches described above might better serve a secondary supportive role for what is the third approach: (3) the re-educative approach (Lewin and Grabbe, 1945). This approach combines the work of John Dewey and humanistic adult education and radical adult education, and incorporates the theoretical and practical work of Lewin, Trist and Emery, and Weisbord into a person-centered/system-centered framework that engages the whole system for rapid change. The themes that resonate within this approach include self-directed change, openness, authenticity, empowerment, individuality, noncompulsory learning, social action, and social transformation, all of which have been thoroughly described in Chapter 2 regarding the work of Rogers, Maslow, Knowles, Illich, Shor, Perelman, and others.

Evolution of Thought on Organizational Change

The goal of this chapter is to outline the general philosophy that specifically spearheaded organizational change as a new concept over the last century. This philosophy has emerged mostly from professors and professionals putting what little theory there was into the practice of actually attempting to change systems. Based on the effectiveness of these practices, new ideas were fed back to the working theories and eventually a body of literature was created. The interaction of this evolving philosophy with practice attempts to create principles that can be applied with greater assurance of results. That selected stream of the evolution of change literature is shared in this chapter.

In order for us to take advantage of the last century or more of wisdom written about change in organizations, it is important to connect the classics in some cumulative way so that we can teach administrators, managers, and executives who are involved as leaders of change that they work in a progressive profession. This chapter reviews the work of Taylor, Lewin, Trist and Emery, Weisbord, and Bunker and Alban. What is revealed is the evolution of a good theory that works for changing organizations. The following section offers a short commentary on the progression of learning in the change process and the two kinds of change, continuous and discontinuous, that are found in the workplace.

Frederick W. Taylor

Frederick Taylor (1911), the father of scientific management, started a new profession in the workplace that combined his experience in mechanical engineering and the act of consulting with all levels at work. In essence, the profession he started is that of organizational change. In his day, he called these professionals "consulting engineers." They could help owners, managers, and workers solve problems together to deal with the rapid pace of change in the 1890s, in large part by examining and clarifying the issues of costs, productivity, and motivation. He began this kind of work, but never really applied it to everybody's satisfaction. Although a systems thinker himself, he seemed to block the application of systems thinking in the workplace. One fundamental flaw in Taylor's thinking was an overemphasis on the person as the cause of low productivity. In Taylor's view of work, a work team meant a rigid, nonoverlapping division of labor among staff experts, managers, and workers, all doing their work and not solving problems together. However, in today's world, where markets, technologies, and organizational systems change rapidly, people must interact in their work environments. Lewin was interested in democratic, large-scale change efforts that involved the person and the system surrounding the person.

Kurt Lewin (1951) added the conceptual tool of tension between the person and the environmental constructs. Being a social scientist (a phenomenologist), Lewin stressed psychological ecology, or the factors in the environment, such as behavioral settings surrounding the individual at work. Here Lewin hoped to identify the immediate determinants of action. His tools were both practical and ethical. Lewin added to Taylor's ideas the concept of environment and aided Taylor's attempt to remove authoritarian behavior at work. Lewin's field theory starts with the position that behavior is determined by the field as it exists at a moment in time. The person and the environment comprise the life space, and this life space represents psychological reality, with a tension involving the dynamic inner-personal construct. In effect, Lewin added social systems to Taylor's thinking. His methods helped shift management thought from mechanical engineering to social-psychological ways of thinking.

Lewin's Principles

The principles from Lewin's writings (Lewin and Grabbe, 1945; Lewin et al., 1945; Lewin, 1947a, 1947b, 1948, 1951) that are important and relevant to the practice of organizational change today include the following:

1. *Understanding the interplay between the work environment and the individual worker is critical for change in organizations.* Any change in the personal growth of individuals within a work group due to training, for example, should have a correlate attempt for social and cultural change within the entire organization. If there is no attempt to change both individuals and the environmental culture of an organization, any change is not likely to succeed. That is why one training session is not likely to bring about significant organizational change. This principle is reflected in the formula $B=f(p, e)$, where behavior (B) change is the function (f) of the person (p) and the environment (e).

2. *To understand the system, you must first seek to change it.* Lewin called this action research. Accurate measurement of environmental and individual perceptions helps to clarify false perceptions and create correct knowledge about problems blocking the performance of individuals. Gathering, measuring, and evaluating this evidence of perceptions must involve all who create the perceptions. For effective change of perceptions to occur, participants involved in change should feel a strong sense of belonging to the group as they participate in the corrective measures to clarify perceptions. Successful organizational changes will more likely occur when workers affected by the change have an opportunity to participate in the process of change as early as possible and as long as is needed for the change to take place.

3. *Wed scientific thinking (action research) to democratic values for organizational change.* Democracy in the practice of change is critical because every work system is a value system as well. It is not possible to have a value-neutral work system. Whereas action research allows for the practice of accurate inquiry and measurement, democracy encourages participants to clarify their own feelings of ambivalence

or frustration as well as their own perceptions of what would or wouldn't work. The combination of action research and democracy creates new energy around accepting new values at work, as well as a sense of belongingness that is necessary for change in organizations. As a rule, the more cohesive the group, the greater the readiness for members to influence others and be influenced by others.

Lewin (1948) contended that it is very difficult to improve productivity if you do things *to* people—it is better to do things *with* them. His re-educative approach was sometimes called an action research approach, which is only a partial use of the principles stated earlier. A re-educative approach was designed to involve and help those with a stake in the problem to accurately define and solve it, because when those affected by the change are less involved, it is less likely that there will be a long-lasting solution.

Lewin's Re-educative Approach to Organizational Change

This re-educative approach is based on the idea of systems changing themselves through a communal effort by the people affected by the change, that is, a whole system engaging in the change of the whole system. The breakthrough vision of this approach, which involves the indispensability of groups as media of effective re-education, was captured by Lewin and Grabbe (1945):

Acceptance of previously rejected facts can be achieved best through the discovery of these facts by the group members themselves. . . . Then, and frequently only then, do the facts become really *their* facts (as against other people's facts). An individual will believe facts he himself has discovered in the same way that he believes in himself or in his group. The importance of this fact-finding process for the group by the group itself has been recently emphasized with reference to re-education in several fields. . . . It can be surmised that the extent to which social research is translated into social action depends on the degree to which those who carry out this action are made a part of the fact-finding on which the action is to be based.

Re-education influences conduct only when the new system of values and beliefs dominates the individual's perception. The acceptance of the new system is linked with the acceptance of a specific group, a particular role, a definite source of authority as new point of reference. It is basic for re-education that this linkage between acceptance of new facts or values and acceptance of certain groups or roles is very intimate and that the second frequently is a prerequisite for the first. This explains the great difficulty of changing beliefs and values in a piecemeal fashion. This linkage is a main factor behind resistance to re-education, but can also be made a powerful means for successful re-education. (Lewin and Grabbe, 1945)

Trist and Emery Continue Lewin's Work

Eric Trist, working with Fred Emery (Emery and Trist, 1960), an Australian building on the accomplishments of Lewin, Wilfred R. Bion, and Douglas McGregor (1960), created a new group orientation to help people integrate the whole system. Bion, a psychoanalyst and much-decorated World War I tank commander, created a leaderless group method to deal with the tension between cooperation and self-centeredness under stress. In 1957 the Tavistock Institute of Human Relations in London, England, pioneered a form of laboratory training based on Bion's ideas. Trist, an Army psychologist, joined Bion and used the work of McGregor. McGregor was the author of the management classic *The Human Side of Enterprise* and had also founded the Industrial Relations Section at the Massachusetts Institute of Technology and helped Kurt Lewin found the Research Center for Group Dynamics at MIT. McGregor emphasized that groups, if properly used, can only improve decisionmaking and problemsolving because effective groups require informality, openness, frank criticism, self-examination of their own effectiveness, and shared responsibility for work and outcomes.

Trist and Emery worked together in the 1950s in Great Britain. This liaison brought systems thinking to the workplace. Trist, understanding the open systems thinking of biologist Ludwig von Bertalanffy (1950), created a way of thinking about management and change that was a reflection of how it really was in the workplace. He connected the social and the technical systems so that those who do the work get to have the power via information, control, and skills. The open systems idea was that all things, somehow, some way, link up and influence one another in all directions. Cause and effect is not the only possible relationship between force and object, as the effect might be the cause. Taylor assumed that any system could be isolated. Weisbord (1987), in this book *Productive Workplaces,* says that Trist and other Tavistock researchers proclaimed that closed systems are forever closed to the energy they need for survival and that Taylor had no recognition of this. Trist (and Emery), on the basis of Lewin's work, proclaimed the following differences between Taylor's work and their own:

Socio-technical Systems

Trist coined the term socio-technical system (STS) to represent the interaction of people (a social system) with tools and techniques (a technical system). In his system, Trist suggested both systems could be a catalyst for change and improvement. Lewin's core principle was that workers are likely to modify their own behavior when they participate in problem analysis and solution design and are likely to carry out the decisions that are made. The ideas of Trist and Bamforth are similar in their comments about interaction. In an article in *Human Relations* in 1951 entitled "Social and Psychological Consequences of the Longwall Method of Coal-Getting," they define STS as an approach that connects mass-production engineering and a social structure consisting of the occupational roles that have been institutionalized. These interactive technological and sociological patterns are assumed to exist as forces having psychological effects in the life space of the worker, who must either take a role and perform a task in the system or abandon his attempt to work. Together, the forces and their effects constitute the psychosocial whole that is the object of the study. They concluded the study by stating that a qualitative change in the method would have to occur so that a social as well as a technological whole could come into existence. Only if this is achieved can the work be accomplished with the emergence of a new social balance. The term "organizational choice" encompasses composite working, self-regulation, team organization, and maintaining production, along with workload stress and cycle regulation, all of which align interaction between the social and technical systems. This description of organizational choice is further enhanced in some of Weisbord's (1987) writing on STS.

Weisbord calls STS a revolution and quotes from Trist's book entitled *The Evolution of Socio-technical Systems* to explain why: "Information technologies, especially those concerned with the microprocessor and telecommunication, give immense scope for solving many current problems—if the right value choices can be made" (Trist, 1981, 59). What this says to me is that ethics in change must be a constant. Weisbord goes on to report (and he was a newspaper reporter at one point in his life) that Trist coined the phrase STS because he wanted to show that the interaction of people (social system) with tools and techniques (a technical system) results from choice, not chance. Those choices are influenced by the economic, technical, and human values present at the time. Trist emphasized the values of learning, caring, and collaboration as necessary for social change. Weisbord lists some of these values when comparing mining methods:

STS designers work to broaden each person's knowledge of the social and economic consequences and to encourage each worker in developing a range of skills needed to get results. The work group became the focus of change, not the discrete tasks. STS also called for internal regulation by which autonomous work groups could develop a capacity for self-regulation. This, of course, is based on Lewin's suggestion to help people learn self-correction. In other words, get the managers out of the way of controlling learning and change.

Weisbord (1987) sums up this work by stating that informed self-control, not close supervision, is the only way to operate new technologies without making mistakes, for they can be mastered only with the learner's direct involvement. Moreover, Weisbord continues, the future of democratic values, the dignity and worth of each person, free choice and free expression, and social responsibility coupled to personal opportunity depends on what we do today. He recommends that social, technical, and economic systems be integrated as soon as possible. If this can be accomplished using the knowledge of Lewin, Trist, and Emery, we could have the whole system in one room.

In action research or STS you are part of the action and you cannot stand outside the process and tell people what to do. Managers also need to be part of the system and part of the action, and thus the question arises whether there need to be managers at all. Perhaps the biggest problem in today's workplace is the widespread practice of using managers to ensure that work gets done. It would be ironic if after all these years of using managers for supervision it turns out that they might very well be a major cause of low productivity and workplace dissatisfaction. We may yet see both systematic management and systemic learning recognized as necessary for change in organizations. Kochan and Useem (1992) seem to agree.

Learning in Organizations Is Needed for Change

Kochan and Useem (1992) suggest that continued and systemic forms of change practiced by teams may be essential for organizational learning. Yet change is not a natural state for many organizations, and it does not occur automatically in response to cues from some invisible hand. Organizations typically display enormous inertia in some areas, as well they should. Without continuity in reporting relations, completing even the most mundane task becomes prohibitively costly. Yet the costs of failing to overcome the inertia can also be the decline or end of the organization.

Kochan and Useem (1992) believe that continuous systemic organizational change must be integrated and consistent among an organization's major components and designed for the long term to provide a more suitable foundation for cooperation, learning, and innovation. They call organizations that undertake such change "transforming organizations" that can handle the pressure of change.

The systemic change that they propose can take place only when the technological, organizational, and human resources are altered together, since the potential of one segment can be fully realized only when developed in concert with all. Moreover, systemic change involves more than changes within each of these components. It challenges the underlying assumptions, tacit knowledge, and standard relationships that link these different organizational components. For example, this challenge is especially real if organizations avoid risks and organize and manage using short-term, inflexible assumptions.

Furthermore, Kochan and Useem (1992) state that learning is essential for engaging in systemic, continuous change and going beyond the isolated shifts and periodic lurching that can be observed in so many organizations. They also suggest that the organization that has learned how to learn will master the challenges of change. They highlight three mutually reinforcing features of a learning organization.

First, the capability for faster innovation and organizational flexibility must be present, and so traditional organizational forms that stress hierarchical authority, centralized control, and fixed boundaries must give way to organizational designs that rely on work teams, decentralized decisionmaking, and informal networks that bridge formal boundaries. They call these permeable boundaries in an organization that must also foster reciprocal information sharing, shared commitment to sustained cooperation, and a common set of values. Second, the learning organization must have a learning culture that stresses learning about the organization's components and the relationships among them, including production technologies and organization. Third, the learning organization will learn from diversity, not simply manage it or value it. The organization will capture the innovative potential of all participants.

Kochan and Useem note that if the learning organization where Continuous Quality Improvement (CQI) is practiced is to be qualitatively different from and better than traditional organizations, discovery and action cannot be limited to a privileged few at the top of the hierarchy. If everyone in the organization must be prepared for change, then everyone must also be capable of learning and be empowered to act on his or her new knowledge.

Weisbord's Learning Assumptions for Organizational Change

Weisbord and Janoff (1995) suggest that over the last century a learning curve has been traversed with respect to organizational change. In 1900 any change efforts came about by an expert solving problems. This was a "great person" approach to change in which change, whether for good or bad or for acceptance or resistance, occurred and revolved around one person. In the

1950s, the dominant ideology was that everybody solves problems, just not all together. In 1965 attention was focused on experts trying to improve the whole system; often the system endured but not the expert. In 2000 the reigning philosophy is that "everybody improves whole systems." This latest philosophy evolved from the initial attempt of Taylor, the focused work of Lewin, and the workable applications of Trist and Emery. Others were involved, but the key pathfinders along the journey are mentioned above. From this philosophy, Weisbord and Janoff (1995, 69) have recalibrated the principles of Lewin and the insights of Trist and Emery into the seven learning assumptions for organizational change that they use in their constructive action for change in organizations.

1. Each person has a unique learning style. Some learn best by reading, others by doing, still others by discussing or listening. Hence we provide in the Future Search process a variety of methods, not all of which will suit everyone.
2. Each person learns at a different rate. Hence some may be confused or lost in early stages. It is okay not to get it the first time you hear it. Try to be patient with yourself and others.
3. Each person learns different things from a common experience. Hence we encourage the trading of perceptions and acceptance of different feelings and views.
4. Each person learns best from his or her own experience. Hence we urge testing ideas against your own situation and supporting a healthy skepticism toward a one best way to process change in organizations.
5. Each person learns more in one Future Search experience than the world will permit us to apply. Hence we focus on local action within a global context.
6. Each person has the ability to help and teach others. Hence we encourage participation and drawing on each others' expertise as well as ours.
7. Each person benefits from trial, error, and feedback, if given support and a chance for success. Hence we provide opportunities for this to happen in relatively low-risk situations. No one is required to invest in these opportunities.

When using these assumptions for learning in the context of an attempt at organizational change, one can see that the key principle of success for Weisbord's Future Search process, a two-and-a-half-day conference (discussed below in detail)—the principle of getting the whole system in the room and focusing on the future—works because of the assumptions that were derived from nearly a century of work. But there are other constructions that involved large group interventions that give a clearer picture of the history of organizational change (Bunker and Alban, 1997) from the Lewinian tradition.

Large Group Interventions Used in Organizational Design

The need for leadership of change in an organization emerges when the company is able to compete successfully by continuously aligning the strategy, structure, processes, and learning to deal with the needs of incremental change while simultaneously preparing for radical change caused by the discontinuous pressure of the external market. This requires that the organization be designed in such a way to account for competition in a mature market where cost, efficiency, and incremental innovation are vital, while at the same time developing new products and services where speed, flexibility, and radical change are critically important (Lawrence and Lorsch, 1967, 1969; Tushman and O'Reilly, 1996). Both of these notions are easily understood, yet usurping one to make the other more sumptuous may create short-term success but will eventually lead the organization to long-term failure. Leading organizations proactively align their strategy, structure, processes, people, and culture through incremental evolutionary change. This change is punctuated by radical and discontinuous change that requires simultaneous shifting of these elements to deal with sudden changes in technology, regulatory events, changes in the political environment, economic conditions, and competitive shifts in the market (Tushman and O'Reilly, 1996). Management must understand many kinds of self-designing processes (Bunker and Alban, 1997) to deal with this phenomenon (Axelrod, 1992; Beckhard, 1969; Beckhard and Harris, 1987; Bunker and Alban, 1992; Lewin, 1945, 1947a, 1947b, 1948, 1951; Likert, 1961, 1967; Lippitt, 1980, 1983; Weisbord, 1987, 1992; Weisbord and Janoff, 1995; and McLagan and Christo, 1995).

All leaders' decisions that deal with organizational design depend on the performers in the organization and the processes they are allowed to use in enabling them to deal with both kinds of change, incremental and discontinuous. If leaders try to adapt to discontinuities through incremental adjustments, they are *not* likely to succeed. If leaders try to do it alone, they are *not* likely to succeed. If you influence the design of the organizational system, you have exerted a direct influence over the individual performer. Those who apply systems thinking for the entire organization and deal with performance improvement endeavors are called organizational designers. Organization

| 1930 – 1940 – 1950 | 1960 | 1980 – 1990 | 2000 |

Ludwig von Bertalanffy

Kurt Lewin ➤ Fred Emery & Eric Trist ➤ Marvin R. Weisbord ➤ B.B. Bunker/B.T. Alban

FIGURE 7.1 Large Group Interventions

design helps companies to organize themselves and grapple with the complexities of organizational life. An effective leader must have knowledge of organization design if he or she is to have any hope of changing the operation and destiny of organizations in the United States.

In Figure 7.1, we outline the evolution of large group interventions used to facilitate change through organizational design.

Bunker's and Alban's Large Group Interventions

Large group interventions for organizations or communities seeking to change are based on the principles of Lewin, Trist, Emery, and Weisbord and involve a critical mass of the people affected by change in the whole system, including internal employees and management and external suppliers and customers, during the change process (see Figure 7.1). Bunker and Alban (1997) created a number of methods based on the idea of getting the whole system into one room so people can support what they help to create (Weisbord, 1987). The whole-system process of change explained in the next chapter accounts for a critical mass of people who participate when they:

- Understand the need for change;
- Analyze the present reality to assess the current needs;
- Generate ideas about how to change; and
- Implement, support, and follow through on making the change work.

Continuing with the evolution of the philosophy of change as depicted in this chapter, Bunker and Alban (1997) have harvested twelve different kinds of methods for getting the whole system into the room.

Two different forms of this process, known as the Search Conference, emerged.

- The Search Conference (Emery and Purser, 1996)
- The Future Search Conference (Weisbord, 1987, 1992; Weisbord and Janoff, 1995)

Large Group Method	Decision-Making Process	Size of Event
Methods for Creating the Future		
The Search Conference	All equal	35-60, 2.5 days
Future Search	All equal	60-100, 18 hours
Real Time Strategic Change	Consultative	100-2,400, 3 days
ICA Strategic Planning Process	All equal	50-200, 2-7 days
Methods for Work Design		
Participative Design	All present at beginning	Ongoing at work
The Conference Model	All present at beginning	80+, 10 days
Real Time Work Design	All present at beginning	50-2400, ongoing
Fast Cycle/Full Participation Work Design	All present at beginning	120, 10 days
Methods for Whole-System Participative Work		
Simu-Real	Consultative	50-150, 1 day
Work-Out	Employees propose only	20-200, 2 days
Open Space Technology	Not integral to process	50-500, 3 days
Large Scale Interactive Events	Participative	50-1000, ongoing

FIGURE 7.2 Summary of Large Group Methods

Other methods originating out of the Lewinian tradition include two of Dannemiller and Jacobs' (1992) methods:

- Real Time Strategic Change
- Large-Scale Interactive Events

The Institute of Cultural Affairs (ICA) Strategic Planning Process was developed by the Ecumenical Institute of Chicago (Spencer, 1989). The Simu-Real Method was created by Donald and Alan Klein (Klein, 1992), and General Electric's Work-Out Model was created by Jack Welch, the CEO of GE (Bunker and Alban, 1997).

Five additional organizational redesign and work design methods have emerged from Trist and Emery's STS principles. Fred Emery, along with Merrelyn Emery, in attempting to correct the flaws of STS, created the Participative Design Method. Dick and Emily Axelrod (Axelrod, 1992) created The Conference Model, and others include Real Time Work Design created by Dannemiller and Tolchinsky (Bunker and Alban, 1997), the Fast Cycle/Full Participation Work Design (Passmore, 1994), and the Open Space Technology (Owen, 1992).

In Figure 7.2 we provide a summary of each of these twelve models in terms of the decisionmaking process used and the size of the group and time requirements. Additionally, we provide the steps used in each of the models in Figure 7.3.

Methods for Creating the Future (Models 1-4)

Model 1: The Search Conference (Participative democracy with no experts)
- Discussion of our turbulent environment (all perceptions are valid)
- Our systems's history
- Analysis of our current system (rationalize conflict)
- The most desirable system (total community discussion)
- Action planning (1/3 of time spent)
- Implementation (explicated created by those who have to do it)

Model 2: Future Search Conference (Participative democracy with no experts yet all stakeholders seeking common ground)
- Focus on our history (Global, Organizational and Personal)
- Focus on the present: giant mind map of current trends affecting the organization
- Discuss "prouds and sorries" regards the conference theme
- Focus on the future via brainstorming scenarios of ideal future
- Discover common futures across scenarios
- Plan action, take responsibility and follow up

Model 3: Real Time Strategic Change (Highly structured custom design to a particular issue with outside experts)
- Focus on dissatisfaction
- Focus on vision
- Focus on first steps

Model 4: ICA Strategic Planning Process (Planning committee and consultants design events of the stakeholder participation)
- Focus on the question
- Map out a clear, practical vision
- Analyze the underlying contradictions which act as obstacles to the vision
- Set the strategic mission of the vision and plans to remove obstacles
- Design the systematic actions
- Draw up an agreed-upon time line for implementation

Methods for Work Design (Models 5-8)

Model 5: Participative Design (Bottoms up approach, education workshops with senior management)
- Analysis
    Top management opens workshop and shares purpose
    Work units analyze how jobs are currently done
    Participants assess all skills to do the work
- Design
    Work units draw existing work flow and organizational stucture
    Work units redesign for six critical requirements:
- Adequate elbow room
- Opportunity to keep learning on the job
- Variety
- Mutual support and respect
- Accepting one's work as a meaningful contribution to social welfare
- Desirable career opportunities
- Implementation
    Work units hold interim meetings
    Work units develop measurable goals and targets
    Work units clarify training needs
    Work units test the work against six critical requirements
    Work units finalize the design
    Management returns to listen, discuss, and negotiate

(continues)

Model 6: The Conference Model (Based on Future Search Conference for redesign of work processes)
• System-wide preconference education
• Design process for five conferences (vision, customer, technical, design and implementation)

Model 7: Real Time Work Design (Implementation team oversees process and mini-conferences)
• Whole system present at launch and implementation
• Other steps include process and design steps where design team manages process and does the micro work

Model 8: Fast Cycle/Full Participation Work Design (Ratifying design changes in organizations)
• Orientation Events educate and include everyone
  Five meetings
    Future Search meeting
    External expectations meeting
    Work systems analysis meeting
    Work life Analysis
    New Design and Implementation

Methods for Whole-System Participative Work (Models 9-12)
Model 9: Simu-Real (Real time work on current issues)
• Get the system in one room
• Address the task
• Stop action, reflection and analysis
• Decision-making process has three forms agreed to in advance
• Executive
• Ad hoc representative group of stakeholders
• Roundtable consensus

Model 10: Work-Out (Problem identification and process improvement)
• Choose a troubled work process for discussion
• Select an appropriate cross-functional, cross-level group to convene
• Generate recommendations from work teams to improve work flow and eliminate unnecessary work
• Ask for a volunteer or teams to follow through on recommendations
• Meet with management and negotiate
• Conduct additional meetings as needed for follow-up

Model 11: Open Space Technology (Discussion and exploration of system issues with the least structured of interventions)
• Divergent process
  Whoever comes are the right people
  Whatever happens is the only thing that could happen
  Whenever it starts is the right time
  When it is over, it is over
• Large group creates agenda of topics
• Interest groups form around topics
• Periodic town meetings with one facitator

Model 12: Large Scale Interactive Events (Uses same process as Real Time Strategic Change).

FIGURE 7.3   Steps in Each of the 12 Models

For the purposes of this book, Future Search will be the only method detailed in Chapter 8 as it is the most developed with the largest number of successful events. Also, it is the most accessible for use by many organizations and institutions. The section on Weisbord's constructive action summarizes the foregoing methods of getting the whole system into one room.

Weisbord's Constructive Action Through Future Search

So what is Weisbord's Future Search Conference? Weisbord and Janoff (1995) suggest that the Future Search Conference is a constructive action, as it is a building block of theory and practice for a house that will never be finished. They view it as a progress report from a learning laboratory that has spawned literally thousands of constructive action projects. The learning that results from a Future Search Conference has three uses:

- Future Search processes lead stakeholders to create a shared future vision for their organization or community.
- Future Search meetings enable all stakeholders to discover shared intentions and take responsibility for their own plans.
- Future Search can help people implement a shared vision that already exists by building aligned strategies for getting there.

Chapter 8 unpacks the Future Search Conference in detail.

Conclusions

Organizational change involves developing a process to support both organizational learning and individual learning (Senge, 1990; Drucker, 1993; Garvin, 1993; Watkins and Marsick, 1993; and Dean and Ripley, 1997). The Future Search process described in Chapter 8 prevents the design of an organization from becoming stagnant and allows it to shift its design to meet the demands of a changing business environment. Though this process is dynamic, there are some principles that stand firm and upon which a leader can build an organization that lasts. These principles are interpersonal communication, equity, fairness, free speech, team work, learning, and relearning. Also, an understanding of organizational change is essential for leaders who desire to positively influence their enterprises as they lead change in their organizations by aligning a better interaction of the many elements in the system.

Practice of Organizational Change

Peter J. Dean

This chapter examines why leaders of change in organizations need to be aware of the different kinds of change and how to integrate them into one process. At different times and for different reasons, organizations and institutions require different kinds of change. Sometimes organizations need a systematic and continuous application of standard processes that require leaders of change who coach, facilitate, nudge, and shape experience to incrementally improve learning, performance, and workflow. This approach to change does patch things together, but the lack of infrastructure for learning and performance improvement shows clearly when the critical and sudden need for change arises.

Sometimes organizations need a radical and systemic application of change that involves everyone and that happens rapidly. More and more, this state of readiness to change things radically at any time has become a way to compete in business. According to De Geus (1997), organizations and institutions often don't perform well because their managers and administrators focus only on the economic activity of producing goods and services and forget about their organizations' true nature. That true nature is that the organization is made of a community of humans who must be allowed to learn and adapt to changes. Incremental change processes focus on cost containment and efficiency, many times to the detriment of the community of employees. The other kind of change, whole-systems involvement, considers the community of humans as key stakeholders and critical to the speed, flexibility, and innovation of change. In Chapter 7, the philosophy of this kind of change was discussed. In this chapter, I will examine the process to bring about whole-systems change within the working community of humans. The process is called Future Search, a process that involves both continuous and discontinuous change. The principles of this practice are necessary tools for the HRD professional.

Organizational Change

To function as a leader of organizational change, HRD professionals must turn knowledge about change into know-how for accomplishing change. This is done by integrating the success factors for change into action plans for implementing and managing change (Ulrich, 1997). The first step is to have a clearly defined change model. A model identifies the key factors for a successful change and the essential questions that must be answered to put the model into action. Specific questions determine the extent to which key success factors exist within an organization. The seven key success factors are:

- *Leading change:* Having a sponsor of change who owns and leads the change initiative.
- *Creating a shared need:* Ensuring that individuals know why they should change and that the need for change is greater than the resistance to change.
- *Shaping a vision:* Articulating the desired outcome from the change.
- *Mobilizing commitment:* Identifying, involving, and pledging the key stakeholders who must be involved to accomplish the change.
- *Changing systems and structures:* Using management tools (staffing, development, appraisal, rewards, organization design, communication systems, and so on) to ensure that the change is built into the organization's infrastructure.
- *Monitoring progress:* Defining benchmarks, milestones, and experiments with which to measure and demonstrate progress.
- *Making change last:* Ensuring that change happens through implementation plans, follow-through, and on-going commitment (Ulrich, 1997).

To resolve the paradox of change, the change leader must transform the seven key success factors from a theoretical exercise into a managerial process. Using the following questions, the capacity of the seven factors for change in a given organization can be profiled. Ulrich (1997, 73) believes that leaders of change should answer these questions to ensure the availability of the resources needed for implementing and managing change.

- To what extent does the change have a champion, sponsor, or other leader who will support the change? (Leading Change)
- To what extent do the people essential to the success of the change feel a need for change that exceeds the resistance to the change? (Creating a Need)
- To what extent do we know the desired outcomes for change? (Shaping a Vision)
- To what extent are key stakeholders committed to the change outcomes? (Mobilizing Commitment)
- To what extent is the change institutionalized through systems and structures? (Changing Systems and Structures)
- To what extent are indicators in place to track our progress on the change effort? (Monitoring Progress)
- To what extent do we have an action plan for getting change to happen? (Making Change Last)

One of the keys to this area of expertise for change leaders is to allocate resources in an efficient and effective manner. This requires change leaders to maintain the correct balance between work demands and resources allocation, identifying legitimate demands on employees and helping them focus by setting priorities. Employee relation expertise enables change professionals to identify creative ways of leveraging resources so employees do not feel overwhelmed by what is expected of them.

Organizational Change Professionals' Responsibilities, Competencies, and Areas of Expertise

Organizational change professionals have two primary responsibilities: to implement and manage change and to enhance resilience (Kotter, 1996; Conner, 1992).

Implementing and Managing Change

Change professionals are responsible for implementing and managing change. This stems from a need to make certain that change is supported at the operational level of the organization. In other words, employees must support change or it does not become a permanent part of the organizational culture.

Organizational change professionals do not implement change, employees do. However, they must be able to *get the change done*. By identifying and profiling key factors for change, they lead employees through the necessary steps for increasing change capacity. The probabilities of implementing and managing any change initiative improve dramatically when these seven success factors and their corresponding questions are assessed and discussed (Ulrich, 1997). HRD professionals leading the change should ask questions that reveal underlying assumptions.

Enhancing Resilience

Although organizational effectiveness implies continuous change and development, employees, senior managers, and executives differ in their ability to adapt to or recover from change. This is one kind of change. The capacity of these members to absorb change without draining the firm or individual energies is referred to as resilience. Change professionals are challenged to strengthen employees' adaptability to change, both personally and professionally. There are two approaches to breaking the downward spiral and, thus, becoming more resilient. First, employees can increase their energy by developing adaptive skills. Second, they can decrease their energy expenditures by accepting the inevitability of change and adjusting accordingly.

As a change professional, you are responsible for discovering ways to help employees strengthen the skills needed to adapt to change and thus remain resilient during change. Moreover, you must create an environment that provides support for change and resiliency. Consequently, your primary responsibility is to help the organization and its employees to increase their resilience by increasing their capacity and ability to adapt to change.

Resilient employees realize when change is inevitable, necessary, or advantageous and use resources to creatively reframe a changing situation, improvise new approaches, or maneuver to gain an advantage. They take risks despite potentially negative consequences and draw important lessons from change-related experiences that are then applied to similar situations. They respond to disruption by investing energy in problemsolving and teamwork, and they influence others to resolve conflicts.

Resilient employees are "positive, focused, flexible, organized, and proactive" (Conner, 1992, 238). They display a sense of security and self-assurance based on their view of life as complex and challenging and filled with opportunity. They view disruptions as a natural part of the changing world, and see major change as a potentially uncomfortable endeavor, yet one that offers opportunities for growth and development. Resilient employees focus on what they want to achieve by maintaining a strong vision that serves both as a source of purpose and as a guidance system to reestablish perspectives following significant disruption. These employees feel empowered during change, recognize their own strengths and weaknesses, and know when to accept internal or external limits. They challenge change and, when necessary, modify their own assumptions or frames of reference. They rely on nurturing relationships for support and display patience, understanding, and humor when dealing with change.

As a way of managing ambiguity, resilient employees develop structured approaches that help them identify the underlying themes embedded in confusing situations. They identify priorities that they are willing to renegotiate during change. If necessary, resilient employees are able to manage several simultaneous tasks. They compartmentalize stress so that it does not carry over to other projects or parts of their lives. They know when to ask others for help and engage in major action only after careful planning. Finally, resilient employees engage change (are proactive) rather than defend against it.

Change Professionals' Competencies

To become an effective change professional, HRD professionals need to develop the following skills. These skills can be used in implementing and managing change and in enhancing resilience.

Business Understanding.   A solid business understanding includes knowledge of business fundamentals, systems theory, organizational culture, and politics. A nuanced understanding of how organizational philosophy guides a firm's strategy and action is an essential attribute of the change professional.

Change Facilitation Skills.   Change facilitation is a process rather than a technique or outcome. Therefore, change professionals direct their energies toward helping employees understand the purpose of change and their roles and responsibilities in implementing it. During change facilitation, change professionals must have the ability to gather employees' opinions, suggestions, and recommendations regarding the best way of generating the desired change in the workplace. In short, change professionals use their relationship and communications skills to encourage participation in the change process. This is done for the purpose of developing support for proposed change while making employees feel more comfortable with the disruption brought about by change.

Interpersonal Skills. At the heart of the change professional–client relationship are interpersonal skills. When change professionals serve as employee champions, they need to be able to demonstrate respect for the personal boundaries and values of their clients. Interpersonal skills such as active listening and questioning help them achieve this outcome.

Employee Relations Skills. Change professionals are in a unique position to serve as employee relations experts. This demands the ability to build collaborative relationships with employees, allocate resources used to improve performance, and make job assignments based on the knowledge, skills, and abilities of employees.

Conflict Resolution Skills. Because of conflicting goals, ideas, policies, and practices in most organizations, it is almost impossible to implement meaningful change. Hence, change professionals need to acquire conflict resolution skills. These skills help change professionals guide executives, managers, and employees through the change process in a way that minimizes resistance.

Conceptual Skills. Change professionals need to have the ability to help clients analyze performance problems, implement change initiatives, and evaluate their thinking about the organizational system (Burke, 1992). To achieve this end, they must develop conceptual skills. These skills are necessary for change professionals to assess and express certain relationships, such as the cause-and-effect and if-then linkages that exist within the systemic context of the client organization. Moreover, these skills help change professionals test solutions and recommendations.

Negotiating Skills. Another important attribute of the change professional is the ability to become an active participant in the problemsolving process. By blending a directive and objective approach, clients are encouraged to define existing problems and test alternatives for an effective resolution to the problem. To execute this responsibility correctly, change professionals should use a partnership approach in focusing their attention on identifying problems and evaluating, selecting, and carrying out alternatives (Gilley and Maycunich, 2000a, 329).

Technical skills. Change professionals must also possess the technical skills to analyze and evaluate change interventions. These skills will help them analyze data gathered during diagnosis, examine solutions, and evaluate the organizational impact of change interventions. They are also essential for developing new initiatives to meet the specific client need and to respond to unforeseen contingencies.

Consensus- and Commitment-Building Skills.   As consensus and commitment builders, change professionals need the ability to monitor their clients' readiness and commitment to change. Turner (1983) provides several questions to help demonstrate this skill:

- How willing are the members of the organization to implement change?
- Is upper-level management willing to learn and utilize new management methods and practices?
- What types of information do members of the organization readily accept or resist?
- What are the members' attitudes toward change?
- What are the executives' attitudes toward change?
- To what extent will individual members of the organization regard their contribution to overall organizational effectiveness as a legitimate and desirable objective?

Analytical skills.   Advanced analytical skills are also needed so change professionals can generate information, analyze it, distinguish among problems, symptoms, and causes, identify solutions to problems, and recommend an appropriate solution(s). These skills are developed from experience in dealing with difficult situations throughout an organization.

Objectivity.   Change professionals must be able to remain impartial regardless of their personal values and biases and in spite of an organization's culture, traditions, and vested interests. This quality is often referred to as objectivity (Hale, 1998). This skill is often difficult for internal change professionals to master because of their perspective. Unfortunately, it is almost impossible to effectively address most organizational issues without applying this skill. In fact, the ability to remain objective enables change professionals to become the social conscience of the organization and is perhaps the greatest single benefit of the change professional role (Gilley and Maycunich, 2000a).

Intuition.   Burke (1992) argues that intuition is important for change professionals. Intuition allows them to recognize their own feelings and biases and be able to distinguish their perceptions from those of the client.

Project Management Skills. Every performance improvement intervention, change initiative, and special assignment is a project. Consequently, change professionals need project management skills to lead such projects from beginning to end. These skills overlap with the other skills required of a change professional in that you will need to negotiate the relationship with the project sponsor and clearly define the change initiative (Fuller and Farrington, 1999, 165–166). Additionally, change professionals are responsible for analyzing the risks to project completion and for engaging in contingency planning to help minimize those risks; they also write requests for proposals and select and manage employees. They need to make certain that the project's requirements are being fulfilled, that people working on the project are aware of their roles and responsibilities, that timing and scheduling of the project are going according to plan, and that the budget is within limits. Another responsibility is managing communications among you, the employees, and senior managers, as well as among employees themselves.

Change Alignment. Change professionals have a thorough understanding of the dynamics associated with the change process (Gilley et al., 2001). Far too many change efforts have attempted to design a fail-safe, lock-step change process without adequate focus on the overarching organizational behavior elements of the equation. These efforts are futile. "There are no sure-fire instructions which, when scrupulously followed, make change succeed, much less eliminate or solve the problems accompanying any change process" (Jick, 1993, 27). Detailed, foolhardy "recipes for success" should be replaced with a broader set of change imperatives that greatly enhance the probability of success for any change initiative.

Forthrightness. True forthrightness is a way of behaving that confirms a change professional's own individual worth and dignity while simultaneously confirming and maintaining the worth and dignity of the employees. Forthrightness is demonstrated when you use methods of communication that enable you to maintain self-respect, personal happiness, and satisfaction. This type of communication allows you to stand up for your own rights and express your personal needs, values, concerns, and ideas in direct and appropriate ways. Simultaneously, you don't violate the needs of your employees while helping them retain a positive self-concept.

Organization Subordination. This is a process by which change professionals place the contributions, involvement, and loyalty of employees above those of the organization. They strive to guarantee organizational subservience to employees' efforts to improve productivity, efficiencies, and approaches that are essential to competitive readiness and organizational renewal. Furthermore, *they get out of the way* and allow employees to work effectively and efficiently, enabling workers to demonstrate creative, insightful, and innovative approaches to business problems and performance difficulties (Ulrich, Zenger, and Smallwood, 1999).

Ambiguity.   Some believe that the change professional's effectiveness depends on his or her ability to tolerate ambiguity (Burke, 1992, 177–178). Since every organization is different, and what works in one may not work in another, it is important that every change initiative fit the unique circumstances within an organization. Accordingly, to become an effective change professional, you must develop within yourself a comfort level with ambiguity. Too often we have observed managers struggling with this issue from two different directions. On the one hand, control-oriented managers struggle with *analysis paralysis*, a particularly dangerous form of discomfort that will not allow decisions to be made until all the unknowns become known. Though we understand such a malady, it is simply unacceptable in today's organizational context. The notion that decisions cannot be made until all the facts are in and all the variables are known simply will not work given the rapid pace of change in most industries. A second type of struggle is the *backseat driver* approach to management. Here, the decisionmaker appears to be comfortable with delegation and decisionmaking, yet he hovers so closely to "inspect" the performance of subordinates that performance is stifled.

Change Professional's Areas of Expertise

HRD professionals need to develop several areas of expertise to be successful organizational change professionals. These include the following:

Establishing and Managing Client Relationships.   Establishing and managing client relationships is one of the most critical elements in improving organizational performance. This area of expertise is necessary for fostering trust and cooperation between consultants and their clients.

Conducting Analyses.   Nilson (1999) and Rossett (1999b) believe that conducting analysis calls for interacting with clients to determine the business need, performance problem, and expected outcomes. Such an expertise requires performance consultants to communicate with clients about the business in industrial terms and about performance improvement and management in a straightforward and understandable way (Gilley and May-cunich, 2000a, 248).

Identifying Root Causes. Performance consultants need to be able to determine whether the root cause is a gap caused by the organization, its people, their behavior, consequences for performance, feedback, or other environmental factors (Fuller and Farrington, 1999). This expertise is essential when utilizing the human performance system and organizational performance improvement models previously discussed.

Recommending and Implementing Solutions. Rossett (1999b) believes that performance consultants must be able to recommend solutions for eliminating the barriers to performance. This is done by addressing root causes of performance deficiencies, which requires a proficient knowledge of the human performance system and an ability to match interventions with types of root causes.

Evaluating Results. Performance consultants must be able to measure the overall success of the project by determining whether initial performance improvement goals have been achieved and the business issue resolved. Fuller and Farrington (1999) and Swanson (1994) believe that effective evaluation begins during the analysis phase when the decision is made about what to accept as evidence that business goals have been met.

Facilitating Learning. HRD professionals are responsible for helping employees acquire the new skills, knowledge, insights, awareness, and attitudes needed to implement change. These could include problemsolving skills, giving and receiving performance feedback, listening skills, leadership development, goal setting, resolving conflicts, and diagnosing group interactions. Further, Burke (1992) writes that when clients have developed such skills and knowledge, they begin to rely less on change professionals and start applying what they have learned.

Building Partnerships. Becoming an HRD professional requires you to develop an expertise in building partnerships. Such partnerships help professionals decide which change initiatives provide the highest value and have the greatest impact on the organization. They also promote the establishment of working relationships based on shared values, aligned purpose and vision, and mutual support. Furthermore, partnerships are built on the business and performance needs of employees, not on a change professional's career aspiration or professional success. Better management of limited financial and human resources is another reason for creating partnerships.

Facilitating Change. The change professional's final area of expertise is to become proficient in change facilitation. A facilitator is an individual who guides a group toward a destination (Hunter, Bailey, and Taylor, 1994). The destination for a change professional is to bring about a change within an organization. To achieve this objective, change professionals need to gain experience and develop expertise in change facilitation.

Outcomes of Organizational Change Practice

The principal outcome of organizational change is improved organizational effectiveness. Organizational effectiveness can be measured in a variety of ways. Regardless of how it is measured, however, meeting one's responsibility as an HRD professional should result in improved motivational systems, compensation and reward programs, work environment culture transformation, and organizational communications. It should also yield improved employee learning and development, job design, and performance management systems. Other outcomes include better employee conflict resolution and problemsolving skills.

Additionally, HRD professionals are able to help their organization improve its ability to adapt strategies and behaviors to future environmental change by maximizing the contribution of the organization's employees. Thus, by raising organizational effectiveness, HRD professionals are dedicated to developing and maintaining the most important systems and linkages to improve performance and to enhance organizational readiness and competitiveness through learning and change initiatives.

There are, however, several other important outcomes of organizational change. First, change provides opportunities for employees to function as human beings rather than as merely resources in the productivity process. Second, it provides opportunities for each organization member and the organization itself to develop to their fullest potential. Third, organizational change increases an organization's effectiveness by helping it achieve its strategic business goals and objectives. Fourth, it helps create an environment in which employees find exciting and challenging work. Fifth, organizational change provides opportunities for employees and managers to influence the way in which they relate to work, the organization, and the work environment. And sixth, it enables every employee to be treated as a human being with a complex set of needs and values, all of which are important in his or her work and life.

Now that we have considered the talents that change professionals need to accrue during their careers, it is time to bring back into the discussion the other kinds of change that are necessary to bring about successful organizational change. We will also discuss the method of Future Search, the use of which distinguishes a change professional from a linear change professional.

Two Kinds of Change in Organizations

The story of Apple Computer illustrates the two kinds of change, continuous and discontinuous, that an organization experiences. Its history begins with a small group of individuals designing, producing, and selling a personal computer. Yet that was not the only reason for their success. The design of their organization had a high degree of alignment and congruence between the strategy of the organization and the organization design (structure, systems of design, manufacturing, marketing, distribution, accounting/payroll, and processes of critical tasks needed to implement the systems). People had assigned roles and a learning culture based on shared values of innovation, commitment, and speed.

With success and growth several changes began to happen. Apple got larger and needed a different design, so more structure, systems, and processes were added for efficiency and control. The learning *culture* changed to reflect new challenges as new *norms* emerged to show what was important and what would not be tolerated. This slowed creativity and the joy of learning, and stunted employee conversation that had formerly focused on all the potential possibilities. This slowing of creative ventures was partially due to energy being directed into the new learning that had to occur for Apple's continued success. In addition, Apple's strategy changed from a single product for personal computer users with a focused strategy to a broader range of products with a marketwide emphasis to user, educational institutions, and industrial markets. For Apple to ensure congruence and alignment of its organization design and its people with this evolved strategy based on changing markets and technology, new leadership was brought into the company. Founder Jobs was out and Sculley was in.

Other things required change as well. As a product type matures, the basis of competition changes. Early on, competition is based on product variation, while later it shifts to features, efficiency, and cost. When Mac, IBM's OS/2, and Microsoft Windows competed with each other it was based on product variation, until Windows became the industry standard in operating systems. Then competition shifted to cost, quality, and efficiency. This required changes in the design of the organization, and Apple had to once again redesign the congruence among strategy, organizational design (the structure, systems, and processes), its people, and the culture. So now Sculley was "out" and Spindler was "in" to shift operations into a more mature market. When organizational performance came to a standstill, Apple's board of directors then chose Amelio to turn it around. Over this twenty-year period, Apple's incremental change was punctuated by discontinuous change. Each of these different periods in Apple's history required radical changes in the design of structures, systems, processes, people, and learning and leadership skills so that the new strategy would be in alignment with the new design.

The take-away lesson from such experiences in business is that eventually the alignment or congruence of a successful firm, or even of an industry, will be upset by discontinuities. There is a need for more than incremental change in organizations. Regardless of whether you agree with the previous point, there are some guidelines one can follow in applying the knowledge of the two kinds of change when dealing with change in organizations.

Organizational change is a field of practice that specifically engineers a criterion-based, measured approach to bring about change through assessment and analysis of gaps, mostly at the microlevel of the enterprise. Once the gaps are identified, systems are created, monitored, and evaluated to generate results from the human performers (Stolovitch and Keeps, 1992). Rosenberg, Coscarelli, and Hutchinson (1999) contend that organizational change operates from a nonlinear perspective to bring about specific change valued by the enterprise. The creation of the right system is crucial in allowing the people in it to perform optimally.

According to several researchers and authors, the characteristics and knowledge that a professional who is practicing organizational change must possess are as follows:

1. Focuses on the whole system to understand the complexity first.
2. Seeks to discover links between different structures, processes, and systems.
3. Uses both quantitative and qualitative methods as needed.
4. Uses both analysis and synthesis as needed.
5. Uses language to deliver information clearly and for joint understanding.
6. Uses observation, not hearsay, to collect facts.
7. Relies on direct, comparative, and economic measures.
8. Removes non-value-added work (Stolovitch and Keeps, 1992; Dean, 1983, 1993, 1995, 1999a; Dean, Dean, and Guman, 1992; Dean, Blevins, and Snodgrass, 1997; Dean and Ripley, 1997, 1998a, 1998b, 1998c).

Stolovitch and Keeps (1992) suggest that organizational change professionals consider the following approach to deal with the complexity in organizations: apply principles and practices systematically and systemically (i.e., through the total system); ensure that actions are grounded in scientifically derived theories and empirical evidence; be open to all means, methods, and media; and stay focused on the value-added achievements of workers.

The change professional should attempt to align the person with a work-supporting system so that the entire organization consisting of numerous variables can work more efficiently and effectively. In this way, organizational change processes will complement one another in improving the performance of the individuals and the overall performance of the organization

By being more knowledgeable and proficient in using organizational change tools, professionals can better perform their jobs. The change professional often has to correct the consequences of what has or has not been designed earlier, and can learn to assist with the design, redesign, development, or rethinking of the work to achieve a better fit among the purpose, processes, and people of the organization (Hupp, 1998).

Organizational Change Tools

Organizational change has traditionally focused on improving the human dynamics in an enterprise. Change encourages management to look at the informal operating patterns in the substructures, subprocesses, practices, and political arrangements of the organization. This effort directly engages the values, beliefs, and accepted norms of the organization. Thus, such change largely involves interpersonal issues and is intended to examine and change the social processes of an enterprise's culture so it can better adapt to new technologies, markets, and challenges, and to the rate of change itself, with better communications, decisionmaking, and planning.

Over the years, there has been an accumulation of tools and methods for effecting change processes in organizations. Briefly, these include:

- 1940s—sensitivity training for the interaction of the person and the environment.
- 1950s—conflict resolution and team building.
- 1960s—intergroup development and open systems planning.
- 1970s—socio-technical systems analysis and quality of work life.
- 1980s—organization transformation, total quality, and large-scale change with Future Search.

- 1990s—reengineering, large group intervention, transcultural planning, and transnational community building.

Additionally, organizational change operates out of a set of core values. These include the integration of individual and organization needs, choice, freedom and responsibility, and dignity, integrity, self-worth, and fundamental rights. Core values also include cooperation and collaboration, authenticity and openness, and effectiveness, efficiency, interdependence, and alignment. In general, core values manifest a holistic, systemic perspective that encompasses stakeholder orientation and the processes of participation, confrontation, and adaptability.

Organizational change has traditionally relied on the interpersonal strategy of normative re-education without giving attention to the economic, political, technological, legal, and ethical issues that affect the organization. Also, organizational change usually has not used evaluation or criterion-based measurement. Yet it has used powerful interventions. Future Search is one such powerful intervention.

Future Search Process

The remainder of this chapter describes a process of organizational change called Future Search. Future Search can be used as a way to develop a new direction for an organization or to refine the current direction among multiple alternatives. It simultaneously addresses the incremental and whole-system change needs in the vision, mission, goals, objectives, structure, and operation of the organization, as well as internal and external problems, concerns, and issues. As a result, organizational change professionals need to focus on the informal culture of the organization and the development of the potential of the people that is not being expressed in their performance.

Purpose of Future Search

Hupp (1998) believes that work should be designed to coordinate purpose, processes, and people. She attempts to align fundamental parts of the system, not to create the perfect design, but to create a self-adaptive system. The three parts include:

- *Environment (the external context) and strategic direction (the organization's response, its corresponding purpose, and strategy):* The knowledge of the organizational design components of strategy, structure, process, systems, work design, and individual performance.

- *Work process and technology:* The work processes and tools required to produce the organization's products and services and to measure the accomplishment of work.
- *People, organizational structures, and human resource systems:* How people are organized, how authority and responsibility are distributed, and how people are selected, developed, and rewarded.

In Future Search, a self-adapting system such as Hupp's (1998) approach is created to:

- Be increasingly self-regulating and more responsive to its business context.
- Deploy a work process that's fast, focused, and flexible.
- Include members with the collective expertise to plan, coordinate, control, and troubleshoot their own start-to-finish work process.
- Construct jobs that build contributors' ownership and commitment.

Design Principles of Future Search

Hupp (1998) identifies several key design principles. First, change professionals and organizational leaders must *think in wholes.* In other words, the best design for a productive system is one in which each part of the system embodies the goals of the overall system. This also includes the concept of joint optimization, which means that the effectiveness of the whole is more important than the effectiveness of the parts.

The second principle involves creating self-regulating units. Hupp (1998) maintains that units should be sufficiently self-regulating so that they can cope with problems and seize opportunities by rearranging their own resources. Such self-regulating units provide internal coordination and control and guide information and discretion directly to those who need it, when they need it. These units provide "requisite variety," that is, internal flexibility should be appropriate to environmental variability. Additionally, feedback systems should be as complex as the variances they need to control. Further, self-regulating units provide for redundancy of functions (multiskilled contributors) rather than redundancy of parts (staffing to support narrowly sliced, specialized functions). This enhances capacity by enlarging roles, not by adding specialists. As a result, the design process should set "minimal critical specifications." Quite simply, "don't carve in stone what should be left to local discretion."

The third principle involves viewing people as a resource, not as a commodity. To attain this, organizations need to provide jobs that meet Emery's six psychological criteria:

- Elbow room (autonomy)
- Learning (allow individuals to set goals and get direct feedback)
- Variety
- Mutual support and respect
- Meaningfulness (allow doers to "see the big picture" and create something important)
- A desirable future

The fourth principle involves "walking the talk." In other words, organizational leaders and change professionals must demonstrate the "change they want to see" by using a change process that demonstrates and reinforces the desired outcomes. Thus, the design process is more about getting the system to see and adapt itself than it is about perfecting workflow and structure. Redesign should be participative, not representative. That is, redesign should be done by people who must make the redesign work, not by a representative design team working in isolation. Organizational change professionals realize that change is never finished. Consequently, organizations are not making a transition from one stable state to another but are moving from one period of transition to another.

Approaches to Organizational Redesign

Hupp (1998) identifies three possible approaches to redesign. In the first approach, management does it. The primary advantages of this approach include speed and achieving the design that management wants. Quite frankly, if management has already decided what they want, change professionals should not try to manipulate the organization to "read management's minds." The principal disadvantages of this approach include the lack of input from knowledgeable sources and the lack of support from those affected by change.

Another approach to redesign is for an appointed "design team" to implement change. This has several advantages in that it will provide higher quality since the design is completed by those skilled in the work itself. Moreover, grassroots support will increase as a result of the representative approach. On the other hand, several disadvantages emerge when using this approach. Most notably, redesign and implementation are slow when using a highly representative approach. Widespread support may also be lacking since only a small group of employees is involved (and they become isolated over time).

A third approach involves assembling a critical mass of stakeholders during large-scale organizational design conferences. The primary advantage in this case is that it allows a high-quality design process, greater ownership, and speed in decisionmaking and action. The principal disadvantage is that this approach requires that a large group of employees be off their jobs during conferences. It also requires careful planning because it is more demanding and less forgiving to facilitate large "critical mass" groups than small design teams or management groups. Finally, management has little leeway in preparing for change when such a public approach is used. If management has second thoughts, it may blunder in the public eye, as well as in front of its employees.

Benefits of Future Search

The unique benefits of large-scale organizational design conferences that involve the stakeholders are significant. When organizational change professionals redesign work to align strategic direction, work processes, organizational structure, and jobs, they can achieve:

- *Better coordination and information flow.* When change professionals organize work around whole products or services, people who need to cooperate with each other are on the same team, focused on a common goal. (In the past, work has typically been organized around functions, putting people who need to cooperate with each other in different work groups, pursuing function-specific goals.)
- *Reduced costs and cycle time.* When change professionals streamline workflow, they remove or minimize steps that do not add value. This reduces cost, cycle time, and opportunity for error. In addition, when mature work teams plan and monitor their own work, organizational change professionals need fewer managers. The managers who remain can focus on integrating efforts across teams and developing business strategy.
- *Improved responsiveness to customers.* When change professionals organize work around products, services, or customer groups, employees get greater access to customers, become better at anticipating customer needs, and provide better informed, more responsive customer service.

- *More innovation.* When change professionals provide employees with the opportunity and responsibility to improve their products, services, and processes, they shorten the distance between ideas and their implementation.
- *More value added through people.* When employees produce whole products or services, not isolated fragments, they take more ownership over their jobs. Also, jobs that integrate thinking with doing result in greater job satisfaction. Finally, when managers focus on integrating, instead of supervising, they concentrate on getting people to work together across boundaries, not on second-guessing individual efforts. This shifts their focus to adding value, not reworking their subordinates' work.
- *More flexibility.* When the organization deploys a broadly skilled workforce it gets more flexibility than when it deploys a narrowly skilled one.

Precautions of Large-Scale Organizational Design Conferences

Hupp (1998) recommends some special precautions in the use of large-scale organizational design conferences. First, management needs to do the hard work of thinking through what they will and will not accept on the front end. Second, organizational change professionals need to understand that this approach requires them to prepare organizational leaders for comprehensive decisionmaking and problemsolving. Hupp (1998) refers to this as aligning the organization. When this is accomplished, the organization has become an open, learning system where the workers who perform the core processes are invested with the authority and accountability to plan, make decisions, and seize opportunities that are embedded in their processes. This involves a fundamental power shift from hierarchical to participative power and from expert diagnosis and prescription (doing it *to* the line organization) to line contributors examining and adapting their own system (doing it *through* the line organization).

Before organizational change professionals begin the process, they must confirm that management is ready for this shift. They must ensure that management intends to become strategic rather than tactical, integrative rather than empire-building, and resource-brokering rather than resource-controlling. To achieve this end, members of the planning or steering team need to play the role of advocates, not critics, of the process. Since change management involves more than good public relations, change professionals will be challenging stakeholders to work through the real conflicts and polarities that underlie differences, *not* smoothing them over with slogans or feel-good jargon.

If an organization uses large-scale conferencing methodologies, the change professionals need to make sure that the conferences allow enough time and provide forums to engage the real conflict and polarities that exist in the system. They should be skilled in building sustainable agreements among diverse stakeholders.

Finally, change sponsors, advocates, and change professionals need to remember that the ultimate answers are *not* in the methodology, which is simply a tool. The system's stakeholders already possess all the wisdom they need to find their answers. It's the job of the sponsors, advocates, and consultants to get them to discuss the right questions, so they can collectively uncover the workplace knowledge and truth that's already there, buried under organizational clutter.

Phases of the Future Search Process

The process of Future Search can be used in different types of organizations in either the public or private sectors. Described below are the four phases of Future Search.

1. Planning a Future Search Conference

Preliminary planning includes the decision to hold a conference, planning the conference times, and selecting stakeholders/participants, program, and location of the conference(s). The purpose of the conference and how the results will be carried forward must be determined in the planning stage. Planning is critical to the success of the conference.

2. Future Search Conference (2 1/2 days)
  * Getting started
  * Recalling the past
  * Appreciating the present
  * Living the future
  * Confirming common future and potential projects
  * Moving into action

3. Follow-up Implementation (3–6 months)
  * Make plans more precise
  * Create decisionmaking process
  * Implement project(s)
  * Summarize experiences
  * Make new action plans

4. Follow-up Implementation (1–3 years)
- Implementation of project(s)
- Decision to form a continuous search process

The Four Phases of the Future Search Process

Phase 1: Planning a Future Search Conference

Preliminary planning includes the decision to hold a conference and planning the conference: selecting stakeholders/participants, setting expectations for the Future Search Conference, and then simply deciding on the program, times, and location of the conference(s).

Decision to Hold a Future Search Conference

Consider a Future Search if . . .	Go slow when . . .
A shared vision is needed	Leadership is reluctant
An action plan is needed	Minimum conditions above are met
Other efforts have stalled	Nobody but you sees the need
New leadership is taking over	Leadership wants to force it in their plan
When key transition is at hand	The agenda is preset
Opposing parties have no good forum to meet	They have no planning time
Time is growing short	Everybody but you wants it

Choosing Participants

They should be the stakeholders affected by the planning.

1. Include stakeholders who have a special interest in probable outcomes.
2. Participants do not have to be experts in the planning situation.
3. Prepare people to be comfortable in groups with mixed rank and status.

Conditions for Participation

1. All participants must attend all activities.
2. A Future Search Conference is not a convention for speeches or testimonials.
3. Participants should not be disturbed in the process by outside activities.
4. The process is best facilitated from a location away from daily disturbances.
5. All opinions and perspectives of participants must be respected by all the participants.

Expectations of Outcomes

1. Consensus generation with creative strategies and collaborative approaches.
2. Awareness of shared vales and commitment to change.
3. Enjoying the learning from each other.
4. Integration of cultural, regional, and value differences.

Phase 2: Future Search Conference (2 1/2 days)

Framework of Principles

The conference is unlike a participative meeting. It involves a cross section of the whole system, which allows more diversity and less hierarchy than is typical in participative meetings. It provides an opportunity for each person to be heard and to learn from others. Future scenarios are put into a global perspective before taking action on a local scene later on in the process. People self-manage themselves and use dialogue as the tool to help each other find common ground where differences are honored but not necessarily reconciled (Weisbord and Janoff, 1995). Thus, the framework of the process includes:

- The whole system, or representation of that system, present in the room at one time.
- Global and historical context that allows the work to occur in the context of the larger environment.
- Focus on the *future* and *common ground*.

- Self-management and dialogue versus problemsolving and conflict management.

Future Search Working Agreements

These agreements should be posted on the wall and visible at all times throughout the 2 1/2 days. They are as follows:

- Conference participants are responsible for:
  —providing information/meaning
  —self-managing in small groups, and
  —generating future scenarios/actions
- Conference manager is responsible for:
  —setting times and tasks
  —managing/facilitating/gatekeeping large group discussions, and
  —keeping the purpose "front and center"

Ground rules to be used in the process from beginning to end include:

- All ideas are valid
- All information is posted on flip charts
- Observe time frame
- Discover common ground and possibilities for action
- Differences will be acknowledged and understood but not worked through
- Listen to others—every voice is important

These ground rules should be posted so that they are in view at all times throughout the 2 1/2 days.

Self-Managing Roles

- *Discussion leader* assures that everyone is heard who wants to be heard within the time available. It is important that the discussion leader "Accept each other's reality as fact for that person." If this is done well, then there is meaningful dialogue and participants can discover common ground for action. Also, the discussion leader and the time keeper help each other keep the participants on task to finish on time.

- *Time keeper* keeps the participants aware of the time left and signals what time there is remaining to the person who is talking. This avoids grandstanding and unequal allocation of time among participants. Time keepers make sure that group tasks are completed on time and he or she monitors the group reports.
- *Recorder* writes on flip charts the group's work in the participants' own words. Often the recorder needs to ask participants to restate lengthy ideas in a more succinct manner.
- *Reporter(s)* presents group results in the time allotted. This role can be shared among many of the participants.

Awareness of the Future Search Conference as a Change in Paradigm

The conference manager needs to be mindful of the tacit task of seizing teachable moments to point out that the participants are probably experiencing pulls from two different paradigms of working together. This is one of many ways that the Future Search process itself gives the group the energy it needs to complete the conference. That experience is then hopefully carried over to the workplace and the follow-up meetings. These two paradigms can be explained by the following breakdown.

OLD	NEW
Things break down over time	Can always self-organize to create anew
Equilibrium is desired	Two kinds of change happen all the time
Structure is made by us	Structure is always unfolding
Structure gives order	Information gives order
Information is controlled	Information is freely generated

No one can force change on anyone else. It has to be experienced. Unless we invent ways where paradigm shifts can be experienced by large numbers of people, then change will remain a myth. —Eric Trist (quoted in Weisbord and Janoff, 1995, 25)

The other essential awareness that the conference manager needs to keep front and center makes up what is called the core values of the process. Each core value is to be treated equally. When this is modeled by the conference manager, the participants begin to model that behavior. The core vales of the Future Search Process (Weisbord, 1992) include:

- *Epistemology:* The real world is knowable to ordinary people and their knowledge can be collectively and meaningfully organized. Thus, people can create their own future.
- *People:* Employees want to engage their hands, heads, and heart to help create the necessary processes for success.
- *Participation:* The best results come from everyone participating like an equal.
- *Process:* The first three values emerge if the process uses cooperation, empowerment, and shared control and appreciates diversity.
- *Prejudice-Free:* Working together with shared tasks across lines of ethnicity, race, gender, class, hierarchy, and special function breaks down negative stereotypes and minimizes bias.

At the actual Future Search Conference, the agenda, as seen below, should be posted on the wall and visible at all times so participants can keep track of the progress of the process. A typical agenda is as follows:

Typical Future Search Conference Agenda

Day 1, Afternoon (Where We Have Been) GETTING ABOARD
    1:00 pm–2:00 pm Welcome and Introductions
    2:00 pm–6:00 pm
    Focus on the Past (world trends: political, economic, sociological, and technological)
    Focus on the Present (external trends that affect the organization)
Day 2, Morning (Where We Are) PLUNGING THE DEPTHS
    8:30 am–12:30 pm
    External Trends Continued
    Focus on Present Trends (external and internal) That Affect the Organization
    (Group Mind Map)
    Owning Our Actions (prouds and sorries)
Day 2, Afternoon (What We Want To Be) VIEWING THE HEIGHTS
    12:30 pm–3:00 pm (includes lunch)
    Ideal Future Scenarios for the Organization
    3:00 pm–4:30 pm

Identify Common Ground
4:30 pm–end
Present Common Ground on the Future
Day 3, Morning (How To Get There) DIALOGUING THE REAL
CHOICES
  8:30–1:00 pm
Confirm Common Future (reality dialogue)
Action Planning (strategies, structures, processes, systems, competen-
    cies, learning)

Past

The focus on the past, going back over the last thirty years, should always be completed as it sets up the dynamics for the group's involvement. What has happened to the organization over the same time
should be covered, as well as what has happened to each participant over
the same thirty years. Past is a prelude to the future outcomes of the process. It can be completed in many ways, but it should involve all the participants. It is meant to show the common experiences that are shared
and open the group up for more rigorous sharing of information. This
part of the program can be missed, but by the same token it is part of
the process that should never be missed. It is essential for what follows.

Present

The present is then examined. It is at this time that the conference becomes a community in and of itself. The giant Group Mind Map that
gets created in this stage of the conference brings about the recognition
that with the sheer number of forces that impinge on people in the organization no one can deal with it all alone. This recognition of the complexity and hugeness of it all opens up avenues for working on changing
the system.

The Group Mind Map involves the recording of the trends that affect
the future of the group and is particularly important to the process. It is
a wall map where the entire group will place trends affecting them right
now. This is a group brainstorm technique in which there is no evaluation and no censorship. An example given by Weisbord and Janoff
(1995) is as follows: "More cell phones is an example of a trend toward
more frequent communication." The Group Mind Map builds a shared
context of concerns and priorities. The ground rules follow.

Ground Rules for Group Mind Map

- "We all see what we all see"
- Key things impacting culture change in the organization
- Remember: "No evaluation or censorship of any item put on wall map"
- Discover major trends and related trends.

Once the Group Mind Map is complete, then in small groups the participants talk over the trends that are of concern to your stakeholder group. Then make your own map on a flip chart to show how these trends are related and how they affect you. On this new map, note the examples of what you are doing right now in response to these trends and what you want to do that you aren't doing right now. The participants then report back to the larger group in a 4-minute report. This allows the participants to see the most important factors affecting the organization.

Once the reports are completed, the information is used to prepare the "prouds" and "sorries" report on the present. Based on the second set of smaller maps, with new people in the leader roles take the information and do the following:

- List what you are doing right now that you are proud of in your relationship to the task of the Future Search Conference.
- List things you are doing right now that you are sorry about.

As a group, select the proudest "prouds" and the sorriest "sorries" and prepare another report 3 minutes in length to be presented to the whole group. This is the last step in looking at the current reality and is a critical time in the process. Bunker and Alban (1997) suggest that by this juncture participants will have a better understanding of the whole system, internal and external, and it becomes clear that to improve the whole the different parts will have to act with the whole in mind. Now, and only now, can the large group begin to think about the future.

Future

Imagining ideal future scenarios in heterogeneous groups is next. Ask the participants individually to put themselves ten years into the future. Ask them to visualize the organization they would really want as if it exists now. Then ask them to list on single sheets of paper the accomplishments that were completed in those ten years that caused the ideal future to happen. Then, on a flip chart, list the major barriers you had to overcome and the opportunities you worked for those accomplishments. Ask each group at this point to choose a creative way to present all of those futures to the larger group, such as in a skit, drama, or TV special. Next, we attempt to discover the common ground across all of these futures.

To focus the group to discover their common ground, simply ask of the desired themes in the ideal scenarios, What Do You Want? Ask them to record these desires. Have the smaller groups report back to the larger groups these themes as well as how they might be achieved. The result is a long list of what is wanted and how it might be achieved. From this collection comes the common future desired by the whole conference. In the large group, prepare a list of themes that make up the common future agenda (what is wanted) and a second list of the ways to work toward it (how it is to be achieved). These are agreed upon by a consensus of the large group. A third list is created of themes that are not agreed upon but are felt to be strong candidates. These lists are then merged into one list. At this time, the conference manager must seek to understand what the group really wants. Also, the point must be made regularly that the participants should move ahead only on what they can agree on and are willing to support. That means that each person must be willing to take action to support the point. All points are accepted and heard, but some may not be reconciled. People can and should work toward their preferred goals, whether or not supported by the whole conference, only not during the conference as democracy dictates. The purpose here is to base the conference on joint action from consensus and then plan common futures.

The next steps are relatively easier. Brainstorm short- and long-term action steps. These include steps you can take right now. Also, list what is needed and the due dates of the series of actions. Then set times for follow-up meetings.

Phases 3 and 4: Follow–up Implementation (3–6 months and 1–3 years)

Conditions for Success Following the Future Search Conference

Organizations that are capable of undergoing significant change must be able to recognize the barriers to change and the ways to encourage support for change. Weisbord and Janoff (1995) suggest that these follow-ups be planned as reunions that include newcomers and newsletters. Follow-ups are a critical component of the process, because the power of the bureaucratic system in the organization has a tendency to slow down or stop the momentous effects of the Future Search.

Barriers That Stimulate Resistance to Change

Change-capable organizations must recognize the barriers to change and the ways to encourage support for change. Weisbord (1987) identified several barriers that stimulate resistance to change:

- Failing to be specific about a change
- Failing to show why a change is necessary
- Failing to allow those affected by the change to be involved in the planning and process
- Using personal appeal to gain acceptance
- Disregarding a work group's habit patterns
- Failing to keep employees informed
- Failing to allay employees worries about failure
- Creating excessive work pressures during change
- Failing to deal with anxiety over job security

Weisbord (1987) provides several ways to encourage support for change. They include involving employees in planning the change, providing accurate and complete information, and giving employees a chance to air their objections. Other ways include always taking group norms, values, beliefs, and habits into account as change moves along, making only essential changes, and learning to use problem-solving techniques.

Future Search Allows the Two Kinds of Change to Emerge

The need for incremental change originates from attempts at cost containment, efficiency improvements, and local-level innovation. Incremental change requires systems and processes that can undergo continuous change. Yet incremental change and the resulting continuous change are punctuated by the need for discontinuous change, which requires a simultaneous shift in strategy, structure, process, people, and learning (Tushman and O'Reilly, 1996). The major drivers for discontinuous change include organizational performance problems, technological advances, competitive shifts in the market, regulatory events, and political events. The Future Search process allows the organization to deal with both kinds of change by allowing the entire system to adapt with speed, flexibility, and radical innovations.

Inflexibility in organizational design leads to rigid assumptions about power and risk avoidance in communication. These are old habits that will not work anymore. Hammer and Champy (1993) suggest that this inflexibility comes from the fragmentation of the workforce through specialization, a rigid hierarchy, and the control of work not being in the hands of the workers. To deal with the inflexibility of these organizations, Kochan and Useem (1992) suggest continuous, systemic organizational change that is integrated and consistent among an organization's major components and applied over the long term to provide a more suitable foundation for cooperation, learning, and innovation. Galbraith and Lawler (1993) state that organizations need to design themselves through innovation and process improvement. They also suggest that successful organizations will be those that can better design their organizations to meet the new realities of the business environment. Kochan and Useem (1992) believe that "learning" and "learning how to learn" are the essential capacities for an organization to better design itself. Gilbert (1996) and Dean (1999a) suggest that organizational design should emerge from individuals operating at different levels within an organization. From these different contexts, a more accurate overall perspective of organizational needs and change opportunities can be gained and therefore subsequent redesign would be more effective. These varied perspectives include:

- Philosophical—the ideals under which the organization operates.
- Cultural—the larger environment in which the organization exists.
- Policy—the vision and missions that define the purpose of the organization.
- Strategic—the plans designed to carry out the mission.
- Tactical—the specific duties that achieve the strategies.
- Logistical—the support system (resources, information, incentives, etc.) that enables workers to carry out duties.

Whatever the suggestions are for design and change from these many vantage points, a central idea will emerge and loom large as a critical need. By ambitiously attempting to create an enterprise that is aligned on all of these variables, Future Search facilitators hope to harness the individual value-added aspects listed above. The organization as a consequence will then perform better and compete more successfully in the global marketplace. Improved performance comes about because the community of humans are learning and adapting to change (De Geus, 1997). Future Search is one practice by which to accomplish this.

Conclusions

This chapter described organizational change practice and the Future Search process, suggesting how they might work together to change organizational systems.

If change professionals can influence the design of the organizational system, they can influence how that system operates, and that operation in turn has a direct influence over individual performers. In this way, organizational change professionals directly influence the performance of the individual.

It has been said many times before that the most important person who controls the safety and success of an ocean liner is not the captain, the engineer, the navigator, or the person at the wheel. The most important person who controls the destiny of the ship is the designer, the person who begins the process in which everyone else plays a subsequent role. In the same way, an organizational change professional must avail herself or himself of all the tools and technologies that are available to bring about the desired and needed results. Collectively, these tools and technologies can help an organization attain the vision of the designer of the organizational change.

Professionals who practice organizational change help companies redesign themselves and address the complexities of work and life in a large organization. These professionals can use the model of the Future Search process to help them examine and understand the variety of issues and opportunities that most organizations are confronted with in the twenty-first century.

Strengths and Weaknesses of Organizational Learning, Performance, and Change

Jerry W. Gilley and Laura L. Bierema

Each of the professional practice domains of HRD has their respective strengths and weaknesses. Strengths provide insight into the advantages of each domain, while weaknesses reveal areas of concern for HRD professionals.

Strengths of Organizational Learning

The practice and philosophy of organizational learning make several contributions to workplace development, including the principle that learning is a fundamental and unique HRD process, a precursor to change, and that it is developmental, potentially transformative, informal, and grounded in social justice.

Learning is fundamental to every aspect of human resource development since many HRD initiatives seek individual, group, or organizational change. Organizational learning, unlike performance or change programs, does not require particular credentials (such as an understanding of a model, or process such as TQM) or a certain hierarchical level to do well. Everyone has the capacity to learn—regardless of title or rank. Yet one might argue that the most effective learning happens among the ranks of employees, but is never captured or shared by management, and is thus of little benefit to the organization as a whole.

LEARNING	PERFORMANCE	CHANGE
	Strengths	
✔ Drives change on all levels (individual, group and organizational).	✔ Provides a framework for continuous improvement.	✔ Offers a key process for organizational survival.
✔ Provides a developmental framework for understanding learners and learning processes.	✔ Incorporates a wide variety of intervention strategies.	✔ Emphasizes organizational renewal capacity.
✔ Holds the potential to foster transformation.	✔ Promotes a results-oriented approach.	✔ Encourages a developmental philosophy.
✔ Happens formally, informally and incidentally.	✔ Encourages a productivity-focused approach.	✔ Improves the organizational and performance management systems.
✔ Commits to issues of social justice.	✔ Embraces an organization centered approach.	✔ Perceived as a trouble shooting process.
✔ Fosters a long-term development strategy—career development.	✔ Embraces systems theory.	✔ Takes both a product and process focus in interventions.
✔ Encourages the integration of the disciplines of the learning organization.	✔ Encourages strategic thinking.	
✔ Promotes learning partnerships.	✔ Promotes the improvement of HRD professionals' credibility.	
✔ Enhances developmental readiness.	✔ Embraces a mission-integrated approach.	
✔ Addresses employee depression.	✔ Promotes linking interventions to the organization's strategic business goals and objectives.	
✔ Encourages personal and professional growth through lifelong learning.	✔ Emphasizes using comprehensive, systematic, and sequential performance improvement models.	
	Weaknesses	
✔ Focuses on the individual (not organization).	✔ Aligns closely with corporate interests.	✔ Tends toward "change for the sake of change."
✔ Views learning as a panacea.	✔ Applies linear, mechanistic measures of success.	✔ Adopts a deficiency attitude toward employees.
✔ Promotes training for training sake philosophy.	✔ Situated in human capital theory.	✔ Fails to develop an organizational commitment to lasting change.
✔ Perceived as non-productivity oriented.	✔ Tends to suffer from analysis paralysis.	✔ Fails to provide organizations with the tools to adjust to ever-changing conditions.
✔ Promotes a "training makes a difference" approach.	✔ Adopts an anti-training stance.	✔ Fails to address the assumptions underlying the need for change.
✔ Promotes a restrictive and specialized approach to employee development.	✔ Fails to embrace humanism.	✔ Fails to identify the common errors of organizational change efforts.
✔ Focuses too much effort on low value-added activities.	✔ Perceived as manipulative.	✔ Fails to address the myths associated with organizational change.
✔ Encourages the belief that "employees should enjoy training."	✔ Perceived as too bottom line focused.	
✔ Encourages a "fix employees' weaknesses" approach.	✔ Perceived as too profit and productivity driven.	
	✔ Encourages an organizational focus instead of a people focus.	

FIGURE 9.1   Strengths and Weaknesses of Organizational Learning, Performance, and Change

Change is a core value of most organizations seeking performance improvement and development. But change transpires only when learning occurs. Some have argued that learning should be the primary goal of organizations and that effective learning processes will improve performance and generate change as a by-product (Owen, 1991; Senge, 1990).

Learning philosophy and theory provide a developmental framework both for understanding the learner and the learning process and for designing educational programs that will be meaningful and will transfer to the targeted context. Learning is developmental, lifelong, free, and often done in spite of management's wishes. Just as learning precedes change, so too learning philosophy and theory create the infrastructure to foster development that is meaningful to the individual and the organization.

Learning has the potential to foster transformation in both thinking and action, and thus is the most powerful process for influencing development, performance, and change in any context. Considering that most organizations are ill-suited or resistant to self-reflection, learning offers the process, and often the space, to engage in reflective practice about thinking and action. Action learning programs provide one such structure and, in a sense, give employees permission to reflect.

Learning is not synonymous with training, particularly since much of the learning that takes place in organizations is informal and incidental (Marsick and Watkins, 1990) and not captured to share lessons with other individuals or groups. A significant amount of learning happens through peers, mentors, and observations and is often not viewed as a key source of development in organizations.

Another unique feature of learning philosophy and practice is its interest in and commitment to social justice. Because learning philosophy considers asymmetrical power relations and how privilege is reproduced through thought and action, it is the primary process available for eroding unfair organizational and societal structures that may function to marginalize women, people of color, and people of lower economic strata.

Several other strengths can be identified for the organizational learning domain.

Strength 1: Fosters a Long-Term Development Strategy—Career Development

Organizational learning professionals have the opportunity to enhance organizational effectiveness through a long-term development strategy known as career development. This is a process designed to improve performance capacity via individual employee growth and development. Career development enables employees to grow and develop beyond the fundamental skills, knowledge, competencies, and aptitudes used in their current job assignments. Organizational learning professionals can provide learning and change activities that improve employees' skills, competencies, knowledge, and aptitudes by viewing enhanced organizational effectiveness from an individual perspective while remaining dedicated to overall organizational enhancement (a systems approach).

However, some learning professionals fail to understand the connection between learning and change and overall organizational development. These terms are often used interchangeably, which leads to increased confusion and misapplication of each process. Career development helps employees analyze their abilities and interests to better match human resource needs for growth and development with the organization's needs. To illustrate, career development can be defined as an organized, planned effort comprising structured activities or processes that result in practical career management actions between employees and the organization (Gilley and Maycunich, 2000b). Thus, it involves learning and change activities such as those that are instrumental in the individual development process. For example, *learning and change* actions help employees obtain basic knowledge, skills, and competencies to perform effectively in their current jobs. *Educational activities* provide a means of career advancement and mobility, and *developmental activities* enable employees to reach their full potential.

Within the system of career development, employees are responsible for career planning, whereas the organization is responsible for career management (Simonsen, 1997). These two separate but related processes combined form organizational career development, a partnership between the organization and its individual employees (Gilley, 1989). Once established and optimized, improved organizational effectiveness results, which is one of the primary strengths of the organizational learning orientation.

Strength 2: Encourages the Integration of the Disciplines of Learning Organizations

One of the principal strengths of the organizational learning domain is a heavy reliance on the fundamental disciplines espoused by Senge (1990). He identifies five disciplines that represent defining characteristics of learning organizations and that become the primary focus of organizational learning professionals. They include the following:

- Personal mastery results from the acquisition of individual expertise and proficiency through education, formal learning activities, and work experience.
- Mental models encompass values, beliefs, attitudes, and assumptions, forming one's fundamental worldview.
- Shared vision, a cornerstone of learning organizations, represents the collective perspectives of employees and evolves from their understanding of the firm's mission and goals.
- Team learning encourages communication and cooperation, leading to synergy and respect among members.
- Systems thinking involves examination of and reflection upon all aspects of organizational life, such as mission and strategy, structure, culture, and leadership.

Strength 3: Promotes Learning Partnerships

Another strength of the organizational learning domain is the establishment of learning partnerships within an organization. Learning partnerships result from the collaborative efforts of managers and employees to maximize learning and its outcomes. Marquardt (1996, 54) maintains that managers are obligated to develop learning partnerships characterized by planning, application, and reflection. Planning involves a mutual effort by learning professionals and employees to determine the gap between the learner's existing knowledge and skills and those demanded by the learning opportunity. Together partners develop learning objectives and an actionable plan to accomplish those objectives, and complete any necessary prerequisite learning.

According to Gilley and Maycunich (2000, 105), "application requires long-term commitment on the part of both parties. A learning professional's primary responsibilities include coaching the learner based on learning needs (job-specific, functional, adaptive), providing the learner with needed opportunities, making certain the learner has access to references and tools, and providing guidance and feedback when needed." Learners are responsible for applying the knowledge and skills gained, utilizing available resources, reflecting on the current task being learned, and asking for assistance and feedback when needed (Marquardt, 1999, 88).

Strength 4: Enhances Developmental Readiness

Another strength of the organizational learning domain is that learning professionals are masters at preparing people for change, which is sometimes known as developmental readiness. This occurs as a result of a concentrated, continuous, nurturing effort on the part of learning professionals, organizational leaders, and managers to: convey the value and benefits of change to employees and the organization; create an environment that encourages risk-taking and allows mistakes; provide employees with the knowledge and skills necessary to facilitate positive change; correlate change with growth and development; and reward personnel for change efforts. In short, learning professionals understand that individual actions (such as change, growth, and development) lead to similar actions at the organizational level.

Strength 5: Addresses Employee Depression

The organizational learning domain can be used to combat employee depression, which is a psychological condition brought about by underutilization, apathy, and alienation of employees who feel they are not perceived to be vital, contributing members of the organization (Ulrich, 1997). Other psychological dimensions of employee depression include feeling overwhelmed, lost, or fatigued as a result of excessive work demands or productivity requirements. In either case, employees feel less energized or unappreciated.

Ulrich (1997) contends that addressing these feelings of inadequacy or excessive work requires organizational learning professionals to strike a balance between the two. Of course, the solution is to adopt an organizational learning philosophy of employee enhancement. With this in place, employees can exert control over their careers, reestablish commitment to the organization, participate in challenging work, engage in collaborative, team-oriented activities, share in a culture that fosters personal improvement, and receive the performance feedback and support necessary to motivate continuous growth and development. All of these strategies, Ulrich (1997) contends, address employee depression. Furthermore, we assert that these actions comprise a central, core component of the organizational learning approach to improved organizational effectiveness.

Strength 6: Encourages Personal and Professional Growth/Lifelong Learning

The organizational learning approach also encourages employees to engage in lifelong learning and acquisition activities for their own personal enjoyment as well as to further the organization. As a result, personal and professional growth and development are enhanced by increased knowledge, skills, competencies, and better attitudes. Educated, well-rounded employees possess insights, qualities, creativity, and unique experiences that enhance their self-concepts and their performance on the job.

Learning professionals help employees recognize performance strengths and deficiencies via utilization of feedback. Analysis of this type is a starting point for performance improvement, growth, and development, as it provides employees with an accurate reflection of their competencies in relationship to other employees and gives them a baseline for improvement. Self-knowledge breeds confidence on and off the job.

Personal and professional growth manifested in improved performance opens the door to career and advancement opportunities. Promotional opportunities yielding additional responsibility, authority, and rewards appeal to motivated employees with an eye toward the future. All of the outcomes are the result of employing an organizational learning orientation.

Weaknesses of Organizational Learning

Although learning is a powerful process, it has limitations: a focus on the individual, treatment as a panacea, lack of infrastructure, and failure to restructure existing power relations in organizations.

Learning-based HRD programs tend to focus on individuals, thus making them less applicable to HRD initiatives that concentrate on the group or organization level. Thus, individualized learning theories are less relevant for tackling organizational issues and may lack strategic focus. Learning is largely humanistic and this philosophy may inadequately address economic or performance concerns in for-profit organizational contexts.

During the 1990s, learning was regularly offered as a panacea for organizational challenges. Unfortunately, learning often gets lip service, but little else. Although Senge's (1990) book *The Fifth Discipline: The Art and Practice of the Learning Organization* has profoundly influenced how learning is viewed and valued in organizations, ironically the model put forth says little about learning other than that it happens and is a positive undertaking.

If organizations are serious about learning, they must understand it and create infrastructure that both supports and captures learning over the long term for individuals, teams, and ultimately the organization. Many organizational structures do not promote learning and some may even prevent it. Learning models must be developed to assist practitioners in designing "learning friendly" environments. Several scholars have provided models for creating learning infrastructure, including Dixon (1994), Marquardt (1996), Senge, (1990), and Watkins and Marsick (1993).

Contemporary learning organization processes offer promise for promoting organization development and change, however, none of the models available offers strategies for restructuring power relations, thus causing them to simply reproduce structures of power that benefit the dominant players, usually white males. A true learning organization not only empowers individuals to develop to their full capacity, it also promotes transformation on individual and collective levels, and reorganizes power relations to promote a higher degree of equitability among all members of the organization.

Several other weaknesses can be identified for the organizational learning domain.

Weakness 1: Promotes a Training for Training's Sake Philosophy

Organizational learning is the domain most closely aligned with the traditional focus of HRD, which is training. As such, some organizational learning professionals believe that there is a "direct cause-and-effect relationship between training and improving performance in the workplace" (Gilley and Maycunich, 1998, 4). Unfortunately, learning that is not reinforced or valued by the organization will be forgotten and never applied. Consequently, training for training's sake in the hope that individual, organizational, and societal development will naturally occur is simply unrealistic. This approach reinforces the activity strategy of HRD, which is the delivery of a plethora of training programs to improve performance and which is so commonly held by learning professionals (Robinson and Robinson, 1989).

Weakness 2: Perceived as Nonproductivity Oriented

Kuchinke (1995, 309) points out that "organizational learning must be managed for performance at the individual, group, process, and organizational levels; learning is omnipresent, yet it must be aimed at improving performance and increasing expertise. A focus on organizational learning is a means to an end; it must be supportive of organizational outcomes and not be an end in itself." Thus, organizational learning should be focused at helping the organization achieve business results rather than learning for learning's sake. Unless this issue is addressed, the organizational learning perspective may be perceived as not sufficiently oriented toward improving productivity.

Weakness 3: Promotes a "Training Makes a Difference" Approach

Many learning professionals are true believers because they honestly think that learning as a separate act can improve organizational effectiveness (Gilley and Maycunich, 1998). When this belief is held, learning professionals accept that there is a direct cause-and-effect relationship between training and organizational effectiveness. However, nothing could be further from the truth since employees are bombarded with problems, circumstances, and decisions that serve as barriers to learning transfer. Consequently, little of the knowledge they gain as a result of participating in learning events can penetrate their mental shields. Without careful and deliberate reinforcement on the job, most of what employees learn is soon forgotten and never applied (Holton and Baldwin, 2001; Broad and Newstrom, 1992).

Weakness 4: Promotes a Restrictive and Specialized Approach to Employee Development

Many learning professionals maintain the belief that training is their responsibility (Brinkerhoff and Gill, 1994). Managers reinforce this belief by washing their hands of the responsibility of developing their employees' skills, thus allowing their training responsibilities to be delegated to professional trainers (Gilley and Boughton, 1996).

Gilley (1998) asks the question, "Who should be responsible for training?" Buckingham and Coffman (1999) answer by suggesting that the person held accountable for employee performance and productivity ultimately should be responsible for training. They also assert that such an individual should also be responsible for conducting employee performance reviews, providing feedback, and confronting poor performance, as well as be held accountable when productivity declines or when the organization fails to meet its goals and objectives. They contend that the person who should be held accountable for each of these activities is the "manager." Gilley et al. (2001) believe that managers lacking the skills essential to adequately train employees should be relieved of their managerial duties and responsibilities.

Although learning-oriented HRD professionals maintain the lion's share of training responsibilities, the unanswered question is, should they? Since such professionals are not truly responsible for employee performance and productivity, should they be responsible for providing employee training? Gilley and Maycunich answer with a resounding "no." They contend that training should be the primary responsibility of managers because they are the only organizational players truly held accountable for employee performance and productivity. They suggest that "organizations need to allow people who have real-world experience—managers—to deliver training. This is the only way learning transfer will be successful. . . . In this way, managers will become the champions of training rather than its gatekeeper" (1998, 5).

Gilley and Maycunich (1998) further assert their position by suggesting that if managers take over the role of trainer, an HRD professional should evolve from trainer into organizational performance consultant and/or change professional. They add that in these roles HRD professionals would support and supplement the efforts of managers as trainers by training them and providing them with well-designed learning interventions to facilitate.

Weakness 5: Focuses Too Much Effort on Activities with Low Value-Added Potential

Some learning professionals spend a great deal of their time managing learning activities. They schedule courses, select training materials, manage enrollments, arrange conferences and workshop logistics, and collect and analyze reaction evaluation forms. Typically, such professionals are simply referred to as trainers. In fact, so much of their time is spent doing low value-added activities that they have little time to spend on transforming the organizational culture to support and reinforce learning. Such professionals operate as though business issues have little effect on learning. They are happy managing learning events and behave as if their efforts are tangential to other operational units within the organization.

Weakness 6: Encourages the Belief That "Employees Should Enjoy Training"

Many learning professionals believe employees should enjoy learning interventions. Such a belief is evident in the use of reaction evaluations (Kirkpatrick, 1995). Many learning professionals rely on these evaluations to determine if employees enjoyed the learning intervention. While learning interventions should be free from negative feedback that reduces employees' self-esteem, learning has a greater purpose if done correctly. They should be designed to improve organizational performance and effectiveness, which sometimes requires difficult and challenging personal reflection that forces employees and management to react and develop new perspectives and possibilities (Gilley and Maycunich, 1998; Brinkerhoff and Gill, 1994).

Weakness 7: Encourages a "Fix Employees' Weaknesses" Approach

One weakness of the organizational learning approach is that many learning professionals believe they are in the business of "fixing" employees. As a result, learning activities are remedial in nature, giving employees the impression that something is wrong with them. Therefore, learning interventions are designed to correct employees' weaknesses rather than building on their strengths and managing their weaknesses (Buckingham and Clifton, 2001; Buckingham and Coffman, 1999; Gilley, 1998; Clifton and Nelson, 1992). Such a philosophy undermines the efforts of HRD professionals and conditions employees to enter learning engagement with a negative and defensive attitude. Consequently, organizational effectiveness does not improve.

Strengths of Organizational Performance

The strengths of the practice and philosophy of performance include a framework for continuous improvement and a broad array of tools for addressing organizational problems. Performance holds continuous improvement as a core value. This is understandable since nearly every consumer seeks products and services that perform well and expects service and product performance to continually improve. Performance practice and philosophy provide the infrastructure and process for improving to meet both internal and external customer expectations.

The performance paradigm casts a wider net when addressing organizational problems than other types of interventions (e.g., training or performance appraisal), and does not view training as the universal remedy for organizational problems. The performance approach also offers several models and tools for addressing organizational issues, which are very useful for both analysis and intervention.

Several other strengths can be identified for the organizational performance domain.

Strength 1: Promotes a Results-Oriented Approach

The organizational performance domain emphasizes achieving organizational results through improving productivity. Bierema (1999) points out that HRD is preparing itself to become an engine that fosters productivity, thus achieving results. While she has serious reservations about this agenda, a results-oriented approach advocated by the organizational performance domain emphasizes organizational effectiveness through a planned holistic approach that utilizes analysis, problemsolving, strategic planning, and systems-based solutions for the purpose of improving organizational performance (Gilley, 1998).

Strength 2: Encourages a Productivity-Focused Approach

Swanson and Arnold (1996, 72) advocate that HRD's principal purpose is to improve performance, which they define as "the organizational system outputs that have value to the customer in the form of productivity attributable to the organization, work process, and/or individual contributor levels." Based on this definition, performance is believed to be a means by which organizations measure their goals. Bierema (1999) adds that performance can be measured through rate of return, cycle time, and quality of output (deliverables). Additionally, it is important to make the distinction between levels of performance. "Performance takes place and can be measured at the organizational, process, and individual levels" (Knowles, Holton, and Swanson, 1998, 117). If performance improvement is the ultimate goal, then learning serves not as an end to human growth, but rather as a means to corporate growth. As performance improvement takes center stage, it is imperative for workplace educators to critically assess their HRD assumptions and practices.

Strength 3: Embraces an Organization-Centered Approach

Swanson and Arnold (1997) believe that the primary difference between adult education and HRD boils down to the locus of control of learning. The adult education locus of control resides with the learner, but in HRD it rests with the organization. Knowles, Holton, and Swanson (1998, 124) support that argument when they state that "because HRD focuses on performance outcomes, the significance of learning control [by the learner] is viewed as secondary by most professionals in HRD." Though some may find this approach unacceptable (Bierema, 2000), "HRD can no longer be merely a training house . . . it must help organizations manage change and improve their competitiveness . . . [and] it must improve employee performance in order for organizations to remain productive and profitable" (Dean, 1993).

Strength 4: Embraces Systems Theory

Typically, organizations are arranged in such a way to describe connections between various departments, both vertically and horizontally.

On the horizontal plane, various departments are indicated, which represents functions such as finance, marketing, manufacturing, customer service, and so forth. On the vertical plane, organizations are divided into subparts of various departments, usually indicating individual titles and specific reporting relationships. . . . Since organizations are organized both vertically and horizontally, they are able to create divisions of labor, departmentalization, spans of control, and levels of authority. Deeply imbedded within these vertical and horizontal intersections is a *culture, work climate,* and *managerial practices* that reflect the interactions between executives, managers, and employees. (Gilley and Maycunich, 1998, 64; emphasis added)

When examined more closely, we discover that all organizations have *policies and procedures* that help structure interactions while providing input into decisionmaking, communications, and accountability. Sometimes what is not observable is the element known as *leadership,* which provides organizational direction, articulation of its *mission,* and the *strategies* necessary in the execution and accomplishment of its mission.

In essence, these components (those italicized) collectively make up an organizational system. Organizational performance professionals focus their attention on the dynamic relationship between these components to enhance productivity and performance. This is achieved by relying on systems theory (e.g., input–process–output flow) and a multiple solutions approach (e.g., performance improvement interventions, motivational systems, environmental factors, selection and retention strategies) as discussed in Chapters 4 and 5. Performance-oriented HRD professionals understand that human beings (employees) are the outward manifestation of a number of internal systems working in harmony. Therefore, they approach organizational problems from both organizational and individual employee perspectives.

Strength 5: Encourages Strategic Thinking

Organizational performance professionals are responsive to their stakeholders needs yet responsible for providing solutions that will address the "real problem" facing an organization. As such, they practice strategic thinking skills in order to avoid reacting before thinking through a request. Rossett (1992) contends that strategic thinking can include a number of things:

1. thinking before reacting
2. listening carefully and selectively to stakeholders' requests

3. filtering suggestions and recommendations through their philosophy of HRD (i.e., performance based)
4. possessing the courage to refuse stakeholders' requests
5. analyzing all requests as requests rather than as commands
6. maintaining consistent guiding principles to ensure credibility.

Failing to do these things can create situations that ultimately produce poor results.

Strength 6: Promotes the Improvement of HRD Professionals' Credibility

Professional credibility can be established in three ways: it can be earned, acquired through shared identities, and acquired through mutually shared goals and objectives (Gilley, 1998, 139). Performance professionals allow all three of these methods to be realized. Holton (1999, 37) points out that some HRD professionals unfortunately have "developmental values and roots,. . . [and therefore] view the notion of performance outcomes and accountability for developmental processes with disdain and avoid it." Knowles, Holton, and Swanson (1998, 115) argue that "it is the increase in performance resulting from HRD that justifies its existence" and is the vehicle by which credibility is established within organizations.

Strength 7: Embraces a Mission-Integrated Approach

Gilbert (1978) first suggested that organizational performance be linked to the organization's mission. Though this appears to be a positive orientation, some believe that such an alignment would minimize the importance of human beings within an organization (Hart, 1992; Howell, Carter, and Schied, 1999). Holton (1999) argues that it is inappropriate to believe that the performance perspective is solely concerned with economic performance. He suggests that performance is defined by and depends on the organizational mission (Bierema, 2000). Since most organizations, however, measure success based on economic returns, it could be inferred that the performance-oriented approach is indeed congruent with all other functions within an organization, which from a credibility and influential perspective is excellent positioning and demonstrates a willingness to be an active partner. As such, performance professionals would be free to influence the organizational culture and make it more responsible to the needs of individual employees and society as a whole, thus aligning it more closely to the organizational learning philosophy.

Strength 8: Promotes Linking Interventions to the Organization's Strategic Business Goal and Objectives

Brinkerhoff and Gill (1994, 77) argue that unless interventions are linked to the strategic business goals of an organization they will not be perceived as valuable. They also maintain that this approach requires a stronger customer focus in the design, development, and implementation of all interventions. Finally, they suggest that measurement is conducted for the purpose of continuous improvement. This inclusive approach allows managers to be equal partners in the performance improvement process.

Strength 9: Emphasizes Using Comprehensive, Systematic, and Sequential Performance Improvement Models

In Chapter 5, we discussed several models that performance professionals can use. These models are comprehensive, systematic, and sequential. As a result, they provide performance professionals with excellent trouble-shooting guides on which to base their practice. They can be used to isolate problems and breakdowns in the human performance system and the organizational system. They can also be used to identify the gap between the current and desired performance states, isolate factors affecting performance, and aid in the selection of interventions used to improve performance and address breakdowns.

Weaknesses of Organizational Performance

The weaknesses of the performance paradigm include a close alignment with corporate interests, a performance-or-else approach, a narrow view of employee development, a tendency toward "analysis paralysis," an antitraining bias, and a language of performativity.

One of the problems of performance-driven HRD is its alignment with corporate interests over human ones. When HRD is exclusively aligned with corporate interests, it functions to preserve asymmetrical power structures that may oppress women, people of color, and lower socioeconomic classes, and may not always have the best interests of individual employees at heart.

The goal of achieving optimal performance is a daunting challenge in the current competitive, global workplace, and there is tremendous pressure to boost performance and keep it high. Generally, business success is measured in tangible, financial terms such as productivity gains, market share, return on investment, intellectual capital, or performance improvement. There is nothing wrong with these measures, but as the performance philosophy of HRD leans more toward these linear, mechanistic "success" measures, the employee may be left at the wayside and the definition of optimal performance may become more rigid and narrow. A focus on organizational performance may decrease the attention and resources directed at individual employee development needs.

Performance models tend to view employee development as an investment in human capital, and as a result demand ever-higher levels of performance from fewer people. Higher performance is an acceptable goal of a business, however, the performance movement risks losing the focus on human development in exchange for productivity gains, and fails to understand that any type of employee development will likely benefit the organization in the long run.

Performance consulting relies heavily on analysis, whether it is focused on the job, the task, or the problem. Sometimes more energy is put into analyzing problems than in solving them. Analysis for performance also tends to be rather deductive, and may miss the big-picture perspective when identifying interventions.

Performance consulting tends to have an antitraining bias, and may not opt for training even when it is the best course of action. Many performance consultants will be quick to tell you, "I am *not* a trainer," which implies a bias against formalized instruction and perhaps even learning. Since training tends to be more individualized, this perspective also suggests greater allegiance to management and organizational interests. HRD practitioners who work as performance consultants risk migrating farther away from their traditional role of helping people grow and improve through their work and may begin to function more as handmaidens of management's strategy. Shortsighted focus on performance may also distract HRD from the ethical and political challenges associated with an ever more complex and globalizing work context. Unfortunately, HRD's drive for performance may minimize the role of human workers and support management's hold on power and control. Finally, the language of performance consulting places it squarely in a behaviorist, capitalist paradigm in its use of terms and practices such as human resources, human performance technology, and performance engineering.

Several other weaknesses can be identified for the organizational performance domain.

Weakness 1: Fails to Embrace Humanistic

Bierema (2000, 290) writes that "HRD professionals wander uncritically through the corporate jungle failing to surface assumptions or assess the systemic impact of their work." Such professionals are perceived as having a results-driven agenda through the advocacy of performance improvement without regard for the human beings who do the work within organizations. Some contend that performance-oriented HRD is not interested in meeting the needs of the individual employee, community, or society as a whole (Hart, 1992; Lyotard, 1984). As such, performance professionals are considered by some critics to be the servants or puppets of organizations because they shun a humanistic philosophy (Cunningham, 1996). Bierema (2000, 286) suggests that "the problem with HRD functioning as a means of productivity, performance, and profit is that is loses sight of what it means to be human. . . . Unfortunately, HRD's drive for performance may relegate human workers to the periphery and enable management's maintenance of power and control." Howell, Carter, and Schied (1999) contend that as long as HRD aligns itself with corporate interests, it will inevitably function to preserve unequal power structures that oppress women, people of color, and lower social classes.

Weakness 2: Perceived as Manipulative

The organizational performance domain is based partially on behavioral theory. As a result of this influence, performance professionals advocate the use of stimulus–response techniques as a means of improving performance. This approach is reflected in the reliance on motivational environmental factors to enhance performance. Critics contend that this perspective is based on a manipulative approach, which is one of the major criticisms of a behavioral-based domain.

Weakness 3: Perceived as Too Focused on the Bottom Line

Korten (1995) asserts that corporate interests regularly prevail over human interests in organizational life. This is because organizational leaders yield to stockholders' interests, customers' demands, and suppliers' requests in their attempt to remain competitive in the global marketplace. Accordingly, performance professionals assemble intellectual capital, align training with mission and strategy, and facilitate optimal performance from employees

(Bierema, 2000). Certainly these are acceptable business goals, but human beings are sometimes neglected as organizations rush to capture additional market share.

Weakness 4: Perceived as Too Profit and Productivity Driven

Some contend that profit- and productivity-driven HRD effectively removes the human from the process. Bierema (2000, 292) points to the "obvious long term costs associated with failure to provide the resources and infrastructure to support whole person learning such as turnover, mistakes and employees leaving to work for the competition and the social costs of such neglect that will impact lives, communities, and the environment." She suggests that performance improvement should be the by-product of individual development instead of the target of HRD professionals. Likewise, Gilley and Maycunich (2000b) argue that profitability and productivity will increase when organizations adopt a developmental orientation, which over time includes improving employee performance.

Weakness 5: Encourages an Organizational Focus
Instead of a People Focus

Knowles, Holton, and Swanson (1998, 122) argue that "when an individual's needs are consistent with the organization's, there is no tension. When the individual's needs are not congruent with the organization's performance requirements, and the organization is providing the required learning experience, a tension exists and inevitably results in some degree of organizational control. For this reason, learning professionals in HRD must balance practices that lead to the most effective adult learning with those that will lead to performance outcomes." Quite simply, organizations control learning as a means to achieve their self-governing needs. Therefore, HRD professionals need to help organizations understand that without qualified and competent employees, their needs will not be met. In fact, short-term performance improvement can be more destructive than failing to achieve the productivity goals that are so critical to organizational success. This is because such achievements can create a work environment full of resentment, fear, and negativity (Gilley et al., 2001), which is counterproductive over time.

Bierema (2000) concedes that corporations cannot exist without profits, but insists that the performance improvement orientation fails to balance human and organizational needs, and has caused HRD to align with organizational interests fully expecting employees to follow suit. Jacobs (1987) reminds us that this does not have to be the case, because human performance is equal to organizational performance. Thus, the needs of employees should be congruent with those of an organization and vice versa.

Strengths of Organizational Change

Organizational change is practically synonymous with survival and is a powerful coping mechanism in an unstable world. Change helps us to function in the permanent state of anticipation of and adjustment to shifts in social, political, and environmental structures. Progress is difficult to make when change does not accompany it, and change helps both individual and collective entities pursue and achieve their visions. Change models are powerful because they adopt a systems perspective and consultants strive to partner with the organization to address challenges and issues.

Several other strengths can be identified for the organizational change domain.

Strength 1: Emphasizes Organizational Renewal Capacity

Another strength of the organizational learning perspective is the focus on continuous growth and development of individual employees. Gilley and Maycunich contend that continuous growth and development is a

> process of never-ending expansion, taking into account new and different things, the outcomes of which are improved renewal and performance capacity. As an individual continues to grow and develop, he or she constantly renews, improving their reservoir of performance capabilities, which can be drawn upon when needed. On a macro level, the final outcome is enhanced organizational renewal and performance capacity. . . . As each individual employee improves his or her personal renewal and performance capacity, the organization's overall aggregate renewal and performance capacity also increases. (Gilley and Maycunich, 2000b, 25)

Over time, organizations enjoy enhanced effectiveness and the capacity to constantly grow and develop, thus avoiding the plateau periods of maturity as well as the slippery slopes of decline.

Strength 2: Encourages a Developmental Philosophy

Another strength of the organizational change domain is the focus on developmental activities used to bring about *change* within an individual. Change occurs as a result of gaining new insight, awareness, and understanding of oneself brought about by critical reflection (Marquardt, 1999; Preskill, 1996; Brookfield, 1987). The outcome of change, which is often referred to as *new meaning,* can be defined as reconfiguration and understanding of oneself (Gilley and Maycunich, 2000b). Whether change is slight or significant, an individual garners a new self-image that filters current realities through an understanding of one's present state. Quite simply, change that brings about new meaning alters an individual to the point where he or she can never return to his or her original state. Consequently, once new meaning has occurred, individuals desire to change the way they interact on a daily basis, which propels individual employees to a higher plane. Employees who are continually evolving fuel organizational evolution.

Strength 3: Improves the Organizational and Performance Management Systems

When change professionals are working to improve organizational effectiveness they do so through two types of consulting activities: change management and performance management. When working to improve the organizational system, the most appropriate type of consulting activity is change management, which is designed to reshape, redesign, and re-engineer the organization. This consulting activity reviews the relationship among leadership, organizational culture, mission and strategy, structure, policies and procedures, management practices, and work climate to see how efficiently and effectively they are working together. Change management consulting examines the impact and effects of the organizational system on the performance management system.

Performance management consulting activities involve the examination of the overall performance capacity of the organization. Performance consulting studies the interplay among components of a performance management system (e.g., performance appraisal, compensation and reward system, learning system, work design, coaching, and career planning) in an effort to determine how employee performance can be improved. This differs from change management consulting in that performance management consulting is designed to improve organizational effectiveness by improving the performance management system and the performance behaviors of each and every employee, whereas change management consulting looks at how the overall organizational system affects performance.

Strength 4: Perceived as a Trouble-shooting Process

One of the best ways of applying the organizational change approach is to think of it as a trouble-shooting process used to identify areas of inquiry or concern surrounding a problem or difficult issue. To isolate problems or breakdowns, electronic technicians use electronic diagrams (schematics), automobile mechanics rely on diagnostic tools, and building contractors refer to blueprints. Similarly, change professionals employ the organizational change frameworks such as Future Search to isolate problems or identify areas which require examination in order to craft a solution for which an intervention can be constructed.

These organizational change frameworks are useful during organizational, managerial, performance, and needs analysis activities as a way of identifying gaps between current and desired expectations. Change professionals use such frameworks to conduct brainstorming activities designed to identify factors that contribute to performance problems or organizational breakdowns. Additionally, these frameworks can be used to assign areas of inquiry during the problem identification phase of a change project. When used to isolate potential problems, one must define relationships between and among various components of the organizational or performance management systems, or identify intervention possibilities, because the potential applications are endless.

Strength 5: Organizational Change Engagements Are Both a Product and a Process

Organizational change engagements are forward-thinking processes, which helps organizational leaders shape the future via intelligent, informed, and innovative actions. They give purpose and direction to an organization by allowing it to ascertain, in advance, what it wishes to accomplish and the means by which to achieve its ends. By providing focus and unity within an organization, it is also the best means to handle external pressures and address customer service activities.

Change engagements allow everyone in the organization the opportunity to participate in decisionmaking, and thus make a personal impact on the organization's future (Hupp, 1998). Consequently, they can be viewed as a way of improving and enhancing the self-esteem of employees. Make no mistake, organizational change engagements are designed to recreate and reinvent organizations by helping them establish a new vision and purpose. Nevertheless, they can greatly improve organizational effectiveness by charting a new course for the organization.

When change professionals participate in organizational change engagements, they will produce an end product—usually a written document that enables all decisionmakers, stakeholders, and influencers to comprehend, analyze, and critique the mission, goals, objectives, and strategies. Conversely, change professionals will use this document to help the organization achieve its desired business results. Consequently, change engagements are both a process and a product (i.e., written plan) interrelated in such complex and overlapping ways that it is almost impossible to analyze one without considering the other (Weisbord, 1992).

Weaknesses of Organizational Change

Organizational change can be problematic when it is not strategic and may simply fall into the old cliché of "change for the sake of change." Organizational change can also be harmful when it is aimed at individuals who must "change" because they are deficient in some way. The notion that people are inadequate and at the root cause of organizational problems raises ethical questions and needs to be challenged. Since structural issues create the bulk of organizational problems, it is unfair to assume that meaningful change is always the responsibility of the individual, or that poor performance is the fault of employees. Some organizational change initiatives have also been found to reinforce the prevalence of organizations that are dominated by white males and to send subtle messages that the perspectives and values of women and people of color are not valued.

Several other weaknesses can be identified for the organizational change domain.

Weakness 1: Fails to Develop an Organizational Commitment to Lasting Change

One of the weaknesses of organizational change is that many organizations will only go through the motions necessary to bring about change even though they desire lasting, meaningful change. Quite simply, many organizational leaders hope that the catalyst for change disappears rather than initiates actions that are required to help their organizations avoid decline.

Much has been written about the importance of change and its relationship to organizational effectiveness. The fact is that occasionally change simply does not work. For example, unfocused, unplanned, superficial change serves as a cotton-candy approach to addressing real operational difficulties (Gilley and Maycunich , 2000b). Although many organizations recognize the need for change, few are able to sustain successful change efforts. According to Ulrich (1997, 157), there are ten reasons why superficial efforts to change often fail to achieve real change: (1) not tied to strategy; (2) seen as a fad or quick fix; (3) short-term perspective; (4) political realities undermine change; (5) grandiose expectations versus simple success; (6) inflexible change design; (7) lack of leadership about change; (8) lack of measurable, tangible results; (9) afraid of the unknown; and (10) unable to mobilize commitment to sustain change. Each of these represents a weakness for organizational change and becomes a challenge for organizational change professionals.

Weakness 2: Fails to Provide Organizations with the Tools to Adjust to Ever-Changing Conditions

Patterson (1997) suggests that organizational change efforts fail to achieve desired business results because of an organization's inability to adjust to ever-changing conditions. He further contends that such organizations are unable to adapt to change because they maintain faulty assumptions related to change activities. For example, he suggests that organizational leaders often believe that their firms are rationally functioning systems that adjust strategically to changing conditions. Patterson argues that this is simply not the case. He asserts that organizations operate in their own best interests, often sacrificing long-term, systematic change (which can ultimately improve organizational effectiveness, competitiveness, and profitability) in favor of immediate or short-term results.

Weakness 3: Fails to Address the Assumptions Underlying the Need for Change

Another weakness of the organizational change approach is the failure to address the assumptions underlying the need for change. According to Conner (1992, 7), organizations have an immeasurable impact on how employees view themselves in relation to change. From their experiences, most employees accept several unconscious assumptions about organizational change. Although firmly held, these assumptions are based mostly on fears and prejudice rather than fact.

Patterson (1997) suggests that one such faulty assumption lies with leadership's belief that organizational change can occur without creating conflict in the system. He asserts that such an unrealistic belief increases expectations among employees that cannot be achieved. Ultimately, such "assumptions are demotivating, creating long-term negative effects on employee morale and performance. Consequently, employees are not motivated to grow and develop or actively pursue career opportunities. When these conditions exist, the type of organizational change required to remain competitive is in jeopardy" (Gilley and Maycunich, 2000b, 28).

Weakness 4: Fails to Identify the Common Errors of Organizational Change Efforts

Another weakness that can negatively affect the success of organizational change professionals is the failure to address common errors associated with organizational change efforts. Kotter (1996, 16) identifies eight such errors to organizational change efforts that result in predictable consequences: (1) allowing too much complacency; (2) failing to create a sufficiently powerful guiding coalition; (3) underestimating the power of vision; (4) undercommunicating the vision; (5) permitting obstacles to block the new vision; (6) failing to create short-term wins; (7) declaring victory too soon; and (8) neglecting to anchor changes firmly in the corporate culture. Failing to address these common errors can lead to several negative, often costly consequences. They include:

- new strategies aren't implemented well,
- acquisitions don't achieve expected synergies,
- reengineering takes too long and costs too much,
- downsizing doesn't get costs under control, and
- quality programs don't deliver hoped-for results.

Weakness 5: Fails to Address the Myths Associated with Organizational Change

The myths held by organizational leaders and change professionals are another weakness associated with organizational change. When these myths are not appropriately addressed, they become barriers to the successful implementation of change within organizations.

Some common myths associated with organizational change include believing that it is impossible to understand why people accept or resist change, and that bureaucracies cannot really be changed (Block, 1999). Others include that change will always be mismanaged, that organizational efficiency and effectiveness inevitably decrease when changes are attempted, that management is inherently insensitive to problems caused during the implementation of change, and that what leaders say about change should never be confused with reality (Gilley and Maycunich, 1998). "Some believe that those who help implement changes are heroes, while those who resist are villains. Finally, there are those misguided individuals who believe that employees are prone to resist any change that is good for the business" (Gilley and Maycunich, 2000, 288–289).

Patterson (1997, 7) believes that ten myths permeate organizational change activities as compared to the realities that exist. The following compares these myths and realities:

MYTH	REALITY
People act first in the best interests of the organization.	People act in their own best interest.
People want to understand the "what" and the "why" of organizational change.	People want to know how change will affect them.
People engage in change because of the merits of change.	People engage in change to avoid or minimize personal pain.
People embrace change when they trust their leaders to do the right thing.	People view change with a great deal of skepticism and cynicism, even though they outwardly appear supportive.
People opt to be architects of the change affecting them.	People opt to be victims rather than architects of change.
Organizations are rationally functioning systems.	Most organizations operate irrationally.
Organizations are wired to assimilating systemic change.	Most organizations opt to protect the status quo.

MYTH	REALITY
Organizations operate from a value-driven orientation.	Most organization react to outside pressure rather than to their guiding principles and values when initiating change.
Organizations can effect long-term systemic change with short-term leadership.	Most organizations implement long-term change with short-term leadership.
Organizations can achieve systemic change without creating conflict within the system.	Most organizations are unrealistic about the amount of conflict that occurs as a result of change and naively expect change to be accepted wholeheartedly by employees.

Change professionals are better prepared to help their organization and its employees adapt to change when they proactively address these myths. Conversely, these myths can lead to disaster if not appropriately understood and handled.

Conclusions

Each of the professional practice domains has their respective strengths and weaknesses. It is important that HRD professionals identify them and react accordingly.

Epilogue

This book has introduced the philosophical frameworks and practical applications of the learning, performance, and change domains of human resource development. As the field of HRD emerges, it is imperative that HRD professionals question assumptions regarding their role, responsibility, and approach to HRD practice while also understanding the roots of HRD thought and action. Reflecting on philosophy and values gives the practitioner insight into how one's beliefs affect choices, commitments, and actions. To that end, this book seeks to provide a better understanding of the assumptions that influence contemporary HRD practice. We believe that by naming and understanding the various philosophical perspectives influencing HRD that future choices, commitments, and actions made by HRD practitioners will be more conscientious and integrative.

It would be nice, and certainly easier, for HRD professionals if we were to provide a prescription for integrating the perspectives of learning, performance, and change into an enduring, infallible mode. Unfortunately, or perhaps fortunately, no such magic potion exists. Just as the field of HRD is diverse, so too are its applications, values, and practices. Instead what we recommend is that HRD professionals engage in the hard work of assessing their own values and philosophical stances. We also believe that effective, conscientious professionals will not rigidly align himself or herself with a particular philosophical orientation, but rather will incorporate elements of the three domains into practice. Finally, we believe that careful reflection on and clarity of values makes difficult intervention decisions easier. Paralleling the Chinese proverb, "A wise man makes his own decisions, and an ignorant man follows the pubic opinion," we also advocate that HRD professionals not limit themselves to the dominant voices of theory and practice, but strike out to find a philosophical practice that meets their individual values.

Indeed, HRD professionals make decisions every day about issues that affect individuals, teams, organizations, and even society. Sometimes these decisions are made without reflection on the values underlying beliefs or with foresight about the consequences of organizational intervention. To quote Isaac Asimov: "No sensible decision can be made any longer without taking into account not only the world as it is, but the world as it will be." This pragmatic stance describes the philosophical orientation that will lead the profession through the twenty-first century and beyond.

References

Ainsworth, D. (1979). Performance technology: A view from the Fo'c'sle. *NSPI Journal,* 18(4), 3–7.

Alkon, D. L. (1992). *Memory's voice: Deciphering the mind–brain code.* New York: Harper-Collins.

Apps, J. W. (1973). *Toward a working philosophy of adult education.* Syracuse, N.Y.: Syracuse University Publications in Continuing Education.

Argyris, C., and Schon, D. A. (1980). *Organizational learning: A theory of action perspective.* Reading, Mass.: Addison-Wesley.

Argyris, C., and Schon, D. (1996). *Organizational learning II: A theory of action perspective.* Reading, Mass.: Addison-Wesley.

Aronson, E. (1995). *The social animal* (7th ed.). New York: Freeman.

Axelrod, D. (1992). Getting everyone involved: How one organization involved its employees, supervisors and managers in redesigning the organization. *Journal of Applied Behavioral Science,* 28(4), 499–509.

Beckhard, R. (1969). *Organization development: Strategies and models.* Cambridge, Mass.: MIT Press.

Beckhard, R., and Harris, R. (1987). *Organizational transitions: Managing complex change* (2nd ed.). Reading, Mass.: Addison-Wesley.

Beder, H. (1989). Purposes and philosophies of adult education. In S. B. Merriam and P. M. Cunningham, eds., *Handbook of adult and continuing education,* pp. 37–50. San Francisco: Jossey-Bass.

Berke, G. B. (1990). *How to conduct a performance appraisal.* Alexandria, Va.: ASTD Press.

Bierema, L. L. (1996). Development of the individual leads to more productive workplaces. In R. W. Rowden, ed., *Workplace Learning: Debating the five critical questions of theory and practice.* New Directions for Adult and Continuing Education, No. 72, pp. 21–30. San Francisco: Jossey-Bass.

Bierema, L. L. (2000). Human resource development for humans: Moving beyond performance paradigms on workplace development. In S. B. Merriam, ed., *2000 handbook of adult and continuing education*. San Francisco: Jossey-Bass.

Bierema, L. L., and Berdish, D. M. (1996). Creating a learning organization: A case study of outcomes and lessons learned. In E. F. Holton, III, ed., *Proceedings of the Academy of Human Resources Development 1996 Conference*, pp. 1–17.

Bierema, L. L., and Cseh, M. (2000). Evaluating HRD research using a feminist research framework. In P. Kuchinke, ed., *Proceedings of the Academy of Human Resources Development Conference*.

Block, P. (1999). *Flawless consulting: A guide to getting your expertise used* (2nd ed.). San Diego: Pfeiffer.

Bloom, A. (1987). *The closing of the American mind*. New York: Simon and Schuster.

Bowditch, J. L., and Buono, A. F. (1997). *A primer on organizational behavior*. New York: John Wiley & Sons.

Brethower, D. M. (1999). General systems theory and behavioral psychology. In H. D. Stolovitch and E. J. Keeps, eds., *Handbook of human performance technology: Improving individual and organizational performance worldwide*, pp. 67–81. San Francisco: Jossey-Bass.

Brinkerhoff, R. O. (1987). *Achieving results from training*. San Francisco: Jossey-Bass.

_____. (1998). Measurement phase: Evaluating effectiveness of performance improvement projects. In D. G. Robinson and J. C. Robinson, eds., *Moving from training to performance: A practical guide*, pp. 147–174. San Francisco: Berrett-Koehler.

Brinkerhoff, R. O., and Gill, S. J. (1994). *The learning alliance*. San Francisco: Jossey-Bass.

Broad, M., and Newstrom, J. (1992). *Transfer of training. Action-packed strategies to ensure high payoff from training investment*. Reading, Mass.: Addison-Wesley.

Brookfield, S. D. (1985). Analyzing a critical paradigm of self-directed learning: A response. *Adult Education Quarterly*, 36(1), 60–64.

_____. (1987). *Developing critical thinkers: Challenging adults to explore ways of thinking and acting*. San Francisco: Jossey-Bass.

_____. (1992). Uncovering assumptions: The key to reflective practice. *Adult Learning*, 16(1), 13–18.

Buckingham, M., and Clifton, D. O. (2001). *Now, discover your strengths*. New York: The Free Press.

Buckingham, M., and Coffman, C. (1999). *First, break all the rules: What the world's greatest managers do differently*. New York: Simon and Schuster.

Bunker, B. B., and Alban, B. T., eds. (1992). Large group interventions [special issue]. *Journal of Applied Behavioral Science*, 28(4).

Bunker, B. B., and Alban, B. T. (1997). *Large group interventions: Engaging the whole system for rapid change*. San Francisco: Jossey-Bass.

Burke, W. W. (1992). *Organizational development: A process of learning and changing*. Reading, Mass.: Addison-Wesley.

Caffarella, R., and Merriam, S. B. (2000). Linking the individual learner to the context of adult learning. In A. L. Wilson and E. R. Hayes, eds., *Handbook of adult and continuing education.* San Francisco: Jossey-Bass.

Caffarella, R. S. (1994). *Planning programs for adult learners: A practical guide for educators, trainers and staff developers.* San Francisco: Jossey-Bass.

Carnevale, A. (1984). *Jobs for the nation: Challenges for a society based on work.* Alexandria, Va.: American Society for Training and Development.

Cascio, W. F. (1995). *Managing human resources: Productivity, quality of work life, profits.* New York: McGraw-Hill.

Cervero, R. M., and Wilson, A. L.(1994). *Planning responsibly for adult education: A guide to negotiating power and interests.* San Francisco: Jossey-Bass.

Checkland, P. B. (1972). Toward a system-based methodology for real-world problem solving. *Journal of Systems Engineering,* 3(2), 87–116.

Clark, M. C. (1993). Transformational learning. In S. B. Merriam, ed., *An update on adult learning theory.* New Directions for Adult and Continuing Education, No. 57. San Francisco: Jossey-Bass.

Clark, M. C., and Caffarella, R. S. (1999). Theorizing adult development. In M. C. Clarke and R. S. Caffarella, eds., *An update on adult development theory: New ways of thinking about the life course.* New Directions for Adult and Continuing Development, No. 84, pp. 3–8. San Francisco: Jossey-Bass.

Clark, R. E. (1999). The cognitive sciences and human performance technology. In H. D. Stolovitch and E. J. Keeps, eds., *Handbook of human performance technology: Improving individual and organizational performance worldwide,* pp. 82–95. San Francisco: Jossey-Bass.

Clifton, D. O., and Nelson, P. (1992). *Soar with your strengths.* New York: Delacorte.

Conner, D. (1992). *Managing at the speed of change.* New York: Villard Books.

Cross, K. P. (1981). *Adults as learners.* San Francisco: Jossey-Bass.

Cunningham, P. M. (1982). *Contradictions in the Practice of Non Traditional Continuing Education.* In. S.B. Merriam, ed., *Linking philosophy and practice. New Directions for Continuing Education,* No. 15, pp. 73–86. San Francisco: Jossey-Bass.

Cunningham, P. M. (1996). Race, gender, class, and practice of adult education in the United States. In P. Wangoola and F. Youngman, eds., *Toward a transformative political economy of adult education: Theoretical and practical challenges.* DeKalb: LEPS Press, Northern Illinois University.

Dannemiller, K., and Jacobs R. W. (1992). Changing the way organizations change. A revolution in common sense. *Journal of Applied Behavioral Science,* 28, 480–498.

Darkenwald, G. G., and Merriam, S. B. (1982). *Adult education: Foundations of practice.* New York: HarperCollins.

Dean, P. J. (1983). Guidelines for the implementation of change by a change team. Unpublished manuscript, University of Iowa, Iowa City, Iowa.

_____. (1993). *Re-engineering the business enterprise by organizational redesign.* Unpublished manuscript, Pennsylvania State University, Great Valley, Penn.

_____. (1995). Examining the practice of human performance technology. *Performance Improvement Quarterly, 8*(2), 68–94.

_____. (1999a). Designing better organizations with human performance technology and organization development. In H. D. Stolovitch and E. J. Keeps, eds., *Handbook of human performance technology: Improving individual and organizational performance worldwide*, pp. 321–334. San Francisco: Jossey-Bass.

_____. (1999b). *Performance engineering at work.* Washington, D.C.: International Board of Standards for Training, Performance, and Instruction, IBSTPI Publications, and International Society for Performance Improvement Publications.

Dean, P. J., and Ripley, D. E. (1997). *Performance improvement pathfinders: Models for organizational learning systems.* Washington, D.C.: International Society for Performance Improvement Publications.

Dean, P. J., and Ripley, D. E., eds. (1998a). *Performance improvement interventions: Methods for organizational learning. Instructional design and training. Volume Two.* Washington, D.C.: International Society for Performance Improvement Publications.

_____. (1998b). *Performance improvement interventions: Methods for organizational learning. Performance technologies in the workplace. Volume Three.* Washington, D.C.: International Society for Performance Improvement Publications.

_____. (1998c). *Performance improvement interventions: Methods for organizational learning. Culture and systems change. Volume Four.* Washington, D.C.: International Society for Performance Improvement Publications.

Dean, P. J., Blevins, S., and Snodgrass, P. J. (1997). Performance analysis: An HRD tool that drives change in organizations. In J. J. Phillips and E. F. Holton, III, eds., *Action: Leading organizational change*, pp. 199–216. Alexandria, Va.: American Society for Training and Development Press.

Dean, P. J., Dean, M. R., and Guman, E. (1992). Identifying a range of performance improvement solutions—High yield training to systems redesign. *Performance Improvement Quarterly, 5*(4).

De Geus, A. (1997). *The living company: Habits for survival in a turbulent business environment.* Boston: Harvard Business School Press.

Deterline, W. A., and Rosenberg, M. J., eds. (1992). *Workplace productivity: Performance technology success stories.* Washington, D.C.: International Society for Performance Improvement Publications.

Dewey, J. (1916). *Democracy and education.* New York: Macmillan.

Dixon, N. (1994). *The organizational learning cycle: How we can learn collectively.* New York: McGraw-Hill.

Dormant, D. (1992). Implementing human performance technology in organizations. In H. D. Stolovitch and E. J. Keeps, eds., *Handbook of human performance technology: A comprehensive guide for analyzing and solving performance problems in organizations*, pp. 167–187. San Francisco: Jossey-Bass.

Drucker, P. F. (1993). *The ecological vision: Reflections on the American condition.* New Brunswick, N.J.: Transaction Publishers.

Elias, J. L. (1982). The theory–practice split. In. S. B. Merriam, ed., *Linking philosophy and practice: New directions for continuing education, No. 15,* pp. 3–11. San Francisco: Jossey-Bass.

Elias, J. L., and Merriam, S. B. (1995). *Philosophical foundations of adult education* (2nd ed.). Malabar, Fla.: Krieger Publishing Company.

Elliott, P. (1998). Assessment phase: Building models and defining gaps. In D. G.. Robinson and J. C. Robinson, eds., *Moving from training to performance: A practical guide,* pp. 63–77. San Francisco: Berrett-Koehler.

Emery, F. E. (1995). Participative design: Effective, flexible and successful, now! *Journal for Quality and Participation,* 18(1), 6–9.

Emery, F. E., and Trist, E. L. (1960). Socio-technical systems. In C. W. Churchman et al., eds., *Management sciences, models and techniques.* London: Pergamon.

Emery, M., and Purser, R. E. (1996). *The search conference: Theory and practice.* San Francisco: Jossey-Bass.

Feldman, D. C. (1967). A contingency theory of socialization. *Administrative Science Quarterly,* 21(9) 434–435.

Flannery, T. P., Hofrichter, D. A., and Platten, P. E. (1996). *People performance and pay: Dynamic compensation for changing organizations.* New York: The Free Press.

Foshay, W., Silber, W. K., and Westgaard, O. (1986). *Instructional design competencies. The standards.* Iowa City, Iowa: International Board of Standards for Training, Performance, and Instruction.

Freire, P. (1971, 1995). Pedagogy of the oppressed. In S. B. Merriam, ed., *Selected writings on philosophy and adult education* (2nd ed.), pp. 137–147. Malabar, Fla.: Krieger Publishing Company.

French, W. L., and Bell, C. H., Jr. (1995). *Organizational development: Behavioral science interventions for organizational improvement.* Englewood Cliffs, N.J.: Prentice-Hall.

Fritz, R. (1989). *The path of least resistance.* New York: Fawcett Columbine.

Fuller, J., and Farrington, J. (1999). *From training to performance improvement: Navigating the transition.* San Francisco: Jossey-Bass.

Galbraith, J. R., and Lawler, E. D. (1993). *Organizing for the future.* San Francisco: Jossey-Bass.

Garvin, D. A. (1993). Building a learning organization. *Harvard Business Review,* July-August, 78–91.

Geis, G. L. (1986). Human performance technology: An overview. In M. E. Smith, ed., *Introduction to performance technology,* Vol. 1. Washington, D.C.: National Society for Performance and Instruction.

Gibson, J. L., Ivancevich, J. M., and Donnelly, J.H. (1997). *Organizations: Behavior, structure, process* (9th ed.). New York: McGraw-Hill.

Gilbert, T. F. (1978). *Human competence: Engineering worthy performance.* New York: Mc-Graw-Hill.

_____. (1982a). A question of performance. Part I. The PROBE model. *Training and Development Journal,* 36(9), 20–30.

_____. (1982b). A question of performance. Part II. Applying the PROBE-model. *Training and Development Journal,* 36(10), 85–89.

_____. (1996). *Human competence: Engineering worthy performance* (tribute ed.). Washington, D.C.: International Society for Performance Improvement Publications.

Gilley, J. W. (1998). *Improving HRD practice.* Malabar, Fla.: Krieger Publishing Company.

Gilley, J. W., and Boughton, N. W. (1996). *Stop managing, start coaching: How performances coaching can enhance commitment and improve productivity.* New York: McGraw-Hill.

Gilley, J. W., and Coffern, A. J. (1994). *Internal consulting for HRD professionals: Tools, techniques, and strategies for improving organizational performance.* New York: McGraw-Hill.

Gilley, J. W., and Eggland, S. A. (1989). *Principles of human resource development.* Cambridge, Mass.: Perseus Publishing.

_____. (1992). *Marketing HRD programs within organizations: Improving the visibility, credibility, and image of programs.* San Francisco: Jossey-Bass.

Gilley, J. W., and Maycunich, A. (1998). *Strategically integrated HRD: Partnering to maximize organizational performance.* Cambridge, Mass.: Perseus Publishing.

_____. (2000a). *Organizational learning, performance, and change: An introduction to strategic HRD.* Cambridge, Mass.: Perseus Publishing.

_____. (2000b). *Beyond the learning organization: Creating a culture of continuous growth and development through state-of-the-art human resource practices.* Cambridge, Mass.: Perseus Publishing.

Gilley, J. W., Boughton, N. W., and Maycunich, A. (1999). *The performance challenge: Developing management systems to make employees your greatest asset.* Cambridge, Mass.: Perseus Publishing.

Gilley, J. W., Quatro, S., Hoekstra, E., Wittle, D. D., and Maycunich, A. (2001). *The manager as change agent: A practical guide for high performance individuals and organizations.* Cambridge, Mass.: Perseus Publishing.

Goleman, D. (1995). *Emotional intelligence: Why it can matter more than IQ.* New York: Bantam Books.

Guba, E. G., and Lincoln, Y. S. (1988). *Effective evaluation: Improving the usefulness of evaluation results through responsive and naturalistic approaches.* San Francisco: Jossey-Bass.

Guns, B. (2001). Officer's role: Challenges and competencies. Unpublished article by Bob Guns, partner of Probe Consulting in Summit, N.J., and an associate at Pricewaterhouse-Coopers LLP in New York City, lays out some basic challenges that face today's CKOs.

Hale, J. (1998). *The performance consultant's fieldbook: Tools and techniques for improving organizations and people.* San Francisco: Jossey-Bass and Pfeiffer.

Hammer, M., and Champy, J. (1993). *Reengineering the corporation: A Manifesto for business revolution.* New York: Harper Business.

Harless, J. H. (1970, 1974). *An ounce of analysis is worth a pound of objectives.* Newman, Ga.: Harless Performance Guild.

_____. (1986). Guiding performance with job aids. In M. E. Smith, ed., *Introduction to performance technology*, pp. 106–124. Washington, D.C.: National Society for Performance and Instruction.

Hart, M. (1992). *Working and educating for life.* New York: Routledge.

Heron, J. (1989). *The facilitator's handbook.* London: Kogan Page.

Hirsch, E. (1988). *Cultural literacy: What every American needs to know.* New York: Vintage Books.

Holton, E. F. (1999). Performance domain and their boundaries. In R. J. Torraco, ed., *Performance improvement theory and practice*, pp. 26–46. San Francisco: Berrett-Koehler.

_____. (2000). On the nature of performance and learning in human resource development. In W. E. A. Ruona and F. Roth, eds., *Philosophical foundations of human resource development practice. Advances in developing human resources, No. 7,* pp.60–64. San Francisco: Berrett-Koehler.

Holton, E. F., and Baldwin, T. T. (2001). Making transfer happen: An action perspective on learning transfer systems. In E. F. Holton, III, T. T. Baldwin, and S. S Naquin, eds., *Managing and changing learning transfer systems, No. 8,* pp. 1–6. San Francisco: Berrett-Koehler.

Houle, C. (1972). *The design of education.* San Francisco: Jossey-Bass.

_____. (1995). The design of education. In S. B. Merriam, ed., *Selected writings on philosophy and adult education* (2nd ed.), pp. 47–56. Malabar, Fla.: Krieger Publishing Company.

Howell, S. L., Carter, V. K., and Schied, F. M. (1999). Irreconcilable differences: Critical feminism, learning at work, and HRD. Paper presented at the Adult Education Research Conference, Dekalb, Ill., pp. 365–372.

Hunter, D., Bailey, A., and Taylor, B. (1994). *The art of facilitation.* Auckland: Tandem Press.

Hupp, T. R. (1998). Personal correspondence. President, Organizations By Design, Warrenville, Ill.

Jacobs, R. W. (1987). *Human performance technology: A systems-based field for the training and development profession.* Columbus, Ohio: ERIC Clearinghouse on Adult, Career, and Vocational Education, National Center for Research in Vocational Education, Ohio State University.

Jarvis, P. (1992). *Paradoxes of learning: On becoming an individual in society.* San Francisco: Jossey-Bass.

Jick, T. (1993). *Managing change.* Chicago: Richard Irwin Inc.

Kasworm, C. (1983). An examination of self-directed learning contracts as an instructional strategy. *Innovative Higher Education,* 8(1), 45–54.

Katz, D., and Kahn, R. (1978). *The social psychology of organizations* (2nd ed.). New York: John Wiley & Sons.

Kearsley, G. (1986). Analyzing the costs and benefits of training. *Performance and Instruction*, 25(1), 30–32.

Keller, J. M. (1999). *Motivational systems*. In H. D. Stolovitch and E. J. Keeps, eds., *Handbook of human performance technology: Improving individual and organizational performance worldwide*, pp. 373–394. San Francisco: Jossey-Bass.

Kirkpatrick, D. (1995). *Evaluating training programs*. San Francisco: Berrett-Koehler.

Kissler, G. D. (1991). *The change riders: Managing the power of change*. Cambridge, Mass.: Perseus Publishing.

Klein, D. (1992). Simu-Ral: A simulation approach to organizational change. *Journal of Applied Behavioral Science*, 28(4), 566–578.

Knowles, M. (1970). *The modern practice of education: Andragogy versus pedagogy*. New York: Association Press.

Knowles, M. S. (1975). *Self-directed learning*. New York: Association Press.

Knowles, M. S., Holton, E. F., III, and Swanson, R. A. (1998). *The adult learner* (5th ed.). Houston: Gulf Publishing Company.

Kochan, T. A., and Useem, M. (1992). *Transforming organizations*. New York: Oxford University Press.

Korten, D. C. (1995). *When corporations rule the world*. San Francisco: Berrett-Koehler.

Kotter, J. R. (1996). *Leading change*. Boston: Harvard Business School Press.

Kuchinke, K. P. (1999). Adult development towards what end? A philosophical analysis of the concept as reflected in research, theory, and practice of human resource development. *Adult Education Quarterly*, 49(4), 148–162.

Laird, D. (1985). *Approaches to training and development* (2nd ed.). Reading, Mass.: Addison-Wesley.

Lawrence, P. R., and Lorsch, J. W. (1967). *Organization and environment: Managing differentiation and integration*. Boston: Division of Research, Harvard Business School.

———. (1969). *Developing organizations: Diagnosis and action*. Reading, Mass.: Addison-Wesley.

Lawson, K. L. (1998). *The Trainers Handbook*. SanFrancisco: Jossey-Bass.

Lawson, K. H. (1975). *Philosophical concepts and values in adult education*. Nottingham, England: Barnes and Humby Ltd.

LeBoeuf, M. (1985). *Getting results: The secret to motivating yourself and others*. New York: Berkeley Books.

Levinson, D. J., et al. (1974). *The seasons of a man's life*. New York: Knopf.

Lewin, K. (1947a). Frontiers in group dynamics, part 1: Concept, method and reality in social science: Social equilibria and social change. *Human Relations*, 1, 5–41.

———. (1947b). Frontiers in group dynamics, part 1: Channels of group life: Social planning and action research. *Human Relations*, 1, 143–153.

———. (1948). *Resolving social conflicts*. New York: Harper and Row.

———. (1951). *Field theory in social science*. New York: HarperCollins.

Lewin, K., and Grabbe, P. (1945). Conduct, knowledge and acceptance of new values. *The Journal of Social Values*, 1(3), 76–82.

Lewin, K., et al. (1945). The practicality of democracy. In G. Murphy, ed., *Human nature and enduring peace*. Boston: Houghton Mifflin.

Likert, R. (1961). *New patterns of management*. New York: McGraw-Hill.

_____. (1967). *The human organization*. New York: McGraw-Hill.

Lindeman, E. C. (1961, 1995). For those who need to be learners. In S. B. Merriam, ed., *Selected writings on philosophy and adult education* (2nd ed.), pp. 31–36. Malabar, Fla.: Krieger Publishing Company.

Lippitt, R. (1980). *Choosing the future you prefer*. Washington, D.C.: Development Publishers.

_____. (1983). Future before you plan. In R. A. Ritvo and A. G. Sargent, eds., *The NTL managers' handbook*. Arlington, Va.: NTL Institute.

Livingstone, S. R. (1995). Cultural studies in adult education. In S. B. Merriam, ed., *Selected writings on philosophy and adult education* (2nd ed.), pp. 1–6. Malabar, Fla.: Krieger Publishing Company.

Lyotard, J. F. (1984). *The postmodern condition: A report of knowledge*. Minneapolis: University of Minnesota Press.

Mager, R., and Pipe, P. (1984). *Analyzing performance problems* (2nd ed.). Belmont, Calif.: Lake Publishing Company.

Mager, R. F. (1975). *Preparing instructional objectives* (2nd ed.). Belmont, Calif.: Fearon.

_____. (1997). *Making instruction work or skillbloomers: A step-by-step guide to designing and developing instruction that works*. Atlanta: The Center for Effective Performance, Inc.

Maher, F. A., and Tetreault, M. K. T. (1994). *The feminist classroom: An inside look at how professors and students are transforming higher education for a diverse society*. New York: Basic Books.

Marquardt, M., and Reynolds, A. (1994). *The global learning organization*. Burr Ridge, Ill.: Richard Irwin Inc.

Marquardt, M. J. (1996). *Building the learning organization*. New York: McGraw-Hill.

_____. (1999). *Action learning in action: Transforming problems and people for world-class organizational learning*. Palo Alto, Calif.: Davies-Black Publishing.

Marsick, V. J. (1990). Action learning and reflection in the workplace. In J. Mezirow and Associates, eds., *Fostering critical reflection in adulthood: A guide to transformative and emancipatory learning*, pp. 23–46. San Francisco: Jossey-Bass.

Marsick, V. J., ed. (1987). *Learning in the workplace*. London: Croom Helm.

Marsick, V. J., and Watkins, K. (1990). *Informal and incidental learning in the workplace*. London: Routledge.

Maslow, A. (1954). *Motivation and personality*. New York: Harper.

McGregor, D. (1960). *The human side of enterprise*. New York: McGraw-Hill.

McLagan, P., and Christo, N. (1995). *The age of participation*. San Francisco: Berrett-Koehler.

McLean, G. N. (2000). It depends. In W. E. A Ruona and F. Roth, eds., *Philosophical foundations of human resource development practice. Advances in developing human resources, No. 7*, pp. 39–43. San Francisco: Berrett-Koehler.

Merriam, S. B. (1995). *An update on adult learning theory.* New Directions for Adult and Continuing Education. San Francisco: Jossey-Bass.

Merriam, S. B., and Brockett, R. G. (1997). *The profession and practice of adult education: An introduction.* San Francisco: Jossey-Bass, No. 57.

Merriam, S. B., and Caffarella, R. S. (1999). *Learning in adulthood: A comprehensive guide* (2nd ed.). San Francisco: Jossey-Bass.

Mezirow, J. (1978). Perspective transformation. *Adult Education,* 28(2), 100–110.

_____. (1991). *Transformative dimensions of adult learning.* San Francisco: Jossey-Bass.

Miles, R. E., and Snow, C. C. (1978). *Organizational strategy, structure and process.* New York: McGraw-Hill.

Miller, J. G. (1978). *Living systems.* New York: McGraw-Hill.

Mills, G. E., Pace, R. W., and Peterson, B. D. (1988). *Analysis in human resource training and organization development.* Cambridge, Mass.: Perseus Books.

Mink, O. G., Esterhuysen, P. W., Mink, B. P., and Owen, K. Q. (1993). *Change at work: A comprehensive management process for transforming organizations.* San Francisco: Jossey-Bass.

Molenda, M., Pershing, J. A., and Reigeluth, C. M. (1996). Designing instructional systems. In R. L. Craig, ed., *The ASTD training and development handbook: A guide to human resource development,* pp. 266–293. New York: McGraw-Hill.

Murphy, J. R. (1999). Why performance consulting is a mirage. *Training,* 36(5), 103–104.

Nadler, D. A. (1998). *Champion for change: How CEO's and their companies are mastering the skills of radical change.* San Francisco: Jossey-Bass.

Nadler, D. A., Gerstein, M. S., and Shaw, R. B. (1992). *Organizational architecture: Designs for changing organizations.* San Francisco: Jossey-Bass.

Nadler, L., and Nadler, Z. (1994). *Designing training programs: The critical events model.* Houston: Gulf.

Nilson, C. (1999). *The performance consulting toolbook: Tools for trainers in a performance consulting role.* New York: McGraw-Hill.

Owen, H. (1992). *Open space technology: A user's guide.* Potomac, Md.: Abbott.

Passmore, W. A. (1994). *Creating strategic change: Designing the flexible, high performing organization.* New York, John Wiley & Sons.

Patterson, J. (1997). *Coming clean about organizational change.* Arlington, Va.: American Association of School Administrators.

Pedler, M., Burgoyne, J., and Boydell, T. (1991). *The learning company: A strategy for sustainable development.* London: McGraw-Hill.

Perkinson, H. (1977). *The imperfect panacea: American faith in education, 1865–1976* (2nd ed.). New York: Random House.

Phillips, J., and Holton III, E. F., eds. (1995). In *Action: Needs assessment.* Alexandria, Va.: American Society for Training and Development.

Pratt, D. D. (1993). Andragogy after twenty-five years. In S. B. Merriam, ed., *An update on adult learning theory.* New Directions for Adult and Continuing Education, No. 60. San Francisco: Jossey-Bass.

Preskill, H. (1996). The use of critical incidents to foster reflection and learning in HRD. *Human Resource Development Quarterly,* 7(4), 335–347.

Redding, J. (1994). *Strategic readiness: The making of the learning organization.* San Francisco: Jossey-Bass.

Revans, R. (1983). *ABC of action learning.* London: Chartwell-Bratt.

Robb, J. (1998). The job of a performance consultant. In D. G. Robinson and J. C. Robinson, eds., *Moving from training to performance: A practical guide,* pp. 229–255. San Francisco: Berrett-Koehler.

Robinson, D. G., and Robinson, J. C. (1989). *Training for impact: How to link training to business needs and measure the results.* San Francisco: Jossey-Bass.

_____. (1996). *Performance consulting: Moving beyond training.* San Francisco: Berrett-Koehler.

Robinson, D. G., and Robinson, J. C., eds. (1998). *Moving from training to performance: A practical guidebook.* San Francisco: Berrett-Koehler.

Robinson, R. D. (1994). *An introduction to helping adults learn and change.* West Bend, Wisc.: Omnibook.

Rosenberg, M. J. (1996). Human performance technology: Foundation for human performance improvement. In W. Rothwell, ed., *The ASTD models for human performance improvement. Roles, competencies, and outputs,* pp. 5–9. Alexandria, Va.: American Society for Training and Development Press.

Rosenberg, M. J., Coscarelli, W. C., and Hutchison, D. S. (1999). The origins and evolution of the field. In H. D. Stolovitch and E. J. Keeps, eds., *Handbook of human performance technology: Improving individual and organizational performance worldwide,* pp. 25–46. San Francisco: Jossey-Bass.

Rossett, A. (1992). Analysis of human performance problems. In H. D. Stolovitch and E. J. Keeps, eds., *Handbook of human performance technology: A comprehensive guide for analyzing and solving performance problems in organizations,* pp. 97–113. San Francisco: Jossey-Bass.

_____. (1999a). Analysis for human performance technology. In H. D. Stolovitch and E. J. Keeps, eds., *Handbook of human performance technology: Improving individual and organizational performance worldwide,* pp. 139–162. San Francisco: Jossey-Bass.

_____. (1999b). *First things fast: A handbook for performance analysis.* San Francisco: Pfeiffer.

Rothwell, W. (1996a). *Beyond training and development: State-of-the-art strategies for enhancing human performance.* New York: AMACOM.

_____. (1996b). *The ASTD models for human performance improvement: Roles, competencies, and outputs.* Alexandria, Va.: American Society for Training and Development Press.

Rothwell, W., and Cookson, R. (1997). *Beyond instruction: Comprehensive program planning for business and education.* San Francisco: Jossey-Bass.

Rothwell, W. J., and Kazanas, H. C. (1998). *Mastering the instructional design process: A systematic approach.* San Francisco: Jossey-Bass.

Rummler, G. (1998). The three levels of alignment. In D. G. Robinson and J. C. Robinson, eds., *Moving from training to performance: A practical guide,* pp. 13–35. San Francisco: Berrett-Koehler.

Rummler, G. A., and Brache, A. P. (1992). Transforming organizations through human performance technology. In H. D. Stolovitch and E. J. Keeps, eds., *Handbook of human performance technology: A comprehensive guide for analyzing and solving performance problems in organizations,* pp. 32–49. San Francisco: Jossey-Bass.

_____. (1995). *Improving performance: How to manager the white spaces on the organizational chart.* San Francisco: Jossey-Bass.

Ruona, W. E. A. (1999). *An investigation into core beliefs underlying the profession of human resource development.* St. Paul: University of Minnesota, HRD Research Center.

_____. (2000). Core beliefs in human resource development: A journey for the profession and its professionals. In W. E. A. Ruona and F. Roth, eds., *Philosophical foundations of human resource development practice. Advances in developing human resources, No. 7,* pp. 1–27. San Francisco: Berrett-Koehler.

Schneider, B., and Konz, A. (1989). Strategic job analysis. *Human Resource Management,* 28(2), 51–63.

Schon, D. A. (1983). *The reflective practitioner: How professionals think in action.* New York: Basic Books.

Senge, P. M. (1990). *The fifth discipline: The art and practice of the learning organization.* New York: Doubleday.

Sheehy, G. (1995). *New passages.* New York: Random House.

Shertzer, B., and Stone, S. C. (1980). *Fundamentals of counseling* (3rd ed.). Dallas: Houghton Mifflin.

Silber, K. (1992). Intervening at different levels in organizations. In H. D. Stolovitch and E. J. Keeps, eds., *Handbook of human performance technology: A comprehensive guide for analyzing and solving performance problems in organizations,* pp. 50–65. San Francisco: Jossey-Bass.

Simonsen, P. (1997). *Promoting a developmental culture in your organization: Using career development as a change agent.* Palo Alto, Calif.: Davies-Black Publishing.

Sink, D. L. (1992). Success strategies for the human performance technologist. In H. D. Stolovitch and E. J. Keeps, eds., *Handbook of human performance technology: A comprehensive guide for analyzing and solving performance problems in organizations,* pp. 564–575. San Francisco: Jossey-Bass.

Skinner, B. F. (1971, 1991). *Beyond freedom and dignity.* New York: Alfred A. Knopf.

Smith, M. E., and Geis, G. L. (1992). Planning an evaluation study. In H. D. Stolovitch and E. J. Keeps, eds., *Handbook of human performance technology: A comprehensive guide for analyzing and solving performance problems in organizations,* pp. 151–166. San Francisco: Jossey-Bass.

Sork, T. J. (1997). Workshop planning. In J. Fleming, ed., *New directions for adult and continuing education, No. 76*, pp. 5–17. San Francisco: Jossey-Bass.

Spencer, L. J. (1989). *Winning through participation*. Dubuque, Iowa: Kendall/Hunt.

Spitzer, D. R. (1992). The design and development of effective interventions. In H. D. Stolovitch and E. J. Keeps, eds., *Handbook of human performance technology: A comprehensive guide for analyzing and solving performance problems in organizations*, pp. 114–129. San Francisco: Jossey-Bass.

Spitzer, R. A. (1999). The design and development of high-impact interventions. In H. D. Stolovitch and E. J. Keeps, eds., *Handbook of human performance technology: Improving individual and organizational performance worldwide*, pp. 163–184. San Francisco: Jossey-Bass.

Stevens, R. A. The hospital as a social institution. *Hospital and Health Services Administration*, 36(3), 163–173.

Stewart, T. A. (1997). *Intellectual capital: The new wealth of organizations*. New York: Doubleday/Currency.

Stolovitch, H., and Keeps, E. J., eds. (1992). *Handbook of human performance technology: A comprehensive guide for analyzing and solving performance problems in organizations*. San Francisco: Jossey-Bass.

_____. (1999). What is human performance technology. In H. Stolovitch and E. J. Keeps, eds., *Handbook of human performance technology: Improving individual and organizational performance worldwide*, pp. 3–23. San Francisco: Jossey-Bass.

Stolovitch, H. D., Keeps, E. J., and Rodrigue, D. (1995). Skill sets for the human performance technologist. *Performance Improvement Quarterly*, 8(2), 40–67.

_____. (1999a). Skill sets for the human performance technologist. In P. J. Dean, ed., *Performance engineering at work*, pp. 143-172. Washington, D.C.: International Society for Performance Improvement Publications.

_____. (1999b). Skill sets, characteristics, and values for the human performance technologist. In H. Stolovitch and E. J. Keeps, eds., *Handbook of human performance technology: Improving individual and organizational performance worldwide*, pp. 651–697. San Francisco: Jossey-Bass.

Stufflebeam, D. L. (1975). Toward a science of education evaluation. *Educational Technology*, 7(14):, 329–344.

Swanson, R. A. (1994). *Analysis for improving performance. Tools for diagnosing organization and documenting workplace expertise*. San Francisco: Berrett-Koehler.

_____. (1995). Human resource development: Performance is the key. *Human Resource Development Quarterly*, 6(2), 207–213.

_____. (1999). The foundations of performance improvement and implications for practice. In R. J. Torraco, ed., *Performance improvement theory and practice*, pp. 1–25. San Francisco: Berrett-Koehler.

_____. (2001). *Assessing financial benefits of human resource benefits*. Cambridge, Mass.: Perseus Publishing.

Swanson, R. A., and Arnold, D. E. (1996). The purpose of human resource development is to improve organizational performance. In R. Rowden, ed., *Workplace learning: Debating the five critical questions of theory and practice.* New Directions for Adult and Continuing Development, San Francisco: Jossey-Bass, No. 72.

Swanson, R. A., and Gradous, D. (1988). *Forecasting financial benefits of human resource development.* San Francisco: Jossey-Bass.

Taylor, F. W. (1911). *The principles of scientific management.* New York: Harper and Row.

Thoresen, C. E. (1966). Behavioral counseling: An introduction. *The School Counselor,* 14(9), 13–21.

Thorndike, E. L. (1931). *Human learning.* Cambridge, Mass.: MIT Press.

Tisdell, E. J. (1993). Poststructural feminist pedagogies: The possibilities and limitations of a feminist emancipatory adult learning theory and practice. *Adult Education Quarterly,* 48(3), 139–156.

_____. (1995). Feminism and adult learning: Power, pedagogy, and praxis. In S. B. Merriam, ed., *An update on adult learning theory.* New Directions for Adult and Continuing Education, No. 57. San Francisco: Jossey-Bass.

_____. (1998). *Creating inclusive adult learning environments: Insights from multicultural education and feminist pedagogy.* Information Series No. 361. Columbus, Ohio: ERIC Clearinghouse on Adult, Career, and Vocational Education.

Tosti, D. (1986). Feedback systems. In M. Smith, ed., *Introduction to performance technology.* Washington, D.C.: International Society for Performance Improvement Publication.

Tough, A. (1979). *The adult's learning projects: A fresh approach to theory and practice in adult learning* (2nd ed.). Austin, Texas: Learning Concepts.

Trist, E. (1981). *The evolution of socio-technical systems: A conceptual framework and an action research program.* Occasional Paper No. 2 (June). Ontario, Canada: Ontario Quality of Working Life Centre.

Trist, E. L., and Bamforth, K. (1951). Social and psychological consequences of the Longwall method of coal-getting. *Human Relations,* 4, 3–38.

Turner, A. N. (1983). Consulting is more than giving advice. *Harvard Business Review,* 61(5), 120–129.

Tushman, M. L., and O'Reilly, C. (1996). Ambidextrous organizations: Managing evolutionary and revolutionary change. *California Management Review,* 38(4).

Tyler, R. (1949). *Basic principles of curriculum and instruction.* Chicago: The University of Chicago Press.

Ulrich, D. (1997). *Human resource champions.* Boston: Harvard Business School Press.

_____. (1998). A new mandate for human resources. *Harvard Business Review,* 76(1), 124–134.

Ulrich, D., Zenger, J., and Smallwood, N. (1999). *Results-based leadership: How leaders build the business and improve the bottom line.* Boston: Harvard Business School Press.

von Bertalanffy, L. (1950). *General systems theory.* New York: Braziller.

Watkins, K. E. (2000). Aims, roles and structures for human resource development. In W. E. A. Ruona and F. Roth, eds., *Philosophical foundations of human resource development practice*. Advances in Developing Human Resources, No. 7, pp. 54–59. San Francisco: Berrett-Koehler.

Watkins, K. E., and Marsick, V. J. (1993). *Sculpting the learning organization: Lessons in the art and science of systematic change*. San Francisco: Jossey-Bass.

Watkins, R., and Kaufman, R. (1996). An update on relating needs assessment and needs analysis. *Performance Improvement*, 35(10), 10–13.

Weisbord, M. R. (1987). *Productive workplaces: Organizing and managing for dignity, meaning, and community*. San Francisco: Jossey-Bass.

_____. (1992). *Discovering common ground*. San Francisco: Berrett-Koehler.

Weisbord, M. R., and Janoff, S. (1995). *Future search*. San Francisco: Berrett-Koehler.

West, G. W. (1996). Group learning in the workplace. In S. Imel, ed., *Learning in groups: Exploring fundamental principles, new uses, and emerging opportunities*. New Directions for Adult and Continuing Education, No. 71, pp. 51–60. San Francisco: Jossey-Bass.

Willis, V. J., and May, G. L. (1997). A chief learning officer: A case study at Millbrook Distribution Services. In H. Preskill and R. L. Dilworth, eds., *Human resource development in transition: Defining the cutting edge. Selected conference proceedings*, pp. 8–19. Washington, D.C.: The International Society for Performance Improvement and the Academy for Human Resource Development.

Wilson, A. L. (1993). The promise of situated cognition. In S. B. Merriam, ed., *An update on adult learning theory*. New Directions for Adult and Continuing Education, No. 57. San Francisco: Jossey-Bass.

Wykes, M. (1998). Performance analysts at Steelcase. In D. G. Robinson and J. C. Robinson, eds., *Moving from training to performance: A practical guide*, pp. 78–94. San Francisco: Berrett-Koehler.

Zinn, L. M. (1983). Development of a valid and reliable instrument for adult educators to identify a personal philosophy of education. *Dissertation Abstracts International*, 44, 1667A–1668A.

_____. (1990). Identifying your philosophical orientation. In M. W. Galbraith, ed., *Adult learning methods*, pp. 39–77. Malabar, Fla.: Krieger Publishing Company.

American Society for Training – Deut (ASTD). Trends that will influence workplace learning and performance in the next five years. *Training and Development*, 72(5), 29–35.

ASTD. The future of workplace learning. *Training and Development*, 72(5), 36–47.

ASTD. The coming of age of workplace learning: A time line. *Training and Development*, 72(15), 5–12.

Index